The Body Impolitic

The Body Impolitic

Artisans and Artifice in the Global Hierarchy of Value

Michael Herzfeld

The University of Chicago Press
Chicago and London

Michael Herzfeld is professor of anthropology at Harvard University. He is the author, most recently, of *Portrait of a Greek Imagination: An Ethnographic Biography of Andreas Nenedakis*, published by the University of Chicago Press, and *Anthropology: Theoretical Practice in Society and Culture*.

The University of Chicago Press, Chicago 60637
The University of Chicago Press, Ltd., London
© 2004 by The University of Chicago
All rights reserved. Published 2004
Printed in the United States of America

13 12 11 10 09 08 07 06 05 04   5 4 3 2 1

ISBN (cloth): 0-226-32913-5
ISBN (paper): 0-226-32914-3

Library of Congress Cataloging-in-Publication Data

Herzfeld, Michael, 1947–
    The body impolitic : artisans and artifice in the global hierarchy of value / Michael Herzfeld.
      p.   cm.
    Includes bibliographical references and index.
      ISBN 0-226-32913-5 (cloth : alk. paper)—ISBN 0-226-32914-3 (pbk. : alk. paper)
    1. Handicraft industries—Greece—Crete.   2. Artisans—Greece.
3. Social stratification—Greece—Crete.   4. Crete (Greece)—Social conditions.   5. Globalization—Social aspects—Greece—Crete.
6. Professions—Sociological aspects.   I. Title

    HD9999.H363 C744   2004
    331.7'94—dc21   2003009663

⊗ The paper used in this publication meets the minimum requirements of the American National Standard for Information Sciences—Permanence of Paper for Printed Library Materials, ANSI Z39.48-1992.

For Meg Alexiou,
teacher, colleague, and friend

Contents

Not for the first time, I find myself deeply indebted to the people of Rethemnos, that long-suffering but wonderfully welcoming town on the north coast of Crete. This time, I owe a special debt of gratitude to the many artisans and their apprentices for their tolerance of my clumsy and ignorant incursions into their working lives and spaces, for their willingness to let me observe and record matters that must have seemed astonishingly mundane to them, and for their frequent hospitality and good humor.

Numerous friends have read the manuscript of this book at various stages and have helped to improve its structure and argument: Vassos Argyrou, Marc Askew, Eleftheria Deltsou, Tracey Heatherington, Ada Kalogirou, Arthur M. Kleinman, Guy Lanoue, Thomas M. Malaby, Vaso Neofotistos, Sonja Plesset, Deborah E. Reed-Danahay, Saipin Suputamongkol, Susan Terrio, and Vassiliki Yiakoumaki. Their critical insights and close readings have been the offerings of true and patient friends. I warmly thank them all, as I do the many others who have listened to presentations I have made on this material over the past decade in numerous institutions around the world. Transcriptions of the tape-recorded interviews were ably done at various times by Panos Tsokas, Pantelis Hatzis, Angeliki Rovatsou, and Mantha Zarmakoupi. Michele Lamprakos skillfully fashioned the line drawings, with appropriate attention to the disguising of identifiable features, from video stills taken from my original research materials, while Steven A. LeBlanc prepared the digital photograph of the wooden paper-holder. At the University of Chicago Press, T. David Brent has repeatedly demonstrated friendship far beyond his editorial role; I also want to express my appreciation for the gentle efficiency of Elizabeth Branch Dyson, for the thorough preliminary manuscript inspection by Catherine Beebe and Claudia Rex, and for the editorial artisanship of Pamela Bruton, whose combination of light hand and eagle eye is an author's dream come true. A special word of thanks goes again to Vassiliki Yiakoumaki, who provided invaluable assistance during the brief phase of the work that I conducted in Khania. To Cornelia Mayer Herzfeld, who was able to accompany me for part of the field research and gave me the inspiration and sense of humor to keep at it, my debt is as always beyond mere words.

The field research, carried out in the summer of 1992 and during 1993–1994, was supported by grants and fellowships from the National Science Foundation, the Spencer Foundation, and the American Philosophical Society. I benefited greatly from a sabbatical leave from Harvard University in 1993–1994, as also from the generous grant of a three-week visiting fellowship—which enabled me to bring this work more or less to its final form—in the Department of Anthropology of the University of Adelaide in 2002. None of these institutions is responsible for the work itself, but without their help it would not have been feasible.

This book is dedicated to Margaret B. Alexiou, superlative teacher of modern Greek culture in my Birmingham days and later my esteemed colleague at Harvard, a true artist of the humanities under whose guidance my still-ongoing apprenticeship has never necessitated the crafty measures described in this book, but who also, with unfailing intellectual generosity, has never let me get away with arguments that made no sense.

The transliteration of Greek is notoriously a political and logistical minefield, in which consistency over the language's long history is a virtual impossibility. In this book, I have opted to use standard conventions for classical Greek but have used a fairly precise representation of the actual sound of modern Greek, and, to avoid further confusion, I have represented *ch* (as in English "chime") in Cretan dialect phonology as *č*. Modern authors are listed in the forms in which they are likely to be most familiar to English-speaking readers (e.g., Prevelakis), but this means avoiding the (sometimes partially) classical conventions often used by libraries (e.g., Prebelakes or Prevelakes). While I use the local form (Rethemnos) of the town in which this story is set, I preserve local people's usage in the translated passages of speech; their occasional choice of the form "Rethimno" may be an index of the formality they wished to give particular points. For Thai, I have opted for a roughly phonemic system.

Chapter One

The Pedestal and the Tethering Post

Globalizing Locality

Artisans and artifice, craft and craftiness: in many cultures of European origin, people associate the idea of manual artistry with cunning and subterfuge, and this association has left powerful marks on many a language. Odysseus the "crafty" *(polytechnos)* was also, at least by etymological implication, "a man of many arts."[1] In English, an artful dodger is a crafty fellow; craftiness itself ideally takes the form of cheating the law at its own game.[2] In Italian, the highly formalized language of fine arts is parodied in a popular phrase, *l'arte d'arrangiarsi*, that is similarly redolent of resistance to formal authority and means "the art of fixing things for oneself."[3] The ingenuity of the artisan is never solely aesthetic; it always contains a component of indirection and guile. Because artisans are artificers, they often stand accused of artifice—indeed, of artificiality. But is artifice not precisely what they are engaged to produce? Their collective reputation is a victim of their own necessary ingenuity.

Yet that ingenuity is the key to their professional and economic survival; today artisans need all the ingenuity they can muster. Once they were deeply respected, the work of their hands a guarantee of worth that was often prized by the rich and powerful, but today artisans face remorseless competition from factory production and its globalization. Where formerly the work of craftsmen's hands acquired value through its transportation over long distances,[4] today the traveling is mostly done by tourists, who, ironically, may discount the work of today's artisans in favor of damaged artifacts hallowed by the wear and tear of distance through time.[5] Worse, the artisans are threatened with categorical "deskilling" in a world that apparently no longer appreciates what it once praised in them. How they deal with the attendant corrosion of their lives is a story that tells us much about the world in which all of us

1

live today—a world in which craftiness has never been the sole prerogative of those whose labor is craft but in which the control and centralization of mass technology have amplified to unprecedented levels the political weakness of those whose competence is specifically local.

In the sullen boredom and limply hanging hands of a carpenter's assistant or in the still, hunched back of an apprentice goldsmith, who knows what resentment and insubordination are smoldering, making him ready to grasp a moment's advantage to challenge the master's authority or surreptitiously siphon off his jealously hoarded knowledge? Who can discern in the jovial face of the artisan, as he deferentially cajoles his customers, the brutal harshness his apprentices and perhaps even his wife may quite consciously attribute to his suspicious fear of modernity and his narrow vision of his own place in the world? And how might we, observers of these tensions, discern in them any sense of engagement with those contemporary forces that seem to suffuse the entire globe with an increasingly homogeneous set of cultural, moral, aesthetic, and political values? What can such close attention to embodiment tell us about the ways in which those larger realities are actually experienced? How might the insight thus generated affect our ability to understand the complexities of globalization itself?

This is a search for the global in the heart of the local—for the hidden presence of a logic that has seeped in everywhere but is everywhere disguised as difference, heritage, local tradition. Some kinds of globalization are hard to miss. We can see them in the logos that sprout predictably in every city in the world, the familiar products that we can buy anywhere from Saskatchewan to Singapore, the assumption that people will know how to use those familiar objects and services no matter where they live. But what of those other varieties of globalization—the ones we cannot see but that we can indirectly sense and often implicitly assume? Why do people from vastly different cultures appear to share some surprisingly similar values, at least in deciding what is a fitting way of disporting themselves on the international stage? It used to be that anthropologists had to work hard to combat the idea of a universal set of values. Today, however, at the very moment at which anthropologists have more or less successfully made the case for ethical diversity and relativism, some attitudes appear to have become universal after all. Notions such as efficiency, fair play, civility, civil society, human rights, transparency, cooperation, and tolerance serve as global yardsticks for particular patterns of interaction. Startlingly, even "diversity" can become a homogeneous product. So, too, can tradition and heritage: the particular is itself universalized.

The increasingly homogeneous language of culture and ethics constitutes a *global hierarchy of value*. This hierarchy, which clearly succeeds to the values promulgated worldwide by the erstwhile colonial powers of Europe, is everywhere present but nowhere clearly definable. Its very vagueness constitutes one source of its authority, since, while it often appears as a demand for transparency and accountability, it is itself protected by that besetting vagueness from any demand that it account for itself. Whether as the most arrogant Eurocentrism of the kind that automatically assumes pride of place for Western "high culture" (itself an opaque concept despite a superficial gloss of obviousness) or as a less direct but ostensibly more liberal assumption that some ways of doing things are simply more decent or more useful than others, it represents the most comprehensive and globally ramified form of common sense—the ultimate expression of cultural authority.[6]

This global hierarchy of value therefore entails a strongly reified—although, again, usually implicit and diffuse—notion of culture. That reification betrays a European and colonialist origin, in that it springs from the massive preoccupation with the definition of spaces and concepts that characterized the emergence of the modern nation-state in the heyday and aftermath of colonialism. Even those essentialist discourses that are deployed against it (such as the "Asian values" touted by Singapore's leaders) cannot escape the logic of culture-as-possession that both reinforces the concrete quality of the identity thus promoted and concomitantly favors the commodification of ethics and aesthetics.[7] Despite these rhetorical claims to permanence and absoluteness, however, it is a hierarchy of shifting signifiers and indices, since upheavals in the distribution of power worldwide, as well as cultural changes within the major centers, may cause revaluation and redefinition at any time. More constant than any particular set of its expressions is the comfortably vague sense—the common sense—that, at any given moment, people know what it is, that they know what the good, the beautiful, and the appropriate are. As in any system of ethics or aesthetics, its constancy lies above all in the assumption of a consensus that papers over differences and changes and declares them irrelevant to the main business at hand.

Against this homogeneity-producing semiotic legerdemain, however, we must set the persistence of local differences at the level of everyday practice and interpretation.[8] The language of universal morality can be manipulated to conceal, as well as to deprecate, such localisms. In its outward appearance, the rhetoric of the global hierarchy of value is perhaps a more subtle kind of globalization than that of company logos and fast food. It is, after all, not obviously associated with special interests. It is not always immediately visible to us because, having invaded local universes of common sense ("local worlds"), it creates the sense of universal commonality. This is a common sense that is no less cultural than the local versions it appears to supplant but that, for reasons of scale and power, is better equipped to hide that contingency and so to make itself completely invisible.[9] Ever potentially subject to contestation but also imbued with a daunting air of irrevocability, the global hierarchy of value has emerged from processes of world domination that colonialism began and that international commerce and the international arrangement of power bid fair to complete.[10]

One aspect of these processes is the way in which certain places, ideas, and cultural groups appear as marginal to the grand design. These are the places and cultures that do not fit the design to perfection; the more they protest its domination, the more they seem to confirm their own marginality. They are the characteristic preoccupation of anthropology, a discipline that has long seemed to be fascinated by highly localized cultural phenomena.[11] Does this mean that, in today's globalized world, anthropology itself is marginal and unimportant? On the contrary, it is by dint of this comparatively microscopic focus, I suggest, that anthropology—with its intimate knowledge of alternative conceptual universes and local worlds—offers one of the few remaining critical vantage points from which to challenge the generalizing claims of the global hierarchy of value. It is in such places that we can see how marginality itself is actively produced, and reproduced, in the lives and bodies of those who must bear its stigma.[12]

The key questions concern what forces are determining what will be marginal and what will be considered significant. *Who* is responsible for that hierarchy; who are its agents? How do these agents subject the physical existence and moral worlds of ordinary people to a logic that renders them subordinate? In order to explore these issues, I shall examine some very marginal spaces. These are the bodies and lives of a socially weak class of people—artisans and their apprentices—in a politically and economically marginal town on an island (Crete) of Greece, which many regard as one of the most marginal countries in Europe. The apprentices often come from poor hinterland villages, from among school truants, and from orphanages. They thus represent extremes of marginality in several different respects. Artisanal apprenticeship here does nevertheless resemble comparable institutional arrangements in other parts of the world. To the extent that the local cultural specificities that I shall describe constitute an extreme case, they highlight important aspects of global inequality that employers and workers in other parts of the world are better positioned to conceal or moderate. They also alert us to the ways in which local culture both plays into, and yet no less frequently subverts, the increasingly potent ideology that posits a global system or hierarchy of value.

Greek artisans and their apprentices are marginal; but, paradoxically, they are nonetheless upheld by the state as exemplars of national virtue and tradition. Craft production in Greece is very much part of a nationalized and commodified folklore, associated with the emergence of national consciousness and glorified as the repository of ancient skills and qualities. In this respect they are a microcosm of the whole country as it faces the consequences of being saddled with an ancient heritage; craftspeople know, however, that their engagement with tradition is a double-edged sword. It exalts them, to be sure; but it also serves to marginalize them from some of the most desirable fruits of modernity.[13]

Who, in fact, "they" are and what makes them artisans are not easy questions, especially since many crafts deemed traditional in the international art and tourism trades are produced in the home and are locally viewed as the very antithesis of professional labor. Should women who extend the weaving of their trousseau items to the commercial sector be so classified? In Greece, at least, they are almost invariably not included in the class of "technicians" (tekhnites), who constitute the closest category to that denoted by the English term "artisans." Women who produce leather goods for pay in small workshops do qualify for inclusion; but then what of the young women who work as assistants to hairdressers? When in the course of fieldwork I asked friends about "apprentices," I was often told both about these girls and about the boys who were once similarly employed as apprentices to barbers, so that the implication appeared to be that any trade in which apprentices learned manual skills (as opposed to accounting or over-the-counter trading) should be deemed artisanal.

From this brief summary, it is clear that the category of artisan is situationally defined and that it is also partially—but again inchoately—gendered. Most of the apprentices we shall be considering in this book are boys. One reason for this may be a still-lingering sense that women who perform manual labor for wages are placing their reputations at risk by spending too much time exposed to the public gaze.[14] A further reason is that the historical burden of male solidarity in the craft guilds that existed in Greece during the Ottoman period has left a legacy of male exclusiveness, which the departure of Islamic norms did little to temper; even in many parts of Western Europe, where men were incorporated into some guilds by ritualistic but nonetheless often unpleasant forms of hazing, "it would have been an odd family that would have been willing to see a daughter enter so male-oriented a life."[15]

Yet another explanation is that women often discover that for them greater power does not easily accrue from competing in the normatively male arena of craft workshops, but that they can acquire that power through the achievement of higher educational credentials. Some young men affect to disdain that option on the grounds that too great a privileging of the mind over the body demeans their manhood (and perhaps also because this turns their admissions of having failed the requisite examinations into triumphant boasts). But educational achievement is also, and in consequence of that moral exaltation of body over mind, fraught with ambiguity for women almost as much as for men: while power in the wider national context is certainly seen to grow from the acquisition of literacy and theoretical knowledge, this evaluation gets reversed in the local context, where theory must give way to the authority of embodied experience. To the extent that men who become highly educated can play in larger arenas, they sacrifice some degree of moral—if not political—authority in the local sphere. By sacrificing the purity of their local allegiance, in other words, they gain access to economic and social resources that those who are unambiguously artisans cannot usually hope to attain.

Greece and the Genesis of Pure Tradition

All this is a reflection of larger dynamics of power, in which the country as a whole is subject to multiple pressures. The Greeks' marginal status in the "Western civilization" of which they are supposed founders, and yet in important respects also the victims, rudely batters their everyday lives at every turn: internationally embarrassed by successive government scandals and acutely aware of their dependency on the European Union, of which Greece is a member state enjoying nominally full equality with the others, they find themselves derided for an obsession with whether or not they are "really European" that is itself the product of a "crypto-colonial" set of aesthetic and ethical norms.[16]

The global hierarchy of value appears more widely distributed even than would be the case if it appeared only in those countries that represent the historical remnants of direct colonial rule. Several countries that were never (or only briefly) formally colonized by modern Western powers—Greece, Turkey, Thailand, Japan, and Nepal come especially to mind—have proved no less subject to its capricious domination, which was often so well disguised that it paradoxically generated local claims to exceptional standards of liberty. The Thais claimed the specific meaning of "free" for their national name; the Greeks celebrated the independent spirit of the very bandit-guerrillas, known as "thieves" (kleftes), whom the newly constituted Greek authorities made it their first order of business to suppress.[17] This covert cultural domination seeps insidiously into modern forms of expansion as well. As Maurizio Peleggi has pointed out in his examination of the Thai heritage industry, an exoticized tradition there became engaged "in the representation and commodification of itself as an object of desire" with considerable political significance.[18]

Today's cultural shots are as likely to be called by an international corporate enterprise as by even the most powerful of governments. But older patterns remain astoundingly durable; even former colonies that arguably have become colonial powers in their own right (the United States is perhaps the most obvious candidate for this description) almost obsequiously reproduce the idea that "Europe" is the source of "high culture." Greece, which has had to adopt the idea of Europe as the touchstone of value in order to lay serious claim to statehood, clearly endorses this perception to the hilt at the official level. But it may not sit very well with ordinary people, whose sympathies evidently often lie more with the bandit-guerrillas of the fight for independence than with the authorities who variously tried to control, co-opt, and suppress them; indeed, twentieth-century historical and political debates about Greek entitlement (or otherwise) to the European mantle continue to hinge, at least symbolically, on whether these historically shadowy fighters should be seen as successors to the heroes of Thermopylae or to the irregulars who flourished throughout the decaying Ottoman Empire.

Greece is a country created and lauded by the West for virtues that were to a great extent invented in the West: the glories of classical culture, intensely studied and reformulated in such universities as Göttingen and Oxford during the Enlightenment, were imported during the Romantic era into Greece, now under a Western-imposed Bavarian monarchy and bureaucracy.[19] In Athens, a partially Albanian small town dragged into modernity by being made the national capital, the florescence of neoclassical architecture signaled the reconstruction of the present as a living past, but the local architecture (and especially those aspects of it that seemed to recall the Ottoman period) was demolished as quickly as possible.[20] Domestic spaces nonetheless retained nonclassical interiors, often with distinctly Turkish-sounding names for the various features, in contrast to the classical names of the exterior ornament. In language, above all, ordinary speech was increasingly condemned as both decadent and foreign, a medley of Turkish and Slavic influences, and was replaced for legal and educational purposes by the newly created puristic language. Music, art, and folklore—everything was reclassicized in a formula created in Germany, Britain, and France. Only the Orthodox Church, which watched these developments with great unease and feared the rise of a new paganism, escaped the official neoclassicism; but its latter-day critics maintain, with some justification in a Weberian sense at least, that its formal establishment as a national church bureaucratized it as a "Protestant" institution and forced it into a mode that discarded the mysticism of true Orthodoxy.[21]

Greek independence was thus highly conditional. The bourgeoisie that emerged out of this situation was beholden to the West; the religious authorities imitated the rationalism of the West; and the academic establishment, especially during periods of military rule, faithfully reproduced the self-demeaning ideology of Greece the European ancestor as the prime instrument of its own—highly conditional—status and power. The blithe, nationalistic occidentalism of the political right wing and its bourgeois followers, as well as the adulation of its Western admirers (many of them engaged in political and ideological support work), remained dominant until the closing years of the twentieth century. This occidentalism continues to represent a powerful majority view, reinforced today by a sense of defending the European frontier against Islam and the remnants of Communism in the name of neoliberal values and institutions.

Yet the critical alternatives remain ever present, not only as an intellectual (and not always very effective) exercise but also as part of everyday lived experience. There is much in daily life that does not fit the ideology, although much, too, has changed beyond the point of no return. It is precisely because such features are to be found in the margins of Greek society that we must turn there to identify and understand them, just as we must examine the concentric marginality of Greece itself in order to understand "Europe" as a historical construct. Too much of the current social-science writing on Europe ignores Greece (and other relatively weak countries) and so necessarily reproduces and endorses a small range of European visions. It assumes that those people who do not conform to such visions are incapable of acting in accordance with European rationality. Internally, as the example of the currency switch from the drachma to the euro shows,[22] the inadequacies of the state apparatus are far less relevant than people's personal competence to deal with new situations by fair means or foul. This is a reading that does not accept at face value the objectivism associated with the spreading bureaucratization of European identity.

Greece thus remains an important and diagnostic arena for the struggle between supposedly universal models of decorum, democracy, and civilization on the one hand and highly localized interpretations of social relationships on the other. Its monuments are arguably the most dramatic example, within a country generally regarded as "Western," of the process Peleggi describes as the universalizing commodification of heritage. But this is what makes it ethnographically a test case: such famous sites as the Athenian Acropolis take on different meanings for local residents determined to contest the dominant interpretation in order to preserve their own vision of things.[23]

Dependency on an encompassing Eurocentrism of perspective is a pervasive, if contested, fact of Greek life. In contrast to the monumental sites of classical antiquity, everyday habits and incidental art forms often met a more destructive response from the self-appointed arbiters of national taste. Here is the ultimate Greek tragedy: that of a country forced to treat everything familiar at the time of the nation-state's foundation as "foreign," while importing a culture largely invented—or at least redesigned—by German classicists of the late eighteenth and early nineteenth centuries. For many decades, and almost without interruption, Greeks were forced to put aside music, art, and language that were deemed too tainted by the "oriental" influences of Ottoman, Arab, Slavic, and Albanian culture; to forget the partially Albanian roots of modern Athens and its environs; to use in elite-controlled contexts such as the schools, the media, and the law courts an artificial language syntactically modeled to a surprising extent on French and German but claimed as a revival of a "pure" ancient Greek that had supposedly been preserved in these quintessentially "Western" languages; and to contemplate the architecture of Bavarian neoclassicists as more genuinely Greek than the homes and churches that had been their cultural setting for many centuries. Although this situation has notably abated since the fall of the colonels' notorious (and notoriously neoclassical) regime in 1974, its influence on current attitudes will take much longer to fade. It is still omnipresent, sometimes as a real concern with living up to the global hierarchy of value it represents, sometimes as an angry shadow of irony that tinges every political and cultural action.

The language of value in Greece is itself very suggestive here, underscoring the peculiar relevance of Greece to understanding the dynamics of the global hierarchy. The Greek term for "value" (*aksia*, the root of the English word "axiology") has spawned a veritable shoal of etymological cognates, all of which are immediately recognizable as having to do with evaluation at once social, cultural, and moral. "Dignity" (*aksioprepia*), "maintenance of standards" (*aksiokratia*), "evaluation" (*aksioloyisi*) by peers—these words, redolent of the purist language (as well as of the religious sense of "worthiness") but today accepted as the normal speech associated with public discourse, all represent fragments of the cultural ethic attributed to classically derived Western ideals. Whereas a baptismal sponsor is hailed as *aksios* with much hearty, smiling approbation for performing a pious duty, the other terms I have mentioned generally accompany sober facial expressions of judgment and authority. They also resonate in every small locality of the country, however, because the etymological root they bear has grown deep into the social soil of agonistic relationships throughout the country; to "be worthy" (*aksizo*) is a reputation that all seek in the face of each other's persistent challenges. And yet, as Christina Veïkou suggests for a northern Greek community, it is precisely this quality that can attract the most destructive kinds of envy.[24] In these communities, it is the attempt to devalue others that actually underscores their standing: they are worthy of one's envy. Such is the true meaning of agonistic relations, in which the most positive of relationships—including political alliances, marriages linking families or clans, business partnerships, and even friendship—are predicated on both past hostility and the constant threat of its reappearance. Locally, value is always unstable. In the highland villages of western Crete the same etymological root can take the explicit form of expressing a self-reliant defiance that is sometimes jocular and sometimes a means of contemptuously dismissing others' claims to social worth: the dialect cognate *ksa* stands for a man's ability to take care of himself, again in the face of challenges from his peers.[25] Such etymological connections serve as convenient hooks whereby globalized concepts and local social ideology latch onto each other. They trace the contours of an encompassing semiotic that informs the particular and the local, so that this brief linguistic snapshot may serve to give a sense of how notions of value are caught up in—but also refracted through—local and regional experience.

Crete exemplifies the paradoxical yoking of the centrality of national ideals with aggressive idiosyncrasy in many ways. The resulting internal tension doubtless owes much to the long and complex process whereby the island was absorbed into the Greek state, as well as to the enveloping and concentric ambiguities of national claims to genuine political and cultural independence from both the Ottoman East and the European West. Crete became part of the Greek state relatively late—in 1913—after a series of setbacks and intermediate stages.

By that time the town of Rethemnos, famed as a city of letters during the Venetian era (1213–1645) and the setting for my account of apprenticeship in this book, had faded to a local backwater, an ironic reverberation of the Western view of Greece as a "sad relic of departed worth," in Byron's famously condescending phrase—a remark that from the outset defines Greece's role in the emergent global hierarchy of value.[26] It may therefore not be entirely accidental that Rethemnos was to become a significant topos in modern Greek literature, as witness the writings of Lilika Nakou, Pandelis Prevelakis, and Andreas Nenedakis.[27] Even in this role, it was portrayed within Greece as a marginal place, by writers who were in varying degrees themselves marginal to the literary mainstream of the country. The town's marginal status, however, serves to underscore important aspects of the cultural and political dynamics that have made it so.

Rethemnos has never been completely ignored by the political centers, whether in Athens or in the larger and more prosperous Cretan towns of Iraklio or Khania. It has, rather, been at the receiving end of a condescension that exposes important aspects of national cultural ideology and official practice. It was (and is) the site of a never-ending contest between local residents and the national conservation authorities over whether its centuries-old domestic and other buildings should be preserved or replaced by modernist conveniences, as happened to a much greater degree in those larger Cretan towns just mentioned; the argument was played out in the language of official discourse, with those who wanted to preserve their old homes (often in the hope of converting them into hotels or restaurants) pleading for restoration funds for their "Venetian houses" while those more in favor of a clean sweep demanded permission to demolish what they contemptuously called their "Turk-houses."[28] That argument itself illustrates the degree to which the language of neoclassicism and a pro-European understanding of the global hierarchy of value had long since pervaded popular perceptions and thought, setting the social price on a wide range of cultural capital, shaping the very spaces in which people lived out their lives, and affecting the way they decorated those spaces, the food they ate, the utensils they used, and the manners and habits with which they accorded meaning and value to these lived realities. The "social life of things" is not a story about material goods alone but incorporates the living spaces, manners, gestures, talk, daily experiences, and habits of the people who variously inhabit, use, and make all these "things."[29] Social existence takes place in and through ideologically laden presences, and evaluation—moral, economic, aesthetic, and political—is the attempt to make sense of them in the flow of daily life.

The town's physical fabric bears witness to the continual struggles to define and classify those presences. Among the proud monuments of the Venetian architectural heritage rise Turkish minarets and domes; the shabby cement-faced homes of poor rural migrants vie for space with smart boutiques, a few of them sporting stucco parodies of classical architectural features. Many of the older buildings are of ambiguous identity: built by local masons in a common style that lasted from the Venetian until well on into the Ottoman years, most of them lack clear construction dates—which is what gives so much play to the tastes, economic interests, and ideological outlooks of their owners in determining their fate. Over the years, decisions about what was to be preserved and what demolished were enhanced or undermined by the locals' taking matters into their own hands, as they manipulated the official ideology—according to which anything oriental was by definition a mark of evil—to suit their intentions and immediate needs. In either eventuality, however, local decision making followed norms generated in the national capital and in the universities of Western Europe. Both compliance and resistance confirmed the town's marginality to the march of modernity, even, or especially, with regard to the preservation of heritage.

Embodiments of Marginality

In the same way, the conduct of the body takes place in a space tugged in two, mutually opposed social directions. One sees aggressive traditionalism in dress, stance, and gesture. At the time of my fieldwork, in the early 1990s, one elderly man from the fabled southwest of the island who liked to strut ostentatiously along one of the busiest shopping streets of Rethemnos still sported the black headkerchief and white boots that are considered distinctive emblems of his native district and its heroic traditions, as he passionately but secretively drummed up support for a Cretan battalion to go and fight for the national cause in Macedonia (and angrily refused to discuss it with me because, he claimed, I was undoubtedly a spy); he also blithely ignored persistent whispers that he had not behaved so heroically or patriotically during the real privations of World War II. Others, lawyers and merchants for the most part, wear well-cut (and locally produced) suits, their wives sporting the current idioms of bourgeois respectability from Athens and abroad. Casual dress mostly follows Western European and North American styles, but there is always a sprinkling of (mostly older) men and women partially dressed in the distinctive garb—turbans and jodhpurs for the men, headscarves and dark skirts for the women—that marks them as villagers from the hinterland, in town for a day of perhaps frustrating encounters with supercilious bankers and bureaucrats or for a shopping spree that will also eventually take them to the watering holes of their urbanized covillagers now living in Rethemnos, where they gulp down rounds of nose-tingling grappa and nibble tiny roast potatoes drenched with fresh lemon juice and salt or the glistening, tiny, mixed black and green Cretan olives.

One Rethemniot man, a self-professed intellectual and self-published author who lived largely off inherited wealth and his merchant brother's assistance, tried to have his cultural identity both ways. He swaggered around town in what was almost a parody of Cretan ideals of masculine comportment, his head nodding sagely at his own ponderous pronouncements and his impatient scowl dismissive of others' opinions and good name, his pace measured and heavy as though he were still wearing the heavy boots of his village forebears, and his speech peppered with self-praise and criticisms of what he saw as the unmanly—that is, unaggressive—body stance (*kormostasia*) of more self-effacing citizens. He deliberately avoided wearing a necktie in the daytime but once claimed that he always wore one when night came on because, during the more dangerous hours when men would drink and disreputable people roamed the streets, the necktie was a sign that the wearer was not looking for trouble. He was ready for any fights that might come his way (clearly, he could afford to leave no room for doubt on that score), but those confrontations would not be his fault. On the one hand, he sought to maintain a pugnacious braggadocio that, in the villages, would usually presuppose the probable intervention of others when matters became dangerously tense. On the other hand, and as a balance, he affected a studied nonchalance that he hoped would make even a sketchy display of violence unnecessary.[30]

A troubled navigator of the shoals between the Scylla of masculine village tradition and the Charybdis of urbane modernity, member of a family of artisans that had attained merchant status, this man remained uncomfortable with a bourgeois identity that had nevertheless given him the space for the intellectual pursuits and accompanying recognition he evidently craved; indeed, the recognition has created within the bourgeois world of Rethemnos's merchant elite a space in which, by defying the conventions that would have had him put his shoulder to the wheel of his family's clothing business, he could lay claim to the status of intellectual in a manner that also allowed him to play the role of Cretan male. His constant belittling of the famous Cretan writer Nikos Kazantzakis, who has become something of a cult figure in the domestication of Cretan masculinity, was all of a piece with this attitude. His use of a necktie was thus more than a symbol of Western cosmopolitanism; it was also his rejoinder to a violent masculinity he preferred to disdain in practice if not in theory. In short, he laid claim to a masculinity both deeper and somehow more sophisticated than that of ordinary folk. In this sense, a demonstrative rejection of traditionalism employs traditional idioms to breach the walls of modernity. But modernity always comes at the price of a deep sense of lost innocence and of surrender to overwhelming cultural odds.

What this man expressed verbally and embodied in his gestures, stance, and dress, others—those less fortunate economically—seek by emphasizing their role as skilled and respected craftsmen and citizens of a town known in Venetian times for its learning and arts. Many of them do know that specific history, and the sense that Rethemnos is a place of cultural dignity is keen. The artisans range from building laborers, ironworkers, and carpenters to pastrycooks and goldsmiths. Their options, although somewhat varied according to craft and experience, are a great deal more limited than those of the merchant-turned-writer I have just described. These artisans have been gradually edged aside by the creeping gentrification of their familiar streets and workplaces and by the emergence of industrial and "artistic" sectors, with which they are obliged to compete from a position of acknowledged social disadvantage. Many of them are drawn from the supposedly wild hinterland villages, which are despised by the more established small-town bourgeoisie. Their apprentices are often school truants and dropouts. They have relatively few options in choosing where to work in a society in which the introduction of machine tools has also reduced the numbers needed to maintain the production of even the most obviously "traditional" craft objects. (At an earlier date, the much larger number of boys then eager to learn a craft similarly placed them at the mercy of employers, who sometimes paid them nothing at all and certainly never paid the insurance contributions that they were legally required to provide.) Moreover, the whole institution of apprenticeship as currently practiced in Rethemnos marginalizes most of the apprentices themselves by thwarting their ambitions of achieving mastery and instead reducing them to the level of unpaid or poorly paid unskilled laborers. In the process, it also marginalizes their employers by gaining them the reputation of unscrupulous child exploiters living beyond the law.

This illegality is embedded both in the widespread absorption of school truants into the apprentice population and in economic realities. Nowadays it is often cheaper and easier to hire illegal immigrants from Eastern Europe, some of whom are highly skilled, than to take on apprentices. Among the carpenters' assistants, for example, one may find the occasional "Albanian"; many of these migrants are Greek-speaking, Orthodox Christian economic refugees from the southern part of Albania, often of mature age, and although they come with only rudimentary skills, their eagerness to learn and their desperate need of subsistence put them entirely at the mercy of local contractors. I encountered two Poles—one a woman—working in leather. Young local apprentices are expensive to maintain at the best of times, given the waste of materials and time lost in correcting mistakes before they can learn even the rudiments of a craft, especially where apprentices (especially those who work for goldsmiths and tailors) must first spend a great deal of time experimenting repeatedly with cheap substitute materials on dummy objects before they can be trusted with the real thing. To this burden the employer must add compulsory insurance payments equivalent to those to which any fully trained worker would be entitled, but which the (often illegal) migrants are willing to forgo as the inevitable cost of employment.

Insurance payments become substantial when an apprentice reaches the age of eighteen. One artisan tried at this juncture to give his apprentice tools to take home, so that he could keep him on but out of sight—and perhaps also keep the apprentice from learning the more advanced techniques. The apprentice did not fall for the unctuous compliment that he was now a full master craftsman in his own right and so could work alone, but stormed out of the shop; he soon found employment elsewhere at a much lower wage but with some prospect of continuing to learn the trade. In the long run, he probably made the right decision, but in either case he faced severe limits on his ability to develop a profitable career. Most apprentices today lack any insurance at all; their employment is legally invisible and they are left completely unprotected from accident, negligence, or summary dismissal. One artisan did admit that paying insurance premiums was not against his interests, since he could claim tax relief—but his apprentices are all underage and thus illegal in another way. This is marginality from every possible point of view.

It is, however, a highly palpable marginality. Townsfolk were often quite secretive about other aspects of their lives. They disguised their daily purchases to avoid giving away too many clues about their current economic state, huffily deflected some of my questions because they assumed I must be a spy for the government's historic conservation office, and headed off inquiries into disputes with neighbors by pretending not to notice my interest. The fact that I could be considered a spy both for some unspecified foreign power, as the old warhorse had thought, and for the government itself is highly suggestive; the secrecy with which Rethemniots like to surround even the most trivial facts points to a moral economy that is reproduced at every concentric level of the global hierarchy of value. Intimacy, whether national and cultural or local and social, is jealously guarded, not only against obvious interlopers at the same level but also, and especially, against those who appear to represent an encompassing and potentially dangerous source of powerful intervention. Crossing the boundaries of such intimacies, as anthropologists inevitably do in the course of asking questions, flushes out the startled expressions of a profound suspicion and sense of disadvantage from the undergrowth of amiable and welcoming friendliness and so reveals many of the contours of the global hierarchy that I will be exploring in some of its most intimate realizations in this book.

The sense of pervasive suspicion is sometimes institutionalized to a surprising degree. The tax office, for example, convinced that no one would ever tell the truth, until a few years ago automatically assessed salable property at double the declared value or more.[31] Yet it would be wrong to suppose that outsiders can never gain access to reliable data in such an atmosphere. Sometimes the data emerge from the very circumstances that engender suspicion, as when two rivals pour out information—not necessarily of a damaging variety—about each other. Sometimes, too, acts that technically violate the law or morality have become so routinized that they serve only as demonstrations of the speaker's ingenuity, the folly of bureaucrats, or simply the fact that the ethnographer is once again asking foolish questions about what everyone already knows.

What everyone knows is, in the same logic, that "we" are the victims of some more powerful force. So general was the illegal employment of apprentices, for example, that few if any of the artisans hesitated to be quite open with me. While their injured complaints about the unfairness of government legislation may have been preemptive in categorically absolving them from blame for breaking the law, these lamentations also exposed a deep contradiction between government support for traditional crafts on the one hand and its labor insurance policies on the other. Thus, paradoxically, the artisans, by being uncharacteristically open about their defiance of the law (and evidently confident about the authorities' pragmatic acquiescence), were claiming a *collective marginality* that also expressed a degree of solidarity and intimacy in the face of the state's hostile formalism. Their situation represents a long process of alienation from the law; in Venetian times apprenticeships were contractual,[32] whereas in Ottoman times it was the guilds that provided a powerful institutional sanction for these relationships. Modernity has not been kind to the artisanal trades; perhaps the greatest decline and the harshest marginality appear in the transformation of apprenticeship from respectable idioms of discipline to a precarious living on the wrong side of the law.

In these pages I emphasize the common (but far from universal) anthropological convention of studying marginal groups. The point of so doing is not to dwell on the exotic for its own sake but, on the contrary, to explore the dynamics of power at the center, defined in various ways: the state, the wealthy, the international economic community, the church, the educational system. In an earlier study conducted among shepherds engaged in reciprocal animal theft in the mountainous zone of the Rethemnos hinterland—an area that supplies some of the town's apprentices and with them some diagnostic social attitudes—I argued that the local extremes of male self-regard and active flouting of state authority were not so much typical as emblematic.[33] While in no sense could one claim that the villagers' activities corresponded to a recognizably Greek code of social norms in their specific traits, they shed important light on the dynamics of Greek political and social interaction in two key regards.

First, they represented a late persistence, after nearly two centuries of national independence (and nearly a century of Cretan incorporation into the Greek state), of the supposedly typical traits of independence and fierce antiauthoritarianism that official historiography claimed for the heroes of the national revolution, among people who were also widely considered to be the staunchest soldiers in defense of their nation in times of war. Second, they exhibited a structural feature that underlies many other Greek social practices even in circles where the kind of freebooting and insouciant cheek shown by the villagers would be considered rude and inappropriate. This is the pattern whereby initially hostile relationships often mutate over time, and to no one's surprise, into alliances and even friendships: if the shepherds "stole to make friends," and while the conversion of hostile relations between families into marriage ties is well documented,[34] urban sophisticates will sometimes also engage in a pattern of challenge and riposte that foreigners find alarming when they first encounter it. Waiters, informed that they have brought the wrong dish, blame the customer, the cook, or the boss—everyone but themselves—and let the customer know exactly what they think of the impertinence of questioning their competence, but they may well end the evening joining the same customer over a sociable bottle of wine. Academic and professional Greek friends to whom I have recounted experiences of my own in this vein immediately recognize the genre—for a genre it most certainly is, identifiable through a progression from hostility to affability that is entirely normative.

The same people who intuitively recognize the structural commonalities of such situations recoil in horror at the idea that reciprocal animal theft, or any other equally reprehensible naughtiness, might figure prominently in descriptions of the nation's culture. Their reaction, too, exemplifies their entailment in the global hierarchy of value. While it is conventional to display disgust at the antics of the functionaries of state and church alike, and to admire transgressive actions of many kinds in the course of intimate conversations, the public presentation of national self-stereotypes is calibrated to the imagined expectations of the so-called civilized world.

Hegemony and Heritage

Such is the pervasive operation of global processes of cultural domination and change. Above all, it is here that we can discern a classic operation of hegemony, whereby the delicate creatures that we call local worlds are caught in the spider's web of global value and struggle: to protest or attempt escape is exactly what so easily, and so often, leads them to look ineffectual, rebellious, and irremediably inferior. One only has to think of the fate of deskilled shipyard workers in the United States, for example, frustrated into outbreaks of rebellion that bring retribution and further marginalization in their train,[35] to appreciate how successfully the neoliberal economy has naturalized its own rules of tact and conduct as globally self-evident.

No matter how globalized the surface, however, there are always cultural specificities that do make a difference.[36] These are matters of local reception. Anthropologists must be careful not to be seduced by the appearance of global uniformity, lest they themselves become uncritically complicit in propagating the idea of a universal set of values. While few today would support the notion of culture as a static entity defined by strict social and territorial boundaries, it is equally important not to go to the other extreme and dismiss local cultural values—however ephemeral or liable to dramatic change—as irrelevant to our understanding of how global processes affect people's lives. To do so is to buy into the globalizing of value that we should instead subject to critical and empirical examination.

One path through which such a generalization of the global has become an article of faith is the literature on what Eric Hobsbawm and Terence Ranger have called "the invention of tradition."[37] That glib phrase does at least successfully capture the sense of agency that has superseded the old *objet trouvé* understanding of the unadorned term "tradition." The weakness of the model lies in the privileged position it accords elite movers and shakers and in not recognizing that all traditions are in some sense "invented." But it is fair to say that one benefit of this literature has been a growing awareness that the very idea of tradition is a modernist one: people did not, in the past, announce that they were living traditional lives. A corollary of this insight is that "heritage," another term that plays a prominent role in writings about the uses of the past, is a global phenomenon; one might speak of the globalization of the local (or of the culturally specific).

Rethemnos, the site of this ethnographic study, is a case in point. In conserving its Old Town, a jewel of Venetian and Ottoman domestic architecture, government officials and conservation experts tussle with local residents over questions of heritage versus convenience, the entire debate further intensified by the enormous ideological load borne by those two innocent-seeming words "Venetian" and "Ottoman"—proxies for competing ideological claims to a European and a post-Byzantine identity, respectively. Hotels offer exhibits of local handicrafts said to represent ancient techniques preserved in the simplicity of the countryside or reborn thanks to the local artisans' fundamental sensibilities, while tourist shops peddle carefully sugared wedding loaves and simplified versions of villagers' hunting-bags along with copies of classical Greek busts and books proclaiming the antiquity and persistence of local crafts. These are globalized forms of local tradition; they sell worldwide.

The heyday of artisanship is usually located, in both popular and scholarly discourse, at some point during the long history of the Ottoman Empire and thus reproduces a choice between being either the repository of ancient skills maintained as a sustained act of cultural resistance against the foreign occupiers of Greek land or the incarnation of the "oriental" styles of the occupier. Understandably, most artisans and their admirers opt for the first

of these choices; it enables them to locate their productivity at the heart of
Greek claims to having originated European culture in general.

This yoking of artisan status to the mantle of a great past has engendered
a particularly cruel irony. The statue busts, the imitation ancient vases, and
the metal copies of museum exhibits are not their handiwork; their handiwork is, in fact, rarely to be found prominently exhibited in those spaces
to which the tourist guides and officials point as repositories of tradition.
The exceptions—the occasional iron grille, for example, or a new wooden
door—are rarely mentioned as products of local artisanship. One might have
expected historic conservation to have provided the opportunity for a revival
of ancient craft skills. But globalization affects the things that do not happen
as much as those that do. Consequently, in Rethemnos as elsewhere, it is
rare for the local artisans to be comprehensively involved in these conservation efforts at all. In fact, numerous artisans are disappearing or leaving
for cheaper residential areas where the architecture could not by any stretch
of the imagination be yoked to images of traditional lifeways; I have observed the same phenomenon in Crete, in Rome, and in Bangkok, and it
appears to be very widespread.[38] Gentrification, especially in the context of
current labor standards and the rising costs of raw materials, creates impossible conditions for most artisans. Many are completely displaced, while others
transform themselves into artists of highly individualistic merit; yet others
produce unique simulacra of traditional goods; a few resign themselves to
becoming middlemen—sometimes at great profit—for poorer artisans long
since departed from these districts.

In some places, a few artisans become living components of the museum
display, showing off their techniques in specially designated areas in what
most visitors correctly understand as a commercially motivated self-parody.
An attempt to do this in Rethemnos, however, failed precisely because, it
seems, key actors found the very idea absurd; again, I have heard very similar
debates in both Rome (as a basis for reviving a dying market) and Bangkok
(as part of the reconstitution of the old royal city as a national symbol).
The notion of the living museum is far from obsolete,[39] and, even when it
runs into opposition, it represents an already recognizable alternative—not
necessarily an attractive one—to obliteration. But we should be alert to what
it is that such efforts actually "preserve." At stake here is a pervasive notion
of the importance of conserving local heritage, a largely Eurocentric form of
nostalgia that has met very little resistance worldwide.[40] The local has itself
become global.

The traditionality thus framed is contrasted, implicitly or explicitly, with
an equally stereotypical notion of modernity. It nevertheless represents a

double bind: it is itself a modernist invention, yet it often serves as a means of exclusion from the modernist vision and its practical advantages.[41] That exclusion comes very close to bodily experience when people are forced by a nationalistically inclined historic conservation service to live, as Rethemniots often claim, in dark and damp houses defined by what they have learned to call a "Turkish"—that is, rudimentary—idiom of sanitation. The creation of pedestrian zones, while good for some tourist shops, makes access for heavier goods more complicated and is often associated with the re-creation of a paving style that, while vaguely evocative of an older way of life, also threatens to restore drainage to its antique state. Official attempts to encourage folklore performances meet similar circumspection. While many Rethemniots gladly dress up in Cretan baggy pants and waistcoats for a dance show, they are quick to point out how inconvenient such dress forms are for modern living. In the overheated rhetoric of globalization, the local and the traditional are equated with each other as quaint survivors from the shipwreck of cultural history, and living bodies feel their awkwardness and unpleasantness as the loss of comforts only recently learned and enjoyed.

Within that logic, which grounds the idea of a universality of values in an image of irreversible historical process, local particularities easily take on the character of flaws and become as self-confirming as the larger morality that sustains them even as it condemns them. Such condemnations often concern seemingly trivial matters, but it is precisely to these that traditionalists claim attachment, and it is precisely that attachment to the seemingly trivial that exposes them to the greatest risk on the international stage. To take a small but extremely revealing example, the European Union's ban on *kokoretsi*—a Greek Easter dish of stuffed and grilled lambs' entrails—served to highlight the persistence of an "oriental" or "Turkish" cuisine *(kokoreç)* in this marginal European land; when the Greeks protested, they were laughed at as culinary nationalists willing to sacrifice public health to a suspect form of heritage, yet they were also magnanimously—or so it appeared—granted a short grace period before the offending dish had to go.

This is, as it were, the obverse of the globalized hamburger: it is the localist dish that offends a universalized culinary aesthetic. Yet by what standards do we suppose that the dish was really likely to provoke an outbreak of "mad cow disease," as the Eurocrats claimed to fear? Even if the danger is real, was there no other way to control the situation short of a categorical ban? Or is this yet another example of what Mary Douglas so long ago pointed out about "dirt"—that it is a matter of cultural classification rather than biological science?[42]

In that case, we might well suspect that what we are really seeing here is the treatment of marginal cultures that refuse to accept submersion in the global projects of more powerful entities as a polluting presence—a locus of disorder—in the rigidly ordered world envisioned by bureaucrats charged with overseeing the management of the globalization process. And if Greeks respond to the external pressures to abandon a treasured specialty by saying that they will simply "go illegal," as they have so often done before in response to the dictates of successive national governments, where does this leave them in the search for an equal place in the modernist sun?[43] Here the carpenter, confined to a small side street where he illegally spreads out his newly varnished furniture to dry in the hope that he can trust his neighbors not to betray him and that the authorities will not bother with such a minor matter, captures the dilemma of how to maintain "tradition" when the institutional context is hostile to its modes of production but when local social tensions also make trust a fragile and evanescent thing.

People make disparaging comments about their own local cultures because they are already judging them by an intrusive set of standards. The resulting stereotypes, often embodied in increasingly stylized forms of self-presentation, become a form of self-confirming everyday experience.[44] They become consumingly important—the more so, paradoxically, because (and with the result that) people increasingly cease to notice that they are conforming to them at all. Such stereotypes are the source of those seemingly irrational reactions—nationalism, localism, and the like—that in circular fashion lock people collectively into the vise of international condemnation and contempt and lead them to accept these unflattering portraits of themselves.

What hegemony has this power to make people so despise themselves? This is where we begin to perceive the ubiquitous but often unobtrusive operation of the global hierarchy of value. We can track it most easily in workplaces and schools, and above all in the schooling of workers' and students' bodies to various forms of discipline. These are the sites of cultural inculcation in which people have been absorbing a set of hierarchical values that have grown increasingly global in their reach. Paul Willis has rightly noted the "self-damnation" that he perceives as "the taking on of subordinate roles in Western capitalism." His research was conducted in a British state school; although the teachers there exerted their control "through an educational, not a class, paradigm," they were still operating within that larger set of determinisms to which, in the global hierarchy of value, class status and formal logic both belong.[45]

In Rethemnos, the classroom of the state-run technical secondary school is similarly a site that some use to resist the authority of their teachers: those students are noisy, disobedient, rebellious, and disrespectful, and the teachers are unable, especially in the current climate of educational theory,[46] to impose much in the way of the discipline the system—for all its outmoded and ramshackle formality—claims to represent. Indeed, the artisans are far more successful at imposing their authority than are the sometimes dramatically ineffectual schoolteachers.[47] That the artisans' workshops offer so marked a contrast to the schoolroom reflects the class structure of the town. In the schools, the teachers are often poorly paid state employees who have difficulty in maintaining the respect of their upwardly mobile charges to the extent that their village counterparts, working in socially more static conditions, are still sometimes able to do. In the craft workshops, master and apprentice are usually of the same social underclass, marked by the same local idioms of language and the same workaday dress code; discipline springs, not from a formal and deniable system of authority, but from the master's virtually unlimited power to inflict petty physical pain and—a much less petty concern—arbitrary dismissal with the possibility of no alternative employment in sight.

The artisans thus themselves become the agents of the reproduction of sometimes humiliating values and practices in the sphere of everyday lived experience. If the teachers Willis studied were "dedicated, honest and forthright and by their own lights doing an honest job" in trying to help their students escape the oppositional culture of their class, the Cretan artisans are surely much less interested in doing so and, at the same time, less aware that they might actually be reproducing the power structure that has limited their own possibilities for social and economic advancement. It is also unclear that in either case a collective reversal of class relations would ever be possible. Those who successfully manipulate these ideologically individualistic structures to find a way out of their humiliation confirm the encompassing hegemony in the almost inevitable way they must adopt the marks of class distinction in order to maintain that personal advantage.[48] These markers are educational, sartorial, and linguistic, and their very rarity, until recently, fitted them neatly into the individualistic demands of the hegemonic system. Only now, as destitute immigrants appear willing to take on such menial roles (as they have in Greece), is there some prospect of a reordering of social relations; but even this will "ethnicize" the class structure rather than radically overturn its imperious logic.

It was the persistent ideological demands of bourgeois individualism, in my reading, that made it hard if not impossible for the teachers in Willis's account to specify the moral and aesthetic values through which the working-class culture of their wayward pupils reproduced itself. As members of a distinctly more privileged social group that is closely identified with the individualistic ethos of the middle classes, they represented their charges' misbehavior as a personal, rather than a cultural, problem.[49] In this way, willy-nilly, they sidestepped the issue of their own role in its perpetuation; they did not see themselves as participants in a larger process. For the Cretan artisans, however, the immediate issues are significantly different, even if the long-term effects are similar: these masters have every interest in reproducing in their young charges the ideology by which they themselves were trained and by which they continue to live. Why should they want to transform their conceptual universe? Their immediate interest lies in ensuring that the apprentices do not depart from it, even if, in the collective sense, a challenge to its authority might also offer the (albeit unlikely) prospect of a release from their depressed social status.

Those who do escape into "higher" professions thus reaffirm rather than undermine the hierarchical structure of value within the community. While Dorinne Kondo has rightly identified a streak of functionalism in Willis's account, especially (I would add) in the sense that the teachers appear to be as entrapped in the reproduction of the system as are the boys in their charge,[50] the Japanese artisans she studied are much more deliberately engaged in reproducing selves in conformity with a traditionalism that is clearly and openly expressed. In a country where outstanding individual artisans are hailed as national treasures, there are plenty of models for emulation as well as, Kondo points out, resistance and playful rethinking; the variety of these models and of the responses they elicit demands a more open-ended account of the role of human agency in negotiating the complexities of power.[51]

Yet too heavy an emphasis on agency alone can elide the important effects of institutional structures; not least significant of these structures are those of the kin group at one end and the nation-state and even the international community at the other. Kondo's analysis is rich in examples of attempts to bring artisans' lives into conformity with an ideal at once familial and national. No doubt such ideals are stereotypes, but, like many stereotypes, they are entertained by people about themselves; they thus provide stable models both for action and for critical or playful response. Such is the social reality of stereotypes; while we may reject them as tools for anthropological analysis, we should not ignore their forceful presence as locally valued models for everyday life.

National self-stereotypes can be especially exigent. For all the creativity and even eccentricity of individual actors, Kondo's account of Japanese artisans shows how important stereotypes of national selfhood are for them all. Greek artisans, perhaps even more than their Japanese counterparts, depend heavily on their ability to identify with the idea of a national tradition as the basis of their prestige, however conditional and circumscribed that prestige may be. Once such identification is acknowledged, however, we must also recognize the international dynamics within which particular national traditions acquire specific kinds of value; and this, in turn, represents a larger context within which artisans are inescapably enmeshed. At this level, it matters very little how aware they may be of their incorporation into larger value hierarchies, even supposing that one could answer such a question with any degree of certainty. Their strategies, both for success within the system and for escape from it, are equally subject to the evaluation of those around them, an evaluation that springs from persistent ideas about European individualism on the one hand and the assumption of European cultural superiority on the other. Their predicament presents a dramatic cultural contrast with the situation of Japanese artisans.[52]

Questions about value are politically contextual, but the context in question is as much about global consumer ideologies as it is about local forms of capitalism. Asking who says that the artisans' and their apprentices' values need readjusting and what interests such moral philanthropies serve is a way of investigating the invisible structure of that hierarchy as well as its ramifications beyond the local. It allows us to ask why working-class boys compound their entrapment by viewing escape from their class identity as not only difficult but also undesirable. These are also questions that Willis has asked, but asking them in the Greek context reorients the investigation to larger patterns of domination that globally encompass even those massive structures that we recognize as class. These questions concern the worldwide systems of cultural distinction that are sometimes simplistically but revealingly viewed as cultural imperialism and that constitute what I am calling the global hierarchy of value.

In asking questions similar to those Willis posed about the self-reproduction of working-class culture in Britain, I have instead chosen to explore these matters among artisan-instructors who are reproducing their own sense of inhabited class identity, and who are also reproducing a sense of regional and national humiliation, rather than trying to teach ways of escaping any of these concentric forms of domination. British class relations offer a dynamic quite far in its implications from the framework of Greece's peculiarly diagnostic marginality within European identity building. I hope to show here how concentric hierarchies—of class, local or regional cultures, and national identities—reinforce each other's self-perpetuating proclivities and to argue that it is precisely in the apparent dead ends of cultural production, where "tradition" becomes a self-confirming mark of static resistance to change, that we can see how insidiously the effects of expanding capitalism, the aftershocks of colonialism, and the bureaucratic universalization of a single morality fuse in the everyday experiences of working people.

Greece's relative irrelevance to European modernism except as a histori-cal point of origin for it suggests that cultural hierarchy is not simply a matter of greater or lesser sophistication. In fact, it is not a matter of sophistication at all, except in the sense that it concerns the question of who decides the criteria of sophistication. And local people are no longer as passive in their response as perhaps they once were (or at least were thought to be). Thus, by studying the self-crafting that accompanies artisanal production in a corner of Greece largely viewed as all but irremediably traditional, we can, ironically, disinter some of the hidden tyrannies of modernism and show how their reproduction actually, and literally, works. The primary site is that of the worker's body.

Impolitic Intimacies

That body is no ideologically neutral space. The view that southern Euro-peans are somehow less verbal, more grounded in bodily experience than in abstract reason, is disturbingly persistent.[53] Greek gesticulation often strikes visitors as vivid, emphatic, and uncompromising, an unsurprising accompa-niment to the "agonism" long viewed by social anthropologists as the dom-inant feature of local social interaction. It heralds dramatic verbal displays of aggression, voices raised in tones by turns imperious and threatening, and occasionally shrugs of contemptuous dismissal or indifference. Every perfor-mance thus witnessed tends to reinforce the essentializing framework within which outsiders are already predisposed to interpret it; and so the reductive stereotypes persist.

But then where, in such a lively landscape, do we place those drooping apprentices, with their yawning boredom and awkwardly motionless hands? Where do we place the pervasive silence that in many workshops is punctuated only by the master's occasional angry bark of command or the crash of some heavy object fallen from a hapless apprentice's unnerved hands? How does the lad respectfully squatting a few inches back from his master but with his head bent forward in a clear display of serious interest, new to the job and following his master's every move with carefully veiled interest or scurrying to obey his every curt command, become the boastful adolescent grinning over his mischievous adventures when he moves to a new job with many more age-mates able to share in his adolescent high spirits? In fact, there is no contradiction here, only the tension between outward acquiescence and the inner mastery of a body trained by degrees to the arts of professional, social, and physical survival.

The theme of embodiment has generated an ever-expanding and exciting anthropological literature in recent years.[54] Its interest goes far beyond Mary Douglas's original—and important—insight into the relationship (or, better, direct parallel) between control of the body and the normative forms of social control.[55] Work on the body personal is also work on the body politic. The body is the site of memories made materially accessible in complex ways. Some of these memories, and the attitudes they document, can easily be recovered in verbal form. But what of memories and attitudes that, for whatever reason, cannot be so transformed and thus rendered accessible? Should we simply give up on the very idea?

Numerous recent writings would seem to suggest otherwise.[56] Within this general tradition, one issue concerns the embedding of local worlds in national and global systems: the ways in which alternative understandings of heavily verbalized official ideologies underpin both individual and local autonomy and yet also, at the same time and occasionally in quite paradoxical ways, provide the means for maintaining national or even larger forms of solidarity despite social actors' disaffection from its official renditions. This is the apparent paradox that I have elsewhere framed as the problem of "cultural intimacy"—that is, the significance of the knowledge, internal to every national culture, that people are unwilling to share with outsiders because they have come to see it as in some way disreputable. Why do people in relatively weak countries often view the most familiar aspects of their daily lives in such demeaning ways?

In turning to the ethnographic analysis of craft activity, and especially of the training of apprentices, we will be hearing echoes of sources of authority that lie beyond the immediate confines of the workshop, but we will be hearing them with the ears of those who work there. We will be hearing them in contexts of considerable intimacy, which transforms the pontifications of authority into struggles for ascendance in the grubby interstices of everyday experience. The encompassing official contexts—church, schoolroom, state bureaucracy—reflect a long history of bodily management in Europe and elsewhere. Schools, for example, have long been sites for contest between an intrusive, Europeanizing elite and a monastic tradition that did not happily surrender control to the new educational authorities when Greece became an independent state. Artisanal apprenticeship is often closer to religious education than to the intrusive systems that arrived with European domination; in Egypt, for example, where Islamic religious schooling did not sit well with the intrusive forms of education brought by the colonial powers, artisans were also caught up in struggles between local elites and international (predominantly Western) economic forces.[57]

Artisans are spatially confined. The restrictions on their everyday movements, however, do not make artisans irrelevant to considerations of global process, even though a full understanding of their entailment in the larger world may require analysis in a wide range of interlinked places rather than on a single site.[58] Their confinement should be read, experientially as well as morphologically, as a symptom and an index of the way in which their lives have been permeated and encapsulated by processes that they do not control and perhaps do not always clearly perceive.

From the sweaty, tense body of the boy apprentice in a cramped and gloomy craft workshop or on a dusty construction site in a small town on a Greek island to the clangorous scaffoldings of international politics and commerce: is this too hazardous an imaginative leap? On the contrary, by straddling such extremes, and by refusing to accept the imperious self-evidence of their difference, anthropology makes a distinctive contribution to the study of how power operates. In a body politic increasingly subject to international forces, anthropologists must seek out the impolitic body that rejects those forces and yet so often succumbs to their dictates. Detailed and esoteric such analyses may seem; but only they can offset the generalizing and conflating that too often pass today for analyses of culture in the age of the global—popular stereotypes sporting a carefully burnished patina of academic authority.

The Crafty at Work

The analysis that follows, then, is an attempt to identify in one small corner of the world, under the magnifying lens of ethnography, the operation of the global hierarchy of value. This is not to claim that the perspective thereby achieved will afford us the only acceptable or true understanding of that hierarchy. But it will allow us to view the hierarchy from within and below, from the perspective of its subordinate members. It will also place it in the well-documented historical context of a relatively new nation-state, and one in which the tension between orientalist and occidentalist images of the collective self is unusually strong and politically fraught.[59]

How have artisans dubbed "traditional" by a pro-Western elite come to absorb and reproduce the dominant ideology, even as they sometimes contest its often condescending implications for them personally? I suggest that this dependency is in part sustained in craft workshops that reproduce, not only traditionalizing objects, but persons framed as traditional artisans. Their bodies become the site of an extremely comprehensive commodification of stereotypical selves, and this is linked in the popular imagination with ideals of Greekness. The Western European tourists who peer with amused satisfaction into the workshop of a shoeblack-stained, heavily whiskered, and gesturally dramatic cobbler—but do his gold-rimmed glasses perhaps betray an intellect as well?—perhaps fail to realize that at that very moment he may be holding forth on the Marxist interpretation of global conspiracy and the degradation of the working classes; but he, for his part, is quite explicit about both the difficulty that he would face in moving out of his profession and the international economics that keep his fellow citizens in thrall to the mass production of traditional objects and performances. When I remarked that some Rethemniot artisans still employed apprentices (and so were securing the continuation of their crafts), one young man revealingly responded, "As Greeks, we have not yet been obliterated!" It is precisely as Greeks—Europeans made marginal by their role as the bearers of a tradition embodied in the now barely legal institution of apprenticeship—that artisans try to reproduce ideals of authority in their workshops.

The terminology of work relations is revealing in this regard, and it also registers significant changes in local understandings of status and cultural value. The role of master craftsman is a bellwether for changes in the status of crafts generally. Until the 1970s, *mastora*, "master," was a common and very respectful term of address for artisans, used both by their apprentices and by their customers. The apprentices, sometimes even known as "slaves," were at best called "foster sons" (*parayi*), a metaphor understood as thoroughly demeaning because foster children are regarded as unreliable in their affections and as lacking the immediate kinship support group that gives people a clear identity and allows them to demand their social rights without fear of contradiction. A foster son is both under the authority of adoptive parents and yet lacking in the certainty of those parents' support and affection. It is thus perhaps unsurprising that in technical usage the paternalistic terminology of apprenticeship should yield, in an ostensibly politer age, to a more technological modernity. Today, apprentices are usually known as "workers" (*erghates*) or "assistants" (*voithi*). Revealingly, the formal term *mathitevomeni*, "apprentices" (or, more literally, "those being induced to learn"), is rarely used outside academic discussions, perhaps because locally everyone recognizes that the master artisans are less interested in teaching their crafts than in exploiting young labor for a pittance that is justified by the pretense that the lads' mastery is still incomplete.

But if the status of master artisan was once held in high regard and was sustained by an array of cowed youngsters toiling in the workshops with their heads bent over their work and their eyes ostensibly averted from both the

Figure 1 A cobbler and his team (circa 1930). Note the woman using the sewing machine; this was normally a female role. The youngest apprentice is demonstrating keen interest, but the master's stance and posture suggest that this interest is not openly encouraged.

street and their fellow workers, or respectfully ranged alongside their master for a formal photograph (fig. 1), today that status has fallen on hard times. The honorific *mastora*, sometimes used as a prefix with a baptismal name (as in *mastro-Niko*, "Master Nikos"), has come to signal an obdurate traditionalism that has no place in the modern world and is best replaced by terms of formal authority or simply by personal names. One man who rejoices in the fact that his former apprentices still greet him in the old way is engaging in full-scale nostalgia, since he himself has become a successful small-time businessman and can afford to take pleasure in this traditionalist title. Those who more seriously expect to be so called sometimes engage in crude displays of old-style masculinity that make Rethemniots who are more self-consciously modern cringe with embarrassment; one such man, a marble-floor layer, exclaimed that the fragile floor sections had to be handled with great delicacy, "like a woman!" This is not the kind of talk that earns one a seat at the high table of self-proclaimed civilization. When his assistant told him, "*Mastora*, they're all laid out on the side," he just nodded, but said not a word—a classically brusque response, but again, to be sure, not one that would earn him a higher status in polite society.

The address term *mastora* today more commonly conveys a condescending (but also ambiguous) sense of hierarchy, as when a customer in a restaurant addresses the waiter in this way. In other words, the *mastoras* is no longer the superior actor, but the client may still feel the need to express some kind of token respect that nevertheless makes their inequality explicit. For those who are well educated and have left the artisanal world behind them, I was told, the term *mastora* has become a taunt *(koroidhia)*. These semantic shifts index a process in which tradition itself, embodied in the role of the *mastoras*, has been identified, framed, and devalued by its association with the crude ways of yore even as it is set upon a pedestal of national adulation. If the Greeks "have not yet been obliterated," neither has their role as living ancestors and debased exemplars of European identity to which their Western so-called protectors have held them; and members of the elite reproduce this systemic inequality in their relationships with the artisanal class.

Today, in many parts of the world, artisans are treated as the last bearers of true tradition. In some countries, such as Japan,[60] they may even acquire the status of cultural monuments in their own right, living embodiments of a collective heritage. In other cases, as with the artisanal chocolate makers of France,[61] artisans can become the standard-bearers of a conservative national pride. In yet others, of which Italy is an outstanding instance, consumerist media—often backed by government subventions—transform select members of the profession into true "artists" of regional vernacular cultures, which have been reconfigured to support the idea of a transcendent national culture for the tourist trade. This is a curious echo of Fascist manipulations of folk culture under Mussolini, when local material culture was conscripted to serve the interests of a politically controlling ideology of national unity rather than those of straightforward commercial exploitation. Whatever the specific motivations in each instance, examples of such expropriations whereby local artisans become the repositories of a national or regional sense of tradition abound throughout the world.

As David Sutton has wisely remarked, also in the Greek context, anthropologists should be less concerned to identify particular traits as traditional or modern than to describe the political dynamics in which such attributions are made.[62] The rhetoric of tradition and modernity is not only the epiphenomenal expression but one of the most critical instruments of hierarchy. When the terms are presented in tandem, "modernity" usually emerges as the technologically and politically superior term, with "tradition" as the repository of those nostalgic idylls in which only the privileged can afford to indulge; tradition, too, is associated with a nobly picturesque "backwardness." This is the long-discredited anthropological doctrine of survivalism, reconfigured as popular discourse. Thus, when "tradition" appears alone, as the glorious repository of national talents, we should immediately ask why the opposing category has remained unmarked.[63] The pedestal on which such romantic yearnings are displayed may turn out to be something quite different.

To explain the ambivalence of tradition, I invoke Ludwig Wittgenstein's famous image of the duck-rabbit—the sketch that looks like a duck until one turns it on its side, when it becomes a rabbit instead.[64] Context and angle of vision determine interpretation. Thus, when the pedestal of tradition is turned upside down, its platform becomes a fixed concrete base, and the pedestal as a whole is revealed instead as a tethering post. The lauding of skilled workers as traditional artisans similarly both glorifies their achievements and firmly embeds their bejeweled glories in the glittering crown of modernity, from which they cannot escape without catastrophic loss of status. The irony of tradition is precisely that it cannot exist except in relation to a self-serving concept of modernity. Moreover, the predicament of tradition reproduces perfectly that of Greece itself: a country mocked (and often self-mocking) for its supposed obsession with a glorious past that thereby becomes as much a liability—a tethering post—as a mark of distinction, a means whereby more powerful countries praise the Greeks for their great heritage even while they point to the distinctive products of that heritage as evidence of Greek backwardness and especially of the Greeks' alleged inability to escape the childhood of the civilization they supposedly founded. The theory of survivals, that condescending anthropology of the colonialist heyday,[65] remains to this day a fact of global political life.

One might object that the glorification of the traditional is the one reliable means of ensuring its preservation; and indeed this is so. But that act of preservation is a dramatic example of the museumification of living populations that Johannes Fabian has identified as the mark of survivalism in anthropological discourse but that is in fact a pervasive feature of high modernism in general.[66] As Jane Hill has noted in a different cultural setting,[67] the rhetoric of nostalgia is a privilege of power, one that seeks to maintain the status quo by lamenting the disappearance of a supposititious ideal world of mutual respect that was in fact a rigid class structure.[68] Thus, artisans, praised for the individualism and independence of their work, can be recast, at the first sign of trouble, as fractious and insubordinate and as incapable of working cooperatively with those who have their good at heart.

Artisans absorb and reproduce this unflattering portrait. They take pride in their indomitable sense of fractious independence. It furnishes an excuse for personal failure in the three principal zones of official inculcation (school, church, and state bureaucracy) into official discourse, and it serves as an especially strong justification for artisans' frequently expressed antipathy to formal schooling of any kind. One artisan recalled attempts to make him attend a church-run school for orphans: "I didn't like it because the school was repressive—that is, there was a lot of church stuff and blah-blah, doping [of the mind], and I am free and revolutionary by nature. . . . I tell the truth directly and I speak out and don't hide; I talked back and it got me into trouble." This artisan also rejected the priests' control of his mind and body, refusing to accept what he called a "strange homosexuality" on their part. Whatever the truth of this conclusion, it is clear that the speaker was attributing his own failure to advance within the scholastic system to his own aggressively heterosexual masculinity, a value that also undergirds much of the rhetoric about the independent spirit of the Greeks in general.

But this is a positive "spin" on a widespread image of the national character. The converse of this model is hardly flattering to those with a more adamantly modernist perspective. "The spirit of collective action in modern Greece," remarked one politically internationalist and left-wing boot-maker despondently, "is still very much behind; it's not like abroad." Few comments better illustrate the double bind created by the global hierarchy of value. Damned for the very individualism that undergirds their claims to represent a peculiarly European form of tradition, artisans thereby find themselves excluded from a specifically European modernity that they see as coming only from the unambiguously superior but vaguely defined space of "abroad." Politicians also reproduce the encompassing hierarchy in their shattering condescension toward artisans, who have already been so effectively lulled into accepting this logic that they collude in recognizing the "evidence" on which it is based.[69] Artisans fail to hire even their own kin, let alone wage-earning outsiders, and fall out over what to an outsider will always be represented as unimportant matters in which they have invested excessive personal pride—as indeed, so the logic goes, befits traditional artisans. Tradition, it seems, requires tutelage.

One attempted solution, initiated by the government-run National Organization of Small and Medium Businesses and Handicrafts (henceforward NOSMBH), involved setting up seminars for traditional Cretan boot-makers and other artisans. The idea was to get the artisans themselves to teach their crafts. There were three key problems. First, the crafts were to be taught in a manner that was certifiably traditional in its attention to detail and methods

of production, but that in consequence effectively placed its products beyond the economic reach of most tourists; most students would thus experience its long-term effects as simply intensifying their already catastrophic
marginalization in the economic sphere. The other two problems concerned
the pedagogical context. Especially important was the limiting circumstance
that most artisans were completely unused to teaching through verbal instruction; many were also unwilling to treat the seminars as more than an
apparently easy way to make some quick money out of the government and
out of the gullible youthful enthusiasts who signed up. On the other hand, the
students were already school educated beyond the point of being willing to
accept the often abusive behavior of "masters" or the dilapidated conditions
under which they were expected to work. The effort to create the seminars
rapidly came unraveled, confirming the view of both those who had initiated
it and the students who were expected to attend that the artisans were uncouth beyond all possibility of redemption. Not only did this failure confirm
a generic self-stereotype that holds Greeks to be incapable of any sort of
cooperation; it also confirmed the local elite's sense that *these* Greeks were
especially recalcitrant.

These dynamics are given a particularly telling twist by the fact that they
are enmeshed in the national discourse about whether Greeks "are Western"
(or "European") or not. This is explicit: a goldsmith, for example, agreeing
that business partnerships were notably unstable in Rethemnos, contrasted
these, unprompted, with their counterparts in "the Anglo-Saxon countries"
and attributed the difference to "mentality," a popular device for explaining
away differences of status in the global hierarchy of value.[70] In this scheme
of things, Greek artisans—representatives of a tradition defined by a so-
called mentality—are trapped in a time warp not of their own choosing.[71]
One foreign-educated leather designer commented that the Greek attitude
to manual labor would have to change, "so that he won't think that if he goes
to do a job of work he's some kind of humble porter." The notion that manual
labor is demeaning is indeed common in Greece, even though labor is also
seen as more honest than the habits of the lazy drones in the public service
sector; the moral high ground emerges as a weak compensation for political
advantage, but it is all, in the internalization of the global hierarchy of value,
that many artisans feel they have.

From this perspective, the artisans' fate corresponds to the bodily character of what they do. By definition, they are people who work with their hands;
they commonly profess to despise learning from books. They are "people
who craft [in] life"—that is, people who deal in reality rather than abstraction
(the abstract noun derived from these terms means "cottage industry" in the

generic sense)—and, socially, they are "people who struggle for a living."[72] They are aware of their central role in the definition of local tradition; some, too, are quite aware of the ways in which the elite can use this to limit their economic access: "We are the spinal column of the Cretan economy. We're the ones! The craftsman and the 'small and medium operator'[73] and the small merchant. It's we [who perform that role]!" Moreover, they are prepared to boast about it; doing so is the one—very precarious—rhetorical claim they can make on the attention of a state they say grievously ignores them. The state "does not look after us. For them, we're the last hole. But in substance we are not the last hole; we're the base. Despite all that, they take no account of us." There is no doubt that the artisans can quite clearly perceive how the pedestal of tradition serves to limit their hopes for a better life.

Artisans regard the state's neglect of their interests as far from benign; they suspect that it is not accidental at all. There may be some basis to their suspicions, but to understand how that could be the case we must again turn to the wider, international context in which questions of value are negotiated. As societies like Greece come to grips with the problems of giving local form and content to some notion of modernity,[74] leaders begin trying to excise the rude masculinity of a past era from their midst. Yet to do so creates another tension out of underlying paradox: the most intimate part of human existence—the human body—is also the commonest metonym for its most public manifestation. The term "body politic" captures the ironic predicament of every relatively new nation-state, especially one born in revolution against a tyrannical oppressor. That nation-state must now at least appear to impose its own authority—a very public matter—on the spaces of its citizens' privacy that it has "liberated" from the erstwhile oppressor but that the state regards as still bearing the incivility of that oppressor's culture (or lack of culture, in a more explicitly Eurocentric view): domineering maleness, sexual predation, boastfulness, uncouth manners and music, rank self-interest, and disregard for all but close kin. The citizens themselves may not be best pleased by such reforming zeal, which treats the familiar and the intimate as antithetical to the values of officialdom and of modernity.

Citizens' bodies are in fact unlikely ever to become docile, reliable instruments of official ideological claims despite numerous historical attempts to achieve that end—notoriously, in the case of Italy, through the application of a specialized form of "criminal anthropology" and other variants of civic cleansing.[75] To the contrary, the citizens' bodies may represent the very antithesis of everything a government wants to establish—of what Norbert Elias, himself unconsciously reproducing a global hierarchy of value that was already well entrenched when he wrote, called "the civilizing process."[76]

Indeed, they are the ultimate target of that process, which may be a good deal less predictable and unilineal than Elias, again much like the exponents of official state values, appears to suggest. The importance of citizens' bodies as the locus of this intimacy is a challenge for the state, which seeks to control the space in which people move and the meanings they create. The state seeks legitimation in its claims on tradition and in the embodied loyalty of its citizens, even as those claims also subvert the civilizational pretensions of the state. The most irrepressible and irreverent citizens may often be both the foot soldiers and the most impassioned exponents of an ideology of national freedom that both sustains their loyalty to the nation and yet also feeds their insubordination toward the state and its regimes of manners and tact. In Greece, the mountain shepherds of Crete push that tension to an extreme, and their urban artisan kinsfolk are not necessarily very far behind them.

The temptation, however, has always been to focus, not on how bodies *fail* to conform, but on how the state tries to achieve uniformity among its constitutive bodies, institutional and somatic. This does not explain how bodies can convey some pervasive aspects of identity the state would prefer to ignore as unseemly and potentially embarrassing. When a rare social analyst emphasizes individual bodies, it is usually as a site of "resistance" rather than as part of that intimate space of departure from official norms on which the very existence of the nation-state—with its never-ending need to reconcile ostensive unity with internal complexity and diversity—always depends. Thus, for example, Susan Brownell has persuasively shown how the Chinese communist state has regimented athletic bodies in the national cause, and Arthur and Joan Kleinman have richly documented the ways in which individual bodies, displaying what are locally deemed pathological conditions, thereby register the failures of the regime.[77] Yet we still miss, for China as for all other parts of the world, a systematic understanding of how local and national cultural understandings are reproduced in ways that allow citizens to lay passionate claim to national identity even as they disobey the state's laws, misbehave by all the local standards of propriety, engage in ribald and obnoxious acts, and cheat and swindle their way to economic prosperity or political comfort—all aspects of cultural intimacy, that space of disorder that is, paradoxically, necessary to the effective functioning of any bureaucratic state that expects to get the loyalty and a semblance of uniform values out of its riotously multiform citizenry.

The state cannot do without the spaces of cultural intimacy because its most fundamental metaphors—body and family—presuppose the presence of comfortingly familiar social alternatives to propriety. If those key metaphors are to be persuasive, the official world must also at least tacitly accept the existence of a "backstage" space, to expand Erving Goffman's term, in which people can, literally and figuratively, let their hair down.[78] Ethnography in the working spaces where "tradition" is produced, reproduced, and modified, in the midst of a town wrestling with both a comprehensive historic conservation effort and a precarious but significant tourism industry, would seem to offer an especially illuminating view of how those metaphors are grounded in the experience of everyday labor, love, and life.

Chapter Two

Schooling the Body

The Aesthetics of Reproduction

In the noisiest of Rethemnos workshops, where the shrilling of machinery cutting through wood and metal and the acrid stink of shavings and filings may befuddle even the most transient of visitors, apprentices bend to their tasks, fetching heavy wooden beams and lifting objects perhaps half their own size, their regimented silence contrasting dramatically with the mundane racket around them. Many seem meek and wear an expression that shifts uneasily between adolescent resentment of a world they do not yet know how to control and boredom from the deadening routines of work in which, at every turn, they are prevented from taking any interest beyond the requirements of obedience to the master.

Appearances, as we shall see, are deceptive; and the mask of indifference may well conceal lively interest and engagement. Nonetheless, a blend of discipline and boredom predominates. In these workshops, artisans and their apprentices are primarily fashioning objects. They are also, however, simultaneously working—in Susan Terrio's telling phrase—toward "both social maturity and a work identity."[1] They are fashioning selves—or, more precisely, modeling—relations among selves. Apprentices' bodies are trained into a set of what Pierre Bourdieu has called "dispositions," the end product of the processes of systematic inculcation that "sediment" the structures of power and social hierarchy in people's bodily habits, which come to include but do not privilege the basic techniques of craft.[2]

Bourdieu's formulation is an attempt to explain the apparent passivity with which ordinary people accept the dominant norms of their society. It is an extremely important argument, which elaborates the Marxist concept of ideology as "false consciousness" by providing an explanation of both its underlying motivations and its regulative effects. But Bourdieu's model nevertheless suffers from a significant weakness, which it shares with its more orthodox Marxist precursor. He fails to recognize the power of individual agency to overcome the imperatives of such inculcated habits. I do not mean here to romanticize the notion of agency as a thinly disguised version of individualism, which is perhaps most usefully seen as an ideology equating Western identity with the power to make independent judgments and choices. Indeed, in an important sense, Bourdieu's model reproduces the logic of the powerful. In the case of artisan-apprentice relations, it initially seems very attractive precisely because the artisans do appear to be trying to drum a particular kind of passive acquiescence into the hapless youths who work for them. Just as artisans try to keep their apprentices bored, without recognizing (or at least admitting that they recognize) that the *affectation* of boredom can mask a very active and agile interest in what is happening in the craft workshop, so Bourdieu lets inculcation *overdetermine* the ways and reasons of the subordinate.

In this regard, Dorinne Kondo's study of Japanese artisans is extremely suggestive.[3] In a society where machinery may be conceived as an extension of the self, standardization and the capacity to produce aesthetically pleasing objects that conform to dominant conventions are highly valued; deviations are quickly criticized. In contrast to the satisfaction that Japanese artisans may take in their use of machines as extensions of their own selves, for example, Kondo's willingness to settle for an imperfectly wrapped piece of confectionery provoked the kind of critical reaction that some non-Japanese observers would view as repressive uniformity. A strong analogy subsists between the production of objects and the crafting of a selfhood; whereas the Japanese place heavy reliance on ideals of convergence and self-effacement, however, their Cretan counterparts are often more interested in expressing individuality. Huge quarrels break out over accusations of stealing others' designs, especially in the more elaborate crafts such as leatherworking. But a truly proud artisan may desist from accusing his imitators, and it is clear that he actually fears that they will turn the tables on him, so that he will end up accused before his peers of having no recognizably individual skills of his own.

Individuality, however, is not equivalent to originality. Quarrels are not primarily about aesthetic plagiarism but involve a social offense that threatens the accuser's manhood by cheapening his often quite small technical and stylistic improvements and rendering them commonplace.[4] The fact that artisans have no "reinforcement," as one artisan remarked, springs not from an absence of copyright laws so much as from the fact that in an arena of small differences, whether technical or social, reputations are fragile and chimerical; moreover, a violent quarrel may be much more demeaning for artisans in the small-town setting of Rethemnos than in the mountain villages, and it may also end in humiliating physical defeat. Artisans, who must display confidence in order to maintain their reputations, are thus constantly beset by economic and social risks that challenge their ingenuity—their craftiness—and recourse to the excuse of bad luck is only a weak, conventional, after-the-fact attempt to staunch the social hemorrhage.[5] There is in effect no context in which an artisan can claim true originality without risking derision for his pretensions of greatness, just as there are few situations in which a person's social standing is safe from gossip. The social context is also one in which the larger, concentric "realities"—the local arena is experienced as a microcosm of a country beset by tragic flaws of underhandedness and vindictiveness—are inescapably compelling. This concentricity is explicit: "Either you'll kill them or you'll respect them and say, 'That's the reality in Greece, and I have to make a new design each year.'"[6]

The play of imitation and invention is thus clearly a social matter, but it is also, and concomitantly, an aesthetic one (as indeed it is in social interaction, in the sense that everyday performances of the self are judged by criteria of taste and appropriateness). The yoking of aesthetics with something like a claim on absolute originality is a refraction of Western European ideological individualism; there is no universal principle that logically requires that such a connection be made. Even the idea of tradition itself is not simply a modernist conceit but a distinctly Eurocentric one to boot; among the Tiv of West Africa, for example, a highly eclectic pattern of borrowing from other cultures without developing a distinctive Tiv tribal style reflects an ideology of selfhood that recognizes any place as home and thereby suggests radical alternatives to the European model of the territorial national culture.[7] In much the same way, the link between originality and individualism—used by generations of art historians as the basis for separating non-European traditions from "high culture"—is extremely parochial and contingent, an example of the Western proclivity for seeing otherness as an absence or lack of some quality especially appreciated in Western cultures.

In consequence of this ethnocentrism, the local orient of the Balkans suffered at the hands of Western European art historians until well into the twentieth century.[8] The Byzantine aesthetic (to which Cretan artisans are heirs, some more self-consciously than others, and which was certainly incorporated into enduring forms of monastic discipline such as those I will mention) treated works of religious art, not in terms of originality, but as embellishments of a single original painting; such embellishments were admirable precisely in the degree to which outstanding skill sustained a sense of reproduction.[9] The (always male) painter might sign his name, but he was the instrument of a perception rather than the creator. Making such images was, after all, an exclusively divine prerogative. This is why photographic reproductions of icons apparently serve their ritual purposes as well as freshly painted ones; the greater intensity of color that can so easily be produced by mechanical means enhances the significance of the original painting in religious terms. This tension between submission and authorship is still evident in the way in which today's Cretan artisans constantly pronounce themselves happy to have been more than competent but never claim to be artists who have produced something entirely new. Crete had a strong tradition in icon painting during the later Venetian years; it is represented especially by El Greco's teacher Damaskinos, whose art reflects some Italian influence within the constraints of the local aesthetic, but whose themes and motifs remain strictly within the religious canon.

One might perhaps have expected Cretan artisans to have absorbed a sense of originality from the Western European "high art" canon to which they were exposed, and that this would have sat well with their aggressive assertion of individual pride. Instead, it is clear, the Orthodox religious aesthetic prevailed in art, while Cretan male assertiveness has less to do with eccentric individualism than it does with the deft manipulation of clearly defined conventions—an assertive act within what Michael Jackson has acutely pinpointed as "the human struggle to strike a balance between autonomy and anonymity."[10] Every swashbuckling act of animal theft, every daredevil acrobatic step by the man leading a line of his fellows in dance, every clever verse and every matching riposte—each of these demonstrations of masculine competence is an elaboration of recognizable form, to which too precise an adherence sits ill with the aggressive insouciance of swaggering manhood, but from which too great a departure elicits disapproval and contempt. Indeed, the art of being a Cretan man entails constantly balancing on a knife-edge between convention and invention—and making sure that both are fully in sight. Self, craft, and performance—all are realizations of the same historically embedded and culturally distinct tension.[11]

From their lack of interest in pure originality comes the extraordinary willingness of Cretan artisans to produce objects that on occasion resemble almost tauntingly crude copies of fine originals. Those originals may not exist, but the repetitive production of familiar motifs hints at their presence in the collective imagination. A pair of paper-holders each with the bespectacled face of early-twentieth-century Cretan political hero Eleftherios Venizelos, for example, sold to me by a local carpenter, is not merely a specimen of kitsch; reproductions of a face seen in plaster busts and photographic images everywhere on the island, these portraits are also a secular, political version of the religious icon, and, as such, are deformations of the conventional image

Figure 2 Paper-holder with portrait of Eleftherios Venizelos (made about 1994).

that they thereby make more recognizable (fig. 2). What to me makes them rather hideous is analogous to the bright coloring that makes a mechanical reproduction of religious art appealing to the official ecclesiastical aesthetic. What goes for the portraits applies also to their subject: Venizelos is emblematic of the Cretan male who transcends his local origins while remaining true to them. Drawing and redrawing his image is a way of affirming the conventions of a personal aesthetic. One prominent Rethemniot burgher took that embodiment even further by dressing like Venizelos, affecting the same combination of thin-rimmed glasses, goatee, and lamb's wool hat. The art here is to imitate but also to foreground one's competence as an imitator and one's daring at stretching the limits of resemblance, whether in one's own body or in the products of one's hands and the tools they control.

This relationship between convention and production seems significantly different from the confectionery manufacture described by Kondo, and the contrast is instructive. It shows that ideas about originality and aesthetics in craft production, however specific they may be to particular cultural contexts, may nevertheless be alike in reproducing or even influencing the way in which social relations are conceived. The homogeneity that is so often attributed to the Japanese is clearly an ideological construction.[12] So, too, is the ideal of European individualism. It should not come as a surprise that the formal qualities of these stereotypes are reproduced in goods regarded as typical of the cultures in which they are crafted.

Such crafting is also always liable to externally derived processes of cultural and social change. In a study of the reconfiguration of urban space in Bangkok, for example, J. L. Taylor describes the official response when religious figures—wielding the only kind of authority that the state has good reason to fear—offer alternative models of bodily discipline to those already incorporated in the state's endorsement of a particular hierarchy (the Sangha, or supreme monastic council that controls the organization of the official religion of Theravada Buddhism). Under these circumstances, the officers of the state exhibit an air of decided discomfort. This is especially true because these new models, which arise in contexts of the sudden social dislocation that high-speed urbanization and what in another context Douglas Holmes calls "fast-capitalism" have brought,[13] threaten the comfortable family image out of which the entire ideological structure of the Thai state (like that of Greece at various times) is presently constituted. If the project of configuring urban space aims at inducing conformity through the habituation of the bodies of the citizenry to harmony between themselves and the encompassing polity, nonconformist sects that focus on bodily practices represent a very substantial threat to order and stability. Conversely, we may suspect, the maintenance of a concern with "traditional" craft production could serve as a powerful antidote to such insubordination, channeling it into a hegemonic conservatism, at once political and aesthetic, that in many countries seems to attract artisans even (and sometimes especially) when it serves them ill.

Monastic Models

Both Greece and Thailand are heirs to long traditions of monastic discipline with a deep concern with the control of bodily movement and desire. In these traditions, the teacher controls the body of the novice much as the state controls the bodies of its citizens. Thai men all normatively served a period of monastic service (and most still do) as a matter of course; this means that virtually every Thai artisan has experienced monastic discipline directly. Although Greek monasticism tends to be a lifetime vocation, monks are often recruited from poor families such as those from which the artisans themselves come, and monks are frequently local arbiters of disputes; moreover, the monasteries employ local herders and farm workers. Monks are familiar figures in both societies, the respect they inspire tempered by familiarity. It is thus important to see what monastic models might have served to reinforce the habits of discipline characteristic of the artisanal workplace, and what happens to these as the teaching methods of the modern schoolroom replace older models of contemplation, repetitive labor, and backbreaking hours in fixed and thoroughly supervised bodily postures. As early as the fourth century, in the writings of the theologian St. John Chrysostom on the appropriate forms of boys' schooling, we see early echoes of attitudes that still pervade the increasingly marginal spaces of artisanal workshops in Greece. Moreover, the monastic tradition that Chrysostom did so much to formulate exercised a substantial influence on pre-independence Greek schooling, virtually all of which, with the exception of a few privileged urban centers, lay in clerical hands and was well concealed from both the surveillance of the Ottoman authorities and the ardor of Western-trained secularists.

Greek artisanal apprenticeship shares some other, equally obvious features with monastic discipline, not least of which are the suppression of outward sexuality and its subjection to a regime of bodily humiliation through labor. A Rethemniot floor-maker who regarded his thirteen-year-old apprentice as a friend with whom he could enjoy a good time at a local taverna nevertheless insisted that in the old days, the moment an artisan and his apprentice entered any place of work, their mien would be absolutely devoid of affect: "That is, they regarded work as a church. Then you get the respect [sevasmos] that's needed." Allowing for a degree of wistful nostalgia, this artisan's evocation of an older moral order still clarifies the sense that artisanal work, like the disciplined life of the monk, should ideally be beyond the reach of embodied emotion; as with religious devotion, the artisan's sensate body must be suffused with "love" (aghapi, New Testament Greek agapē) for the work, an emotional commitment modeled on the Christian love the name of which it bears.

The early church, as one local scholar has noted,[14] regarded the inculcation of habit—for which it even used the terms later adopted by Pierre Bourdieu, doxa and hexis[15]—as a form of "tyranny," to be abjured when it has originated in evil but to be embraced when it emanates from the church. This self-professed tyranny is an authoritarian model in precisely the sense intended by Talal Asad and, as such, perhaps more typical of a wide range of practices in the Christian world than of even the relatively narrow compass of activities we call religion elsewhere.[16] Asad emphasizes the importance of establishing the cultural specificity of disciplinary practices that, in Western Christianity, are associated with the search for pure theological wisdom. In Greece, by contrast, these practices are instead grounded in a view of humanity acknowledged and even appreciated as flawed and sinful.[17] In consequence, Orthodox ideas infuse everyday life in ways that often depart from state-sponsored ideals concerning the relationship between body and place. In an activity as close to monastic schooling as craft apprenticeship, we should hardly be surprised to find evidence of a pervasive, common idiom of bodily discipline and its social management. One local commentator explicitly speculated that a self-professed communist friend who worked as an artisan by choice rather than necessity, and who frequently extolled the virtues of manual labor, was unconsciously invoking a Christian model. This local awareness of such a connection shows that the idea of a monastic template is not particularly far-fetched. I do not want to overemphasize the significance of religious models; Cretan attitudes may owe as much to Islamic-Ottoman guild practices as to ecclesiastical antecedents, and antiecclesiastical sentiment is strong among many rural Cretans and left-wing urban dwellers. There is nevertheless abundant evidence that in Greece religious understandings of lived space may persist even among those who explicitly declare themselves to be atheists.[18]

Chrysostom's advice to teachers reproduces attitudes toward discipline and punishment that resonate with what happens in the artisanal workshops and in the privacy of the home far more than with the practices of modern schoolteachers. Among these parallels and continuities we should especially note the injunction to use frequent threats of physical punishment but not to carry all of them out; Greek parents today frequently announce, "I'm going to beat you!" but know full well that a reputation for violence against their children will cost them dearly in the social arena.[19] The family provides a source of trust, but it also becomes a place where children learn contrastively to objectify the possibility of distrust instead; when the boys move to their first apprenticeships, these first harsh lessons are amplified and rendered materially consequential. Goldsmiths' apprentices are given a piece of cheaper metal to work; tailors' assistants are set to work sewing a useless piece of cloth. There is no obvious trust here at all; when it is earned, the assistant is already more of a partner than an apprentice.

Even in the harshest of workshops, threats may be reversible. One goldsmith, his exasperation with his sole apprentice's constant absences brought to boiling point by a request to go to Athens for a sports event lasting a full week, told the boy that if he was going to be away so long, he should stay away permanently. The goldsmith assured me that he would never take the boy back. Nevertheless, amid a sense of awkward sheepishness on both sides, return to work he did—although now his wage was replaced by the possibility, depending on good behavior, of "pocket money" *(khartziliki)*.

It is not clear whether the artisan succumbed to pressures from the boy's father, a neighbor and friend, to whom he first thought of excusing the firing by claiming that there was not enough work to sustain an apprentice, or whether the threat would never have been carried out anyway. For practical purposes it does not matter; apprentices have enough experiences of this sort not to worry too deeply when their masters rage at them and conjure up the direst of consequences: they must both fear those consequences and find ways of riding out the threats with at least a semblance of nonchalance, because no master craftsman wants to rely on timid apprentices.

This is especially true today, when even inadequate apprentices are hard to find; theirs is a sellers' market to a perhaps unprecedented degree, a factor that increases the ambiguity of the power relationship between artisan and apprentice. As one disgruntled employer complained, according to a local teacher: "'I'm not telling him off,' says he, '[or] he'll leave.'" The father of the goldsmith's apprentice did tell me that he read his son the riot act—but it is not clear whether he really did or saying that he had done so was simply his way of asserting a claim to parental authority. Perhaps, too, it carried just a hint of the old expectation that fathers should be totally unsympathetic when their sons complain about working conditions, since apprenticeship furthered the goal of eventually socializing sons into full independence and manhood.

A Theology of Insubordination?

From childhood to adolescence, from home to workplace: these are distinct stages in the development of an attitude of deep suspicion toward the social world. The pedagogical model is clearly prefigured in Chrysostom, who claims that the excessive use of corporal punishment induces habituation and thence contempt, undercutting its potential as a deterrent. The idea that threats are pedagogically more effective than conclusive action seems curiously similar to modern Greek attitudes, suggesting that to some extent he countenanced the development of a personality that was not cowed in spirit but only submissive in manner; indeed, Chrysostom argued that the entire family circle, from the father to his slaves, should tease the children of the house so that the latter would learn to control the outward expression of anger.[20]

This reading of Chrysostom emanates from a local source and thus sheds light on contemporary Cretan bourgeois religiosity. It is especially salutary because the scholarly tendency is to "read" Orthodoxy through the lens of a Western, post-Reformation version of Christianity in which such an emphasis on self-presentation would seem duplicitous, if not downright hypocritical. Yet virtually all the ethnographic accounts of Greek society concur on the importance given, quite openly (to underscore a paradox), to social appearances over personal realities and show that this attitude has cosmological underpinnings. It is, after all, God who "wants things covered up."[21] A measure of hypocrisy may be sinful, but not venally so; it is part of the legacy of Original Sin that defines all members of the Christian ecumene in general and all Greeks in particular.[22] And was it not Christ, after all, who sanctified and exemplified the devious Greek who might steal from his neighbors but who shared with them a collective antipathy to everything represented by the bureaucratic authority that destroyed Christ and still imprisons these his humble followers on earth? Is it not the most powerful and active of sheep thieves who have the least pressing need to display aggressive braggadocio, but who instead gain enormous stature by demonstrating the self-restraint of those who can afford it? The social and the sinful are never far apart; both, in this Christian worldview, are dimensions of the blessed imperfection of humanity. And both, as it is important to recall in drawing parallels between the crafting of objects and the making of selves, are the very conditions that enable reproduction. The imperfections of the picturesque are products of a Christianity that has not yet encountered Weberian rationality—a moment that some Neo-Orthodox theologians would like to restore to a central place in national life.[23]

Dissimulation, moreover, is a way of imposing discipline on the self, and self-discipline is especially valued in Greek society as the basis for not revealing too much of one's affairs. In a world of sinners whose humanity lies precisely in that sinful condition, dissimulation is a virtue in its own right. Once we dispense with the false distinction between folk and official religion, the coherence of these teachings with the practical worldview of rural Greeks becomes wholly apparent.[24] The religious assumption that ordinary people are morally flawed had thus become well ensconced long before the arrival of the state and furnished the grounds for the calibration of this self-demeaning perspective to the emergent global hierarchy of value.

Especially suggestive in the local scholar's account of Chrysostom's pedagogical ideals is the exhortation not to elevate the achievements of the mind over the humble creativity of artisanal hands. Local artisans pick up this theme; the more left wing they are politically, the more explicitly they seem to endorse it. One boot-maker, a fluent speaker of English who has traveled widely and is well read in political theory, was especially emphatic that he had chosen to remain an artisan both because his life choices had been limited at the time and because he found manual labor more edifying than constant talk. Others chime in with similar expressions of disdain for the life of the pure intellect, an attitude which for many Cretans has been further exacerbated by the contemptuous labeling of mainland Greeks as "pen pushers" in everyday speech in general and in the writings of Kazantzakis in particular. In expressing this attitude, however, they fall into the trap laid for them by a condescending elite that professes to praise the honesty of manual labor even while socially despising those who perform it, much as working-class Englishmen find such attitudes cheerfully reinforced by their small-town capitalist employers.[25] An obvious internal parallel is the way in which priests enjoin poverty on ordinary people, who in turn deride the church as a "little shop," its clerical managers the true traitors to the teachings of Christ in their sheer greed and venality. Curiously enough, however, Rethemniot artisans are less explicit in attributing the same logic to the secular elite in its exaltation of manual labor; they never praise poverty as a virtue but do frequently speak glowingly of the virtue associated with manual work.

Religion nonetheless plays an important role in this attitude; Chrysostom, for example, is explicit about the importance of submitting the self to a humble social status. The encouragement that the educated lend such contempt for their own world and the exaltation of manual labor serves, it seems, as a means for persuading peasants and artisans that they should be content with their lot—a classic illustration of the operation of hegemony in perpetuating a "culture of poverty," on which it then heaps blame for the predicament of the poor.[26]

At least in Rethemnos, however, the artisans' acceptance of these views is far from comprehensive. The boot-maker just mentioned, for example, is a skilled exponent of conspiracy theories regarding the marginalization of the working poor within his local society, the exclusion of Crete from the centers of Greek power, and the international plots to keep Greece under the West's firm control—concentric oppressions that he connects into a single conceptual argument. In the limply hanging hands of the sullen carpenter's apprentice, therefore, his "helpless perplexity" the antithesis of manual dexterity, there may be visible, not evidence of an abiding incapacity, but, to the contrary, the first stirrings of that capacity for the silent dissimulation of real skills—what Greeks call *koutopiniria*, "dumb cunning"—that marks the male Cretan artisan as a member of his class.

It is a capacity that has long been recognized as both central to everyday survival under various kinds of authoritarian rule (the shadow puppet Karagiozis theater is a particularly clear expression of this)[27] and a barrier to the long-term acquisition of new powers and freedoms. The image of Greeks as antiauthoritarian rebels, prepared to fight for freedom at any cost, gives those in authority a way of explaining away (and often of punishing) the unruliness of the masses even as it lauds the free spirit that their actions exemplify. This is the same logic that makes of "tradition" both a virtue and a deficiency.

The encompassing context for such hierarchies of value is not capitalism alone but the Cartesian rationalism that undergirds it with the clear promotion of the mental over the material.[28] If we are to seek religious models for the artisanal experience, then, we must also probe historically back before the establishment of a formal state religion in the form of the Greek Orthodox Church, and beyond the accommodation of the church with the Byzantine and even the Ottoman authorities in earlier times. We should look instead to the monastic traditions that persisted more independently of temporal power. Chrysostom is thus more relevant to our present purposes than the ecclesiastical writers of the nineteenth and twentieth centuries. The Neo-Orthodox movement, with its attacks on Western rationalism and the separation of mind from body,[29] recovers some of that older perspective. Its perspective is analogous to the Thai dissident monks' rethinking of official Buddhism in that both are reactions to the scientific rationalism and modernism of the secular nation-state.

One problem we encounter in trying to discover the religious models that underlie artisanal pedagogy is that this is a society in which religiosity and masculinity are often at odds with each other. As Charles Stewart has pointed out, however, it would be a serious mistake to take the modern ecclesiastical leaders at face value and accept their—decidedly hegemonic—attempts to delineate the official teachings of religion from a socially grounded notion of "folk practices." Neo-Orthodox intellectuals would probably agree with his rejection of this Cartesian way of understanding religion in Greek society: for them, too, the essence of Greek religiosity is its oneness with ordinary social experience. If the category of "religion" as used by anthropologists has tended to reproduce narrowly Christian definitions, as Asad argues,[30] it is in fact an even narrower vision than he claims, being that of, specifically, a *Western* Christianity that fetishizes reality in contrast to pretense or hypocrisy. Christos Yannaras, a key exponent of Neo-Orthodoxy, even accuses the established church of "Protestantism." In a society where the artifice of dissimulation is central to acquiring social esteem, a religion that gave Western modernity its classic concern with the literal truth of scientific knowledge would never have been viable. That the rationalistic nation-state has so far failed to capture deep social acceptance in significant areas of everyday life is clear from the habit of distinguishing clearly and acerbically between the virtuous nation and the corrupt state.

The artisanal workshops of Rethemnos, deep in the heart of one of the most profoundly antiecclesiastical places in Greece, provide a setting for the nurturing of these attitudes. Truth cannot be reduced to book learning; dissimulation means that one can never know another's innermost thoughts; and the deep historical roots of Greek resistance to authority feed on a mode of knowledge transmission in which the need to cheat and steal one's way to understanding finds no opposition in a religiosity that—unlike its officially proclaimed ideals—extols the virtues of concealment and deception. This is not so much the hegemony of the capitalist system described by Gramsci and Willis, although it serves that hegemony, too. It is the hegemony of local power, vested in the moral authority of master craftsman and local priest, that—at the very moment that it appears to fly in the face of formally constituted authority—reconstitutes authority for its own advantage "on the ground."

Individualistic Bodies

Another angle of analysis is represented by an important literature, this time of a comparative and ethnological character, that focuses on practical epistemology, and specifically on the relationship between craft apprenticeship and the social production of knowledge. This is significant work, and its achievements should not be ignored.[31] At the same time, however, it is also so heavily focused on the transmission of, especially, the esoteric knowledge of craftspeople that it tends to ignore the social contexts in which that process is embedded, and of which it may be a relatively minor segment. At best, that context emerges as a specialized fragment of the encompassing society, with its own normative codes and idioms of performance.[32] John Singleton's fine-grained analysis of Japanese folkcraft potters, for example, focuses on the discipline to which they subject their apprentices; Singleton persuasively argues that these demands "are intrinsically related to traditional Japanese conceptions of obligation, learning, and discipline."[33] Missing from this account, however, is a sense of how far the training of the apprentices might have practical consequences in the larger cultural arena. Is this just one example of "traditional" notions of discipline? Is it perhaps a unique variant on the larger theme and worth studying for its own sake but of little value in rethinking those "traditional Japanese conceptions" in a more comprehensive way? Or is this framing of appropriate work habits—especially in a craft that has been deliberately reformulated as a modernist exercise in tradition—a way of working on the national culture at large and bringing it into conformity with official notions of Japanese tradition and national character?

The transmission of knowledge is a complicated process, and it is perhaps understandable that those who study it tend to view it as a closed system, especially as artisans appear to do so much to close it off from view themselves. Hans Buechler, for example, does argue for a more contextual approach but sees this as a way of illuminating the learning process rather than as a device for opening up larger social questions.[34] Singleton recounts the Japanese potters' reluctance to explain the principles of production to their pupils, forcing them—in an unconscious echo of what we shall be seeing here in a very different society—to "steal" the masters' skills with well-hooded but cunning eyes.[35] Yet to conclude that this secretiveness is typical of artisans because they are concerned about spawning too much competition for themselves, and to leave the matter there, begs the all-important question of what such secretiveness can tell us about the encompassing society's norms and practices. Is it exceptional—an artisans' eccentricity—or do the artisans in fact serve to focus a tendency that is widely diffused throughout the society as a whole?

These questions are of some comparative import; Greece is notoriously an "agonistic" society, whereas Japan has often been stereotyped (even by local commentators) as conformist and consensual.[36] What, then, are we to make of the fact that the idiom of "stealing" the craft persists in both? Do such patterns reflect only economic imperatives, or are they culturally diverse in what they imply? Timothy Jenkins begins to move toward considering such wider issues with a careful dissection of embodied practices among horse traders at French livestock fairs; he shows that the traders' embodied practices (he does not in fact discuss apprenticeship) reflect larger values, which they encapsulate and negotiate in the particular context of these fairs.[37] It is not enough to say that what happens in apprenticeship reflects larger social processes. We must ask whether examining apprenticeship as a limiting or extreme case might help us to identify related tendencies elsewhere in the encompassing society, rather than simply to spot plausible correlations. And we should seek to discover how far and in what ways apprenticeship equips young people to operate more generally in the larger society of which they are members.

Probably the most dramatic departure from the conventional anthropological view of apprenticeship is Jean Lave and Etienne Wenger's

Situated Learning.[38] These authors reject the study of apprenticeship as something intrinsically interesting in and for itself. Instead, they treat it as the site of what they call "situated peripheral learning," whereby a person learns as much about social process in general as about a specific craft by arriving at the margins of a group and discovering through experience what will work and what its social consequences will be. In other words, learning the craft—with all the obstacles that this entails—becomes their model for learning how to be members of their society.[39] Apprenticeship is less concerned with the transmission of craft techniques than with modeling the social values and attitudes within which the craft is practiced.

Apprenticeship, so often idealized as a mentoring process, offers an explanation of cultural transmission, to be sure, but it is less clear precisely what is transmitted. It is also, for some,[40] a powerful metaphor—more comprehensive and less deterministic than that of language acquisition among children,[41] for example—for the work of ethnography. As Lave and Wenger have argued, moreover, apprenticeship is less about teaching (many apprentices will tell you that no one wants to teach them anything anyway!) than it is about learning—learning from a context in which the apprentice is what they call a "peripheral" and "situated" actor.[42] Even this focus, however, useful though it is, remains primarily concerned with the apprentices in their role as emergent practitioners of specific skills. Lave and Wenger's perceptive analysis can resonate throughout the concentric social systems and values over which apprentices may gain a more comprehensive mastery than they ever do over the techniques of a specific craft.

These authors' preference for emphasizing reflexive learning over teaching of any kind—and practice over structure—is a radical and necessary departure. In particular, it challenges the idea of static hierarchy that is built into most descriptions of the process of apprenticeship. In the pages that follow, we shall see that apprentices often learn despite the fact that their masters, far from teaching them, often seem to discourage them quite deliberately from learning anything at all. But what they learn has more to do with survival in an often adversarial social environment than with the acquisition of specific craft techniques. They become effective and knowledgeable members of their respective local communities, in ways that often subvert the ostensible norms of those communities. What they learn, moreover, stands in a metonymical relationship to larger spheres of social antagonism and competition, so that their understanding of the social can afford us considerable insight into orientations at the national level, even among people who have never themselves even so much as entertained the idea of a life in artisanal craft production. Viewed in these terms, apprenticeship emerges as a training in the mastery of cultural intimacy at multiple levels from the most local to the international. It is an inculcation into the management and defense of, in a nutshell, concentric intimacies.

Necessarily, therefore, this analysis is not about the apprentices alone. These budding artisans are crafting, so to speak, crafty selves; and their craftiness is situated in a larger social context in which it is assessed, appreciated, or condemned. Here we return to the rich implications of Kondo's analysis. Whereas her study suggests a straightforward parallel between making objects and making persons, however, what we see in the Rethemnos material is more relational. It shows how the relationships among objects reproduce the relationships among selves. More specifically, concepts of individualism and atomism, deeply rooted in the ideologies of European identity and its opposites, are worked out in the artisans' notions of aesthetic creativity, standards, and reproduction, reinforcing in this way the sense of a direct link between the way in which the members of a given culture apprehend the role of agency and the production of distinctiveness in artisanal objects.

The selves thus seen in production are locally defined as intelligent, but in the "low" sense of cunning rather than with any implication of intellectual refinement. The popular Greek image of the uneducated person's "dumb cunning," an oxymoron embodied in the way the curious eyes of the slouching, superficially indifferent apprentice track the master's every move, captures the selfhood that artisans are willy-nilly inculcating into their young assistants.[43] To have an appetite for work is also to be cunning—one artisan made this quite explicit, equating the two terms—because deviousness compounds the desirability of what life has to offer.

Thus do young men (and a few young women) learn to be Greek, not in the official image of the idealized Hellene (although that bit of cultural camouflage is part of the encompassing package),[44] but in the mold that every Greek claims to be able to recognize in every other Greek: the crafty, wily, plausible, roguish, wheeler-dealer; the adventurous, self-aggrandizing defender of his family's reputation against all comers; the agile expert in the ethical justification of every act that contravenes official morality but serves the interests of household, kin group, and local community; a person whose exploits amuse by virtue of their frequent use of an assumed acquiescence or stupidity; and, above all, a person of great practical ingenuity, cleverly and productively masked by a display of dumb passivity. This is the intelligence of social actors who know the value of dissembling and do not find it either embarrassing or demeaning. They also know that those close to them will understand and appreciate it.

In much writing on apprenticeship, there remains at least a residual assumption that the core of what the apprentices learn is their craft. While that may be the ideology and the ostensible intention, it is commonly not what actually happens. Even when apprentices fail to learn much about the craft, however, they may acquire a good deal of practical social knowledge. Indeed, it may happen that the sheer frustration of apprenticeship prepares them well for a sometimes relentlessly agonistic social milieu. That is certainly what we shall see here. Apprentices are not engaged in a self-defeating exercise in failed learning but instead are constantly balancing between norms and practices in the production of, at one and the same time, material objects and social selves.

Crete is a place where masculinity is associated both with artisanal skills and self-confidence and with rebelliousness and displays of controlled violence. While Rethemniots are less inclined to display their aggression in public than are the armed shepherds of some mountain villages, shouting matches are far from rare and curses and threats abound. Men here do not easily submit to the authority of others, yet they must deal with a society in which others certainly wield greater power than they will ever possess; unlike the mountain villages, where power is sometimes spectacularly evanescent because differences in wealth can be erased by a dramatic raid on flocks or a bad harvest, Rethemnos exhibits relatively durable and distinct class identities marked by dress, speech, manners, and the use of time. It is a world in which working men's rebelliousness may serve to secure them temporary advantages in the immediate struggle for existence, yet it is this very feature that also, and simultaneously, frames them as weak, unmodern, and hopelessly beyond rescue—a category of hopelessly marginal, traditionalist, corrupt, and, above all, crafty people.

In the workshops of the artisans we see youths schooled to this unpromising existence, their bodies reconstructed as sites of both traditional discipline and sullen insubordination. They, quite literally, are the ones who inhabit tradition and who make it a *vioma*, a "thing lived." They are also its principal bearers, although Greece may not have them around in appreciable numbers for much longer. The prospects for apprenticeship, and thus for artisanship as a whole, are suffused with nostalgic gloom. "They've stopped having apprentices and all that. You see, if you go to the barbershop, there's no barber. If you go for a shave, there's no one to shave you. Nothing's left. Think how far men have come down in the world—they get their hair cut by women hairdressers!" Such is the obituary now being written of manhood in the Cretan style, to be read against the counterclaim that, "as Greeks, we've not been obliterated." From either point of view, artisans afford an especially useful point of access to the dynamics of Greek cultural politics because they are strongly associated with the rhetoric of "tradition"—itself a key component of most nation-state ideologies, at once the cornerstone of the European individualistic genius and the antithesis of European modernity.

The Bodily Economy and the Changing Marketplace

A walk down any street in the Old Town of Rethemnos reveals that artisans are still active there. But what one finds is more complex than the tourist agencies' proclamation of traditional arts and crafts might lead one to expect. Much of what the tourist shops sell is not made in Rethemnos at all; the ubiquitous woolen bags, some of them decorated with crude classical motifs or even maps of the island, are usually made in some of the remoter villages and brought to town by middlemen. The little busts of ancient Greek heroes and philosophers are produced in mainland factories; the ceramic coasters are largely from Rhodes; and the hand-painted copies of Greek vases are mostly produced in Athens and other urban centers.

Nor are all the artisans Cretan; a few are not even Greek. One goldsmith, a Syrian who married a local woman, supervises a group of local boys. He speaks Greek fluently and seems at ease with his local customers, yet it is clear that he has brought skills that are more highly appreciated in his native Syria, a country with its own strong sense of handicraft tradition. Such people are exceptions, in part because, until the heavy influx of migrant workers from Eastern Europe after about 1990 and Greece's full integration into the European Union, it was extremely difficult for a foreigner of any origin to obtain a work permit.

In practice, moreover, most people who live in Rethemnos assume that in general the artisans are the bearers of a specifically local, Rethemniot cultural heritage. Thus, another master goldsmith, an elderly Cretan, comes from a family that created several such establishments in Rethemnos; his surname still symbolizes the essence of the craft to those with long memories. Although there are possibly a few exceptions, local master craftsmen represent the craftiness of artisans in another sense as well: through the illegal status of their apprentices and the questionable practices to which they are forced by their extremely tight economic margins. The state is fair game for minor acts of deceit, especially since—as artisans are wont to say repeatedly—that state does nothing to help the artisans as a class. There was particular bitterness about the fact that as Greece entered the European Union the few artisans who were successful in getting bank loans were paying some 37 percent on the loans in bank charges and interest, for which the state gave them a tax discount of merely 13 percent. That "we don't *have* a state" is a constant plaint. It means, not that the state literally does not exist, but that it fails to achieve its own ideals, instead permitting bureaucrats to pursue their personal interests at the expense of the citizenry at large.[45] In this grim view, tax policy toward the artisans appears as a sustained effort to maintain class distinctions between property owners who (in their own view) deserved bank loans and those others (including the majority of artisans) who represented too high a risk for the bankers.[46] From the poorer artisans' viewpoint, moreover, there is no point in distinguishing among bureaucrats, bankers, and the generically wealthy: all are in a grand conspiracy against the poor, a conviction that serves to maintain the strong sense among the elite that the working class really does not understand the nature of economics.[47]

Artisans cope with this situation creatively; when they get caught, they rail against the bullying bureaucratic state and further exonerate themselves from the charge of foolishness by blaming traitorous neighbors. In reality, however, there is an expectation of some tolerance on the part of bureaucrats and neighbors alike. On a side street, partly removed from the officious stare of local officials, the furniture varnishing I have already mentioned violates local zoning regulations; the sharp smell of the varnish mingles with the alluring scents of baking *mousakas* and roasting meat from the restaurant next door. No one objects; minor illegality is a survival strategy that everyone understands and to which everyone expects to have to resort one day. (This is perhaps one result of the fact that Rethemnos has not become gentrified after the fashion of the center of Rome, where complaints about noise can quickly close down a carpentry shop.) But the more active and mechanized carpentry shops are located farther out or next to feeder roads, where the roar and grind of impatient traffic makes their shrilling and screeching and hammering less obtrusive. There are many ways of being crafty.

Machinery often creates the dominant sensory impressions, and here again one starts to appreciate the pressures with which artisanship in Rethemnos must contend. It is clearly going the way of artisanship in every other industrializing society, with larger numbers of individuals manufacturing increasingly simplified products and using ever more mechanized means of production: "Now, instead of taking on lads [as apprentices], we get machines!" This is partly the result of modernist state policies that require expensive injury insurance to be paid on behalf of every employee, a practice that began under the populist-Fascist dictator Ioannis Metaxas and subsequently developed to what for most artisans are ruinously expensive levels.

But these processes have been greatly accelerated by the end of the Greek state's economic protectionism after the collapse of the colonels' regime in 1974 and the emergence of a ruthlessly competitive, neoliberal economic ideology. In today's marketplace, "professionalism" *(epangelmatismos)* has come to mean commercialization and vastly increased numbers of competitors, rather than a concern with the quality of the goods produced or the local needs to be met. Today, villagers who arrive in Rethemnos as apprentices and aim to set up as independent operators imitate those businesses of which they see large numbers—notably jewelry shops, which flourish in part because of tourism—and thus increase the disequilibrium among categories of shops. Now many former artisans have opened shops from which they sell the mass-produced goods made for the tourist trade. Professionalism in this sense is radically different from the situation of specialty artisans in wealthier consumer settings such as expensive New York restaurants, Parisian chocolate manufacturers, Bordeaux vintners, Comasco silk producers, or Maine boatbuilders.[48] It now means a situation in which everyone is trying to enter the commercial profession. Standards of production are often not even at issue.

The number of mutually competing businesses grows rapidly in Rethemnos, which has mortgaged a significant part of its future to downscale tourism. The merchants who engage in this form of free-market competition are all obliged to lower their prices; usually the effects are catastrophic for the majority. Even tourism has shown limited growth, and, as the numbers began to fall again in the 1990s, Rethemniots—even those whose work was not directly with the tourist industry but would be affected by its vagaries—scanned the statistics with deepening gloom. A baker who admitted that there was still plenty of tourism in Rethemnos, and who also saw his profession as lucrative since "people want bread," nevertheless saw that trouble was looming: "It gets that way sometimes, that you are producing bread but you yourself have no bread to eat!" In addition, especially in the food trade, mass-produced goods all too easily displace artisanal products; the difference in price overcomes most concerns with quality.

Part of the problem lies in the changing expectations of customers. This is particularly the case with foreign tourists, who may be less interested in— or less knowledgeable about—the quality of what they eat but who expect to receive a kind of service that is often produced in the form of a simulacrum of local hospitality. This must be performed in a manner that runs counter to the established social habits of the place. Restaurants, shops, and bars, for example, often place a young tout to draw customers inside. While this appears to work for the less adventurous tourists, who (so local people believe) want to be persuaded that they should sample a particular shop, it is despised as the very antithesis of professional behavior by older artisans: "It is very easy to bring people to your shop, without a tout. And why? I [and here he added his locally illustrious family name, that of the jewelers just mentioned] am the reason. How would I bring them? I'd bring them with my own manner. That is, how? You, Michael, come, and you order a beer from me. But just a beer. So, Michael, why should I just bring it to you with nothing on the side? How much would a bit of cucumber that I could serve you cost me? Thank God, poor old Crete has everything. Tomatoes for free—we throw them away!—free cucumbers, free carrots! Eh, how much do they cost, tell me that!"

So older merchants, like the artisans who adhere to an older style of working, rely on that ever significant correlation between the kind of work they do and the persona they project and represent. Under the pressure of the inflated competition brought by the tourist trade, by contrast, when the persona of the artisan is already invisible to the undiscerning foreign visitor, the demand for quantity erodes the skill that is necessary for quality and cheapens the personal quality that is only recognizable in the skill of the craft or service provided. Within an economic system that increasingly demeans it, however, that skill is often the only form of cultural capital that artisans can transform into economic value. The effects of this kind of routinization, which is not unlike the deskilling that we see in artisanal sectors of industrial labor,[49] can be devastating. It is an inexorable march that sweeps all but the strongest along with it, and the neoliberal rhetoric not only expresses but materially contributes to that sense of inevitability.[50]

The process of creeping "professionalism" in this negative sense seems to affect merchants rather than artisans, but it also induces many artisans to become merchants who sell cheap and often shoddy versions of the goods in which they once invested their personal creative pride. It is fueled by the higher status and easier life associated with commercial success. It reflects a process that is also present, in a slightly different form, in the hill villages of the Rethemnos hinterland. There, shepherds and farmers began, in the 1970s, to open coffeehouses in accelerating numbers, in the hope of acquiring greater local authority rather than of making money. The desire to open a village coffeehouse was widely understood as the expression of a relatively benign form of self-regard (eghoismos). This self-regard appeared in the guise of a protocapitalist individualism that nevertheless, in an irony that foreshadowed what has happened to the artisans of Rethemnos, made any real economic advantage untenable, although it did provide the new proprietors with a comfortable and very public space in which to display whatever local authority they had. As a result, while these villagers became flag bearers for the ideology of competition, they were simultaneously co-opted into the lower end of the hierarchy that it created.

The sheer number of coffeehouses that opened virtually guaranteed that none of them would be economically viable, but at least their owners usually remained active in their pastoral or agricultural professions as well. The coffeehouses served as social centers and in many cases did enhance the proprietors' communal status.[51] In Rethemnos, by contrast, artisans who became merchants had no time to maintain their craft skills and so lost out on both counts. Those who failed to make a success of their new ventures were ridiculed, so they lost out socially as well as economically. Some artisanal trades dwindled to the point of virtual extinction; barbers, cobblers, tailors, and saddle-makers were particularly affected as the demand for their services evaporated, either because they were not needed or because (in the case of cobblers and tailors) ready-made products were cheaper and more convenient and fashions became more relaxed. There is an element of desperation in the proliferation of tourist shops, especially as the latter sometimes disgust the very customers they are intended to lure.

There are Rethemniot artisans who understand the dangers clearly. One jeweler and goldsmith, a member of a large family that has owned and managed several jewelry shops and workshops for three generations, favored the competitive expansion of artisanal and merchant trades and suggested that the rush to open large numbers of low-grade souvenir shops was not what real professionalism was all about. On the contrary, he argued, professionalism was a matter of competing in terms of quality, although he phrased it in the locally familiar, agonistic terms: "The real professional is the one who can struggle against others." In either reading of professionalism, however, the key remains the social fact of competition rather than the aesthetic criterion of excellent quality.

This is the language of both the agonistic social values of Cretan manhood and modern market capitalism. It rests on a vision of wide choice predicated on assumptions of individualism (which again matches both the Cretan masculine code and the ideological underpinnings of neoliberal capitalism): if you give customers a choice of ten pieces, they may find nothing to their liking, whereas if the choice is among twenty pieces, the chances improve, because customers want "something different." And those who are unable to produce this degree of variety, which was certainly not a feature of artisanal trades half a century earlier, are tempted to sell their businesses to wealthy operators, most of them from out of town, who see in Rethemnos a place where they can exploit the dearth of alternatives to make a quick and relatively risk-free killing. Locals who thought that professionalism was simply a matter of opening a new shop are rapidly disillusioned, ending up either on the sidelines without a shop of their own or slaves to the increasingly unremunerative servicing of package tourists' search for cheap souvenirs. The jeweler thought that the increased number of cafés in town would similarly improve the quality of the goods and services these establishments provided: "it creates a market [*aghora*], a *piatsa*." But that success is predicated on the assumption that it is acceptable for the weak to go to the wall, and indeed the recent history of Rethemnos commerce is littered with dismal failures that seem to confirm its marginality to the march of economic progress.

The neoliberal vision of "the market" thus sits well with a conventional male Cretan reading of "tradition" in Rethemnos. Just as the proliferation of village coffeehouses appeals both to local values of *eghoismos* and to capitalist ideals of competition, so, too, the image of trade that the competition-minded Rethemniot jeweler advocates, while appearing simply to ape the increasingly dominant ideology of neoliberalism, also invokes and revives older structures of social engagement. The jeweler appealed specifically to the idea of the market square, the *aghora* of the ancient world that he emphasized by glossing it with the Italian-derived term *piatsa* (from *piazza*): it does not seem too far-fetched to suggest that he was at the same time linguistically conjuring into existence an unimpeachably "European" cultural pedigree, from classical antiquity to the land of modern European high style.

This marketplace, however, also recalls older spatial arrangements that the modern neoliberal economy does not specifically encourage. It is an open arena where members of the same craft vie directly with each other while engaging in some degree of sociability. In Rethemnos, there were formerly many such areas in which artisans of a single craft—cobblers, saddle-makers, tinsmiths, carpenters—clustered together; the cobblers' street was famous for the way in which the artisans would start hammering nails in rhythmic unison every time a notably attractive woman started to walk along the street. Even in Athens, the jeweler remarked (no doubt intending to invoke images of greater modernity than Rethemnos could provide), this kind of clustering was once common: "Once we used to say, 'Plug Square.' A square in Athens. Because it was all electrical shops. And those guys all did something like shared business [*kinopraksia*], it seems, they raised some money and advertised together. They'll have said, 'It's a *piatsa*. If you don't find what you want in the first shop, you'll find it next door.' You don't have to run around everywhere." This kind of clustering has more in common with the old trade neighborhoods than with the frenetic competition that characterizes the new "professionalism" of many Rethemnos merchants today.[52]

One alternative to professionalism in this sense is to remain determinedly loyal to an obsolescent skill. That choice, however, can be very costly. Most artisans who maintain their skills find that they are locked into the role of obdurate traditionalists. Garage mechanics are a rare exception; this is one growth area for skilled artisans, especially younger ones able to escape at a sufficiently early age from other trades. Skilled electricians hover somewhere on the borderline between artisanal and professional status; plumbers are evidently unable to escape the humbler designation and were often mentioned to me as examples of an artisanal occupation.

In general, artisanship and modernity appear increasingly to be viewed as categorically incompatible with each other, except in the sense that quaintness can itself become a resource for enterprising artisans in a world in which it seems to be in short supply. This perspective at least represents a more productive response to modernity than the pious cultural obituaries and museumification efforts that various organizations sporadically sponsor. But the overall picture is a gloomy one. In effect, artisans face a chilling choice among accepting their role as the picturesque bearers of an obsolescent tradition, becoming merchants in a rat race that most of them are destined to lose, or joining an international labor force in which the price of modernity is to lose one's identity as a skilled and individual personality—the only remaining claim they have to a place in the sun of that same ideal of Europeanness that has historically brought them to this sorry pass.

Chapter Three

Hostility and Cooperation

A Hostile Relationship

It is a commonplace of the literature on southern Europe that social relations are agonistic—competitive, hostile, and sometimes violent. Even hospitality, which serves as the positive reading of Greek sociability for the purposes of tourism (which is rapidly absorbing the logic of sociability into its own commercial framework), is competitive. People frequently wanted to know what I had eaten at others' houses. They also expected me to maintain a demonstrative and unceasing show of appreciation by swallowing huge quantities of food and drink; only intimate friends ever—but rarely—showed any mercy toward a painfully full belly or accepted satiety as any sort of excuse for faltering. Even when they were less concerned with exercising symbolic domination over the visitor, they were always acutely aware that others might observe or subsequently probe for evidence of their inadequacy as hosts—the ultimate shame.

While the idiom of competition might be thought ideally adaptive in a context of global capitalism, the extravagant forms it takes in Rethemnos do not fare well within the aesthetic economy that has come to predominate along with the neoliberal economy. Even the constant disclaimers ("not that I wish to praise myself," "I want to stand tall in the marketplace," "I've never cheated a client") sound uncouth: their very transparency, in contexts where agonistic pride defines the tone and rhythm of everyday encounters, shows them to be a form of boasting in themselves.[1] Few indeed are those who master the subtle nuances of self-effacement to the point where it allows them to transcend their class origins.

In this respect, a constant feature of Greek social rhythms coincides with the difficult tensions that often subsist between artisans and their apprentices.

These tensions are notorious in cultural settings the world over.[2] We repeatedly learn that while apprentices accept offers of a position in the hope of learning a craft or trade, they soon find themselves thwarted and frustrated. The fear of competition from erstwhile employees, especially when the latter are recruited outside the immediate family or even larger group of kin, has a more or less universal status. Moreover, artisans easily find that apprenticeship serves as a source of cheap unskilled labor, whatever their motives in engaging it in the first place; consequently, they are often reluctant to allow those who work for them to move to more elevated levels of work and, by extension, status and pay. By maintaining potential rivals who are also members of competing kin units in a state of abject humiliation, they stave off the evil moment when others will elbow them aside and take over the management of all their professional secrets.

These forms of hostility, while common in this generic sense, are not universally patterned. To the contrary, they are actualized in the context of very specific local ideas about cooperation and competition. There are also differences among the various trades. For example, in Rethemnos a goldsmith's apprentice is expected to be politer and more softly spoken than a builder's or a carpenter's lad because the decorum of the shop demands this courtesy. The content of confrontation may not differ substantially from profession to profession, but some shadings of style mark an internal hierarchy that, by conforming to the larger pattern, also confirms its validity for the entire society. Goldsmiths, as Rethemniots often pointed out, handle precious metals; they also make artistic objects associated with rites of passage such as weddings and engagements. Theirs is consequently a field of relatively delicate social encounters and higher commercial risks. Since it is also closer to direct commerce, a few highly skilled apprentices escape to the large cities or set up as business operators on their own, and so succeed in elevating their social standing; their gentler manners are one attribute they can ill afford to neglect. Not so the carpenter's or the ironworker's apprentice, for whom the slightest hint of delicacy may be as much of a disaster in his immediate social setting as it is potentially advantageous for the goldsmith's assistant.

One feature that gives artisan-apprentice relations in Greece a distinctive cast is the local ideology of gender. Gender was central to the earliest anthropological work there, and—on Crete in particular—local identity is heavily invested in adherence to the canons of aggressive masculinity. Female apprentices are rare in Rethemnos except among seamstresses and hairdressers, and their relationships with their employers appear generally to be far less competitive and hostile than those among males. In pre–World War II times a few young women trained as cobblers' assistants, with the specific task of sewing the soles to the shoes. One artisan allowed his prepubescent daughter to work in the shop, and she, he pointed out with pride, showed all the potential skill of a male apprentice (and none of the insubordination, we might add); the girl's teacher, however, remarked that she was not doing as well at school as a girl of her intelligence should and thought that this was because her father was forcing her into the role of the son he never had. For his part, the father made it clear that he would not allow her to continue working in the shop after pubescence; at that point, both the risk of a sexual encounter and the fierce disdain of even the most casual passersby mandated her removal from the scene. While he was willing to make an exception for her when she was still a child, and even took pride in her interest and obvious intelligence, he was clearly determined to make sure that he could not be accused of fulfilling his paternal role by allowing her to continue as an artisan into womanhood. That would have been too large a blot on his own reputation.

Another feature in which there is considerable cultural variation concerns the nature of the preexisting relationships between masters and their apprentices. In some parts of the world, artisans employ close kin, and in societies with a strongly patrilineal ideology, such as China,[3] they may sometimes prefer to employ patrikin. Not so, however, in Crete, despite a notable sense of patrilineal solidarity. That sentiment is offset by the embarrassment of admitting that patrilineality plays any role at all. Not only is it seen as a mark of "Turkishness," but the risk that it might be exposed in the breach—as when an artisan fights with the agnates whose son he has just fired from his workshop—is too great to countenance.

Such differences underlie, and sometimes underwrite, patterns of artisan-apprentice interaction that are in themselves very widespread. Anthropologists have generally noted that in many, widely divergent social settings, for example, the fear of training future competitors appears to be directly linked to artisans' unwillingness to teach their apprentices very much at all. Indeed, what the apprentices learn they learn *despite* their masters' attitudes. There is little teaching but a great deal of what Jean Lave and Etienne Wenger appropriately call "situated peripheral learning"—the active acquisition of knowledge about social interaction and values from the margins of production, often in the face of massive discouragement that is itself both the instrument and the object of the apprentices' socialization. This pattern is not unique to societies known for the agonistic quality of their social relations.

Cretan male artisans do nevertheless exemplify the pattern, and the dramatic extent to which they exhibit it is culture specific—self-consciously so, in this age of intensified international contact and travel. They inhabit a notably agonistic society outside the craft workshop as well as within it. The anthropological literature on Greece is replete with descriptions of how men compete for prestige. Indeed, as Ernestine Friedl notes,[4] life in general is portrayed as a "struggle," in which the pitting of human resources against nature and the social competition among people are two aspects of a common disability. Such attitudes are not peculiarly Greek; they characterize the ethos of male workplaces, especially those involving brutally hard physical labor, around the world.[5] In the Greek case, however, the metaphor and experience are both embedded in a larger sense of being heroically under siege, whether as Greeks, as Cretans, or as Rethemniots. Through the embodied experience of grueling work—the struggle to make ends meet that is also a battle against one's social environment as well as to master the implements and materials of one's trade—Rethemniot artisans thereby sustain in themselves a powerful sense of aggressively defending tradition against its enemies.

Rethemnos is a rather genteel place and prides itself on its civility. Nevertheless, a large proportion of its working population originates, often only a generation or two back, in the hinterland villages, which display some of the most dramatic enactments of this agonistic social idiom: the blood feud, reciprocal animal theft, and verbal duels in provocative and derisive verse. Within the bourgeois setting of the town, the attitudes of craft apprentices to their masters often reproduce the agonistic proclivities of those who steal each other's sheep and goats.

There is, to be sure, a tension between these two aspects of Rethemniot social life. On the one hand, the desire to be "European," in a town that was an important center of learning and the dramatic arts during the so-called Cretan Renaissance under Venetian occupation (1213–1646) and that two decades ago became the seat of the humanities faculty of the University of Crete, predisposes many of its inhabitants to affectations of elaborate courtesy and gentility. On the other hand, the pride of an island that has always resisted invaders—or at least has claimed to do so[6]—requires that amour propre be respected at all times and defended to the death on occasion. In the retrospective frame of Greek nationalism, this tension has been recast as a tension between claims to a European and "civilized" identity and the shamefaced but affectionate acknowledgment of "barbarism" within.

This tension extends also to social life. Among those of more sophisticated education or greater wealth, elaborate courtesy and the avoidance of village dialect are the marks of urbanity. But others are less concerned with manners than they are with blaming their failures on neighbors, whose predictable treachery, in an agonistic society where life is lived as a zero-sum game,[7] indicates how far they are from that fondly imagined civilized world. Quarrels are far from infrequent, although they tend to break out less often in public spaces since exposing themselves as uncouth and, above all, un-civilized louts is the last thing both parties want; whereas in village life men defend their reputations with knives and wounding words, in Rethemnos they sometimes do so with excruciatingly correct manners and smug affectations of moral superiority and of a dramatically unconvincing "simplicity," as they call it, of lifestyle.[8] People sometimes end up not speaking to each other; that is considerably more dignified than a raucous quarrel and offers less purchase to malicious tongues quick to exploit any sign of rift—because gentility, too, can be a weapon of fierce rivalry.

Kin, Customers, and Curses

Rethemniots are quick to point out that theirs is a small town. Actions have immediate consequences; people know each other. In this context, especially problematic is the role of kin. Family life has a centrality not much less prominent than in the villages, and residents often visit their rural kin—especially parents and grandparents—on weekends and on feast days. But they also recognize that kin can be a problem. In a self-consciously modernizing society, the tendency to call on kin obligations is an embarrassment; it is also a thoroughgoing nuisance, since loans of this kind are often left unpaid because the borrowers can rely on their kinsfolk's reluctance either to expose the whole kin group to ridicule or to admit that they had been fooled. Yet kinship also provides the only *categorical* source of reliability: one *ought* to be able to rely on kin, and it is precisely this ideological commitment that allows the unscrupulous to exploit kinship ties. The point is amply demonstrated by an inverse example: a wealthy lady asserted that her parents' former servants were "now our closest kin"—by which rhetorical flourish she apparently meant that they exhibited the loyalty of true kin but were restrained from exploiting that link by the inequality that in fact subsisted between them and her. In the final analysis, all acknowledge that the real dangers come from actual kinsfolk who exploit the fear of seeming disloyal to one's own flesh and blood—the only people whose equality with oneself one can never contest in any public space. The closer the relationship, the greater the danger; one man even complained about his own younger brothers, whom he had taken on as apprentices and who demanded twice the pay the other apprentices were receiving while expecting, soon after they had begun working for him, to be recognized as fully seasoned, competent artisans—which they decidedly were not.

But if relations with kin are delicate, so, too, although for very different reasons, are relations with customers, many of whom represent a wealthier and more powerful stratum of local society. Engineers and architects who provide important custom for ironworkers and carpenters, for example, assume a manner of easy camaraderie with the artisans, but it is a manner that thinly disguises an unequal relationship of power. Here, the honorific address, *mastora* (master craftsman), may signal condescension as much as respect, particularly when delivered heartily in an affectedly folksy speech idiom that in reality makes few concessions to the specific forms of local dialect and that is met with studied politeness and carefully articulated formality on the part of the artisans themselves.

Apprentices witness the politeness with which their masters deal with such clients. Rethemnos is economically dominated by a local bourgeoisie of lawyers, teachers, engineers, architects, doctors, and entrepreneurs. These people often hail from the same hinterland as the artisans or are their children; one baker's son, for example, acquired a university degree and then joined a local firm of civil engineers, while his sister became a children's day care manager. The members of this emergent class have invested a good deal of cultural capital—in the form of education, ways of dressing, speech patterns, and modes of public consumption, including both conspicuous consumption (expensive cars and clothing) and affectations of simplicity (expensive food carefully presented as rustic fare)[9]—in placing a distance between themselves and those less fortunate citizens they somewhat condescendingly view as the passive embodiments of a tradition that they themselves both share and transcend.

Thus, the hierarchy is transmitted and reproduced. The artisan whose bullying and ranting leave the boys in his workshop cowering and sullen, or who refuses to let them do anything more interesting than fetching and carrying heavy materials, is himself the target of daily humiliations: by the engineer or architect who lectures him about the materials he knows profoundly from daily bodily contact or who shortchanges him economically in a buyers' market in which the educated can also demand all the external trappings of respect; by the wealthy bourgeois customer who lectures him about the importance of tradition and of his own role in perpetuating it but who also excoriates him for failing to live up to it; and by the local authorities who inspect the working conditions of his employees and threaten his livelihood with crushing fines, even though the artisan knows (or at least thinks he knows) that these petty bureaucrats would be unable to gain any purchase over him at all were it not for the backstabbing local community they are able to mine for incriminating information.

Clients do not always hold the upper hand. Those who habitually default on their debts, for example, can be boycotted without fear of retribution, if only because what they must fear most in such situations is gossip about their failure to pay. Artisans take pride in recounting how they stand up to both defaulters and educated clients who fail to show proper respect. In so pervasively agonistic a society, high status is both a weapon and a target, and those who fail to live up to the obligations that accompany it, and who thereby also show themselves to be both socially and professionally inept, are correspondingly in danger of public humiliation. Artisans must know when to call their clients' bluff and when to accede deferentially to their occasionally peremptory demands.

The double-edged character of this relationship is not lost on the apprentices, who hear numerous telephone calls and witness frequent visits from clients. Most workshops are small, and there is no soundproofing. The conditionality of the customers' power thus suggests an obvious parallel with the sometimes tenuous hold of the artisans over their apprentices, all the more so because the apprentices quickly learn that this authority is far from unchallengeable.

Thus, while artisans expect a degree of formal politeness from their apprentices, both sides acknowledge that this politeness may serve both as a dissimulation of actual feelings and as a cover for sneakily extracting as much information as possible about the performance of the craft from masters reluctant to share their knowledge. At the same time, it is qualified by expressions of growing intimacy when the relationship is a successful one. In years gone by, before World War II, apprentices would kiss the right hands of their masters as a greeting, just as they would those of their fathers, uncles, and godparents. Today, such formalities—which bespeak a potential intimacy grounded in respectful affection—have all but disappeared, although they live on in the imbalance between the masters' language of command and the apprentices' formulae of submission and respect.

Artisans do encourage apprentices to use informal language; for example, a pair of goldsmiths asked their shared apprentice to use the informal singular verb forms when speaking with them, but this agreement collapsed—and its conditional character became entirely clear—when the apprentice was verbally chastised for his unreliable appearance at the workshop. At that point, the apprentice hastily retreated behind the distancing device of the plural—perhaps because polite language offers a small degree of protection from some of the more colorful kinds of verbal abuse his two masters could heap on him. Apprentices in rougher trades, such as carpentry and building, generally use the informal singular, but this simply confirms their lowly and irredeemably rural status: the polite plural remains rare in most Cretan villages even between residents of vastly different status.[10] An apparent reluctance or inability to use the polite plural thus, if anything, tends to increase its users' subjection, in a manner that confirms the reproduction of inequality at multiple levels of social and cultural hierarchy.

The linguistic environment in fact encourages a pervasive sense that artisans can never escape their sometimes humiliating position in society. That view is, paradoxically, strengthened especially by those who do manage to escape (or, more commonly, help their children to escape through education). This is because the few who succeed in achieving bourgeois status take particular care to reproduce the distinctions in which they have so painstakingly invested. They do not sit on the pedestal of tradition; some, at least those who enter the elevated worlds of engineering and architecture or become successful entrepreneurs, help to keep those who have remained artisans firmly on the pedestal by praising their devotion to their crafts. The pedestal thus remains forever a tethering post as well. For their part, most artisans respond with a politeness that often masks resentment and even dislike, although it may also represent genuine, if distant, affection. Since the artisans' business usually depends on the patronage of the local bourgeoisie, they have little choice. Relationships between classes are couched in an idiom of mutuality and respect that nevertheless makes it clear where the real power lies—it is a mutuality, already noted, that is very much on the terms of the local elite. Thus, for example, an engineer who is building a new hotel and wants it decorated with Cretan folkloric and historical motifs, and who lauds his own simplicity of lifestyle while ostentatiously chaffing (and perhaps also implicitly threatening) the artisans who work for him, is yoking affectations of mutuality to an inflexibly hierarchical view of tradition as much in the sphere of social relations as in that of craft production.

An important part of apprentices' training thus lies in observing the ways in which their masters disguise any negative feelings they may have about an inequality that is also reproduced within the workshop, in the relationships between artisans and apprentices. They see their masters respond on the telephone with courteous phrases explaining away delays or calming fussy clients who want to check on every detail, and they hear the masters' comments once the clients are out of earshot. They learn fast that there is a disjuncture between surface manners and actual affect—perhaps an even greater gap, geared to higher stakes, than their relatively restricted home lives had hitherto led them to appreciate. They also learn fast that dissembling is essential to survival. Those who want to learn the trade, for example, take especially good care not to show the kind of interest that would immediately kindle the suspicions of a jealous master: by appearing bored, they gain themselves more freedom to absorb precious information.

Even when the exchanges of pleasantries are cordial, there is no doubt that a principle of noblesse oblige constitutes a key element in the bourgeoisie's cultural capital. Customers show that they have the right and the power to be gracious. Relations are especially sensitive when artisans have to enter the houses of wealthier people. A builder explained to me that he had always warned his apprentices, when they went into such a home in earlier days (when poverty enhanced the temptation to engage in petty theft), "Any apprentice who steals, no master artisan in Rethimno is going to take him on, because he will be [known and defined as] a thief." Such an apprentice would be an impossible liability for any artisan dependent on the goodwill of wealthier customers. Another artisan deliberately left money lying around in order to test the honesty of would-be apprentices, while a motorbike mechanic would test one of his apprentices by sending him to deposit cash in the bank while remaining vague about how much money he was giving him to deposit (he would then wait to see how long it took the boy to return and how much money eventually showed up in the account). This mechanic refused to rehire an apprentice who had been caught stealing on an earlier occasion, telling him that, had he worked in an accounting office, he would have robbed the shop of everything in it![11] In earlier times of great shortage, theft was so common that any sudden acquisition could provoke suspicion. A specialty baker who as a boy apprentice earned a tip for helping a photographer take a large can of oil to his house and then bought a couple of bagels (*koulouria*) recalls how he was immediately accused by his employer's wife of having stolen the money; such stories clarify the deep experiential roots of Rethemniots' mutual suspicion, since virtually any evidence can provoke the most unflattering interpretations, and theft constitutes an all-too-credible charge. Today, with tourism absorbing many young men, who become waiters to make easy money when they might otherwise have opted for the much harder and less lucrative path of apprenticeship, there is the fear that when the tourist economy collapses (as many expect it to do), these youths will resort to theft because, untrained and unequipped to earn a living and untrammeled by a master's discipline, they will be reluctant even to try more honest options.[12] Nor is stealing a male prerogative. One of the few female artisans still active reported that girls who worked for her would sometimes steal half-finished leather goods from her workshop; these incomplete objects were of no use to the thieves—except perhaps as a potential affirmation of cunning in a society where that is a socially valued quality.[13]

Artisans were generally adamant about punishing acts of material theft of any degree of seriousness. Their refusal to keep offenders in their employ gave them an opportunity to make ostentatious displays of their own sense of responsibility—a valuable way of building social capital and an excellent lesson for apprentices as well. (The female leatherworker was inclined to an indulgent view of her girls' small thefts, but she was mostly dealing with very small infractions, which she saw as practical jokes—the sort of insubordination all artisans come to expect of their more promisingly high-spirited apprentices—rather than as acts committed for significant material gain.) Other opportunities for promoting the artisans' own probity were seized as they arose. A builder described an incident in which a boy who worked for him broke the glass of one segment of a many-branched lamp and was then very upset at what he had done. The master swept up the shards of glass and awaited the owner's return. "So as soon as the owner returned, I told him, 'Boss, there's been an accident. We broke the glass of the lamp, so tell me where you bought it—they'll have the spare part—so we can go and get a glass and put it back on. I'll pay for it.' 'Master Dimitris,' he tells me, 'It doesn't matter, these things happen. No problem!' 'No, tell me where you got the glass.' In the end, the boss [i.e., the owner of the house] doesn't let me [pay];[14] he tells me, 'It doesn't matter. The damage is small'—because it wasn't the whole lamp that got broken, just the one bulb; it had four bulbs and just one broke." It would have been demeaning for a wealthy householder to insist on being compensated for such a small loss, but his refusal to accept it also, like the acts of hospitality that show who is in control, served to underscore the hierarchy of the situation. The young apprentice cannot have failed to note that his—and his master's—good fortune was also a form of potential humiliation.

Some artisans are very explicit about the need to teach apprentices the rudiments of good manners. Customers expect a degree of respect, and manners are also a key part of that global hierarchy of value in which relations of power are encoded. That encoding, which has been extensively studied by sociolinguists in Greece and elsewhere,[15] should perhaps not be read as literally as these scholars have tended to do: irony provides a basis for expressing a resentment that cannot be made too overt. Conversely, however, such indirection, no less than excessive bluntness, plays into the prevailing hierarchy of value. Both their politeness and their occasional outbursts of uncouth insubordination serve to lock apprentices ever more firmly into their subordinate position.

The apprentices are clearly not engaging, at least in any generic sense, in a pattern of resistance. It is easy to regard insubordination as a form of subversive activity, and it is also clear that apprentices sometimes see their minor acts of rebellion in that light. At the same time, as resistance their behavior would be remarkably ineffectual; it might more usefully be described as "performances of resentment," which would bring this analysis into line with the concentric motivation (*ressentiment*) of emergent nationalism as described by Liah Greenfeld.[16] The late Alfred Gell, observing some of my video materials, noted that they strongly reminded him of Indian house servants who would slow down their movements so as to upset their masters' intentions; this is particularly interesting in light of the old tradition whereby Cretan artisans would use their apprentices for domestic work (as *fameyi*). Slowing a work rhythm is not very effective as resistance and runs into the same problem as women's ironic mockery of male braggadocio: it not only has little practical effect but provides the stronger party with an excuse to maintain the upper hand.

What these apprentices evince thus has little to do with effective resistance. The performances of resentment that they stage, however, may be a relatively more effective way of communicating *insubordination*, a notion that begs fewer questions about intentions and effects. The effects are in practice quite predictable: they allow apprentices to claim a sense of injured masculinity in specific moments while exposing themselves to a degree of mockery that ensures that they will in fact never be allowed to reclaim their generic dignity altogether. In this sense, their predicament—not as the dupes but as the prey of a hegemonic system—reproduces that of their country as a whole. Whatever they say or do in self-defense tightens the noose still further. It is sometimes best to remain silent; even this is no solution, however, since silence can be malevolently interpreted as stupidity or obstinacy. True resistance hardly seems even an imaginable option here.[17]

Getting Hired: The Politics of Recruitment

Every day, on the main roads leading into Rethemnos from the hinterland, adolescent boys hitch rides with truck drivers to their workplaces in the town. This is the path by which many of them originally came to find their present employers. Many are truants from school or dissatisfied village children lured—like so many young work migrants around the world[18]—by the brighter lights of town. But the really bright lights are not to be found in sleepy, provincial Rethemnos, although the tourists have brought a measure of excitement; they are to be found, instead, in Iraklio and in Athens. Those who come to work in Rethemnos or who were born there and find work with neighbors or friends are tied to the town by family obligations or by sheer poverty; they hope it will prove the first rung on a long ladder of upward mobility, but for many it will represent the most ambitious horizon of possible advancement.

Apprenticeship provides a precarious living. Not only do potential employers usually refuse to pay their apprentices' insurance, but the relationship is fraught with fear: fear of the master artisan first of all but also fear of the tax office, the labor office, and the school truancy authorities. The illegality of most apprenticeship arrangements exposes both master and apprentice to serious legal and financial sanctions. The security that a few Rethemnos-born apprentices enjoy because their fathers and their employers know each other and must coexist in the same community does not extend to the village boys, who must also face a good deal of mockery on account of their uncouth manners and awkward and uneducated speech.[19] Then there is a practical concern on the part of the artisans themselves: an irate employer would more willingly fire an apprentice than risk the wear and tear of daily irritation or botched work. Moreover, an apprentice might find the situation eluding his direct control. One artisan, for example, had a young man and an adolescent boy from the same village working for him. When the older assistant was caught with drugs in his possession and had become completely unreliable, the artisan fired both of them because he felt that the younger boy would be embarrassed to work for a man who had sacked the boy's senior and covillager. The master artisan did not want to deal with the potential effects of that embarrassment, even though he thought the younger apprentice was hardworking and smart. Artisans cannot afford any disruption of routines that have become economically close to unsustainable. While today's apprentices are exposed to marginally less verbal abuse and considerably less corporal punishment, they face increased danger from an unsympathetic state and a runaway consumerist economy.

Apprentices in Rethemnos have never had an easy time. A century ago fathers would often bring their sons of ten or twelve years of age and place them with artisans in the town. Especially in the winding cobblers' street, they would try to arrive on a Monday, when the artisans, sleepy and hung over from weekend drinking and feasting, had little inclination to work and were more inclined to chat with these village supplicants. Frequently forced to try as many as ten shops before they could find an artisan willing to take on a new lad, a father would pay the artisan who finally offered a berth for the privilege of whatever grudging education the lad might sneak from under his taciturn new master's jealous eyes. If the father had no money, he would send village produce: a chicken, perhaps some cheese, or some oil.

The father would ask the artisan to get his son "straightened out" (*na ksestravothi*). This is a revealing metaphor: the lad's pliable body is implicitly likened to the materials of the trade (especially cobblers' nails, which novice apprentices were set to fixing because materials were expensive and in short supply). The emphasis is on physical, rather than mental, inculcation, the body a material component of basic production rather than the locus of a distinctive personal presence. Another revealing analogy between an artisanal instrument and an apprentice's body is the metaphor of the "razor blade" (*ksirafi*) for a novice's sharp mind, the revelation of which in a cobbler's apprentice, for example, used to be the sign that the lad should now acquire his own first *falseta* (small leather-knife). The identification of artisan with instrument is extremely suggestive: it signifies both a stage in the artisan's personal honing and a oneness of body and craft. The metaphor of "straightening out" is doubly instructive because another meaning of *ksestravono* is "make someone able to see properly." This second metaphor may seem an odd choice in a society where artisans actively try to prevent their apprentices from seeing anything at all, but that makes it all the more suggestive an indication that perhaps they are actually trying to teach the apprentices to practice some guile in learning through surreptitious observation—by stealing, as they call it, with their eyes.[20]

Nowadays, it is the effort of "straightening out" a new apprentice that represents the largest investment and the greatest risk: "as soon as you straighten him out, he'll leave you" (*apano ke tone ksestravosis, tha sou fiyi*), just like the nail in a new boot that one has successfully sold. If the phrase also suggests that the apprentice has learned to see properly as well, the apprentice now represents a greatly increased danger, thanks to the knowledge he can carry into a competing workshop. Was the investment of effort worth the returns and the attendant risks? The effort of straightening a shoe nail is small indeed; but an apprentice can represent a considerable commitment on the part of the artisan despite the more or less predictable displays of reciprocal indifference (nicely conveyed, in fact, by the rather trivializing metaphor of the shoe nail). The sense of a deeper investment appears in the further implication of straightening out as a form of moral management; a key concern of fathers used to be that their sons "should not wander about in the streets," a clear allusion, in local parlance, to womanizing, and a master would be as willing as a father to beat any lad he found walking in the street for any purpose other than an errand. In this regard, before World War II little had changed since Chrysostom's day, and the suppression of adolescent sexuality was almost monastic in its severity. This aspect of apprenticeship is clearly no longer operative; the relative sexual freedom that apprentices now enjoy parallels their freedom to switch employers more or less at will, as their masters' physical control over their young bodies dissipates in the mists of reminiscence.

In the past, the promise of that control allowed fathers to push their sons out of the protective embrace of home without much fear that they would become corrupted by the larger society. Fathers had every interest in disposing of their sons by apprenticing them to skilled masters. Not only would a craft trade offer chances of some limited economic advancement, but those chances would be enhanced by working for a comparative stranger—someone who was preferably not even a distant kinsman and who could therefore more freely impose the brutalizing discipline that, both sides agreed, could turn an indulged adolescent son into a true man capable of operating in the world beyond the family home. This transition might be ritually marked. When a cobbler decided that it was time for a novice to acquire his own cutting-knife, the *falseta* already mentioned, he would call in the boy's father and have him watch the boy's first attempts to cut sole and sides and shape his first shoe; the cobbler would not offer a single word of instruction, and the father had to pay for any mistakes the boy made, but this moment marked the transition from novitiate to being a *kalfas* and enjoying a measure of independence within the workshop.[21]

In the past, artisans paid their apprentices "pocket money" (*khartziliki*), if they paid them anything at all. Since the early 1970s, that situation has changed; now the artisans have to pay their apprentices, although they can still expect, as the owners of desirable skills, to get away with refusing to pay employment insurance. This refusal is clearly the result of economic necessity: an artisan's profit margins are minimal, and he will initially lose money to an apprentice's bumbling first steps, waste of precious raw materials, and lack of self-discipline. But at least today it is the apprentices who themselves usually come in search of work, and artisans know that the lads can move on with relative ease if they are dissatisfied. The boys, for their part, learn early on that small-scale but persistent defiance of the law is a normal way of life in their professions.

Matters were formerly far harder on the apprentices. Before the economic boom of the 1970s, no effort was made to consult the tastes of these children of poor families, who would often change trades several times before settling to something for which they had a modicum of aptitude. Some did not even earn the infamous "pocket money"; the best return such exploited youths could expect might be a pair of shoes (known as *kalikoma*) or a suit of clothes at the end of the year, during the festive season, and it would often be several years before they saw any financial reward at all. Humiliating initiation rituals of incorporation in which a new recruit was hazed by being made to bow under the master's workbench, beatings and curses, menial and backbreaking sweated labor involving no skill and therefore no learning, grumpy silence from the master and hostile glares from the older apprentices jealous of anyone who might threaten their own advancement by showing excessive skill or zeal, nights in a stable and daytime at incessant work—the list of miseries that greeted a new recruit is long and sad.

Before the 1970s, artisans were as much in a buyers' market for apprentices' services as they were in a sellers' market for the goods that they exclusively produced in an era before prefabricated products became common and cheap—at which point the now much smaller population of would-be apprentices was again at a disadvantage, since there were also far fewer artisans. Before that point, however, apprenticing the sons of poor families to skilled artisans represented the only easily accessible escape from the grind of harsh rural conditions or poverty in the genteel backwater of Rethemnos, described so eloquently by novelists of the period.[22] Artisans were men of confidence; dissatisfied clients could be sent packing with impunity. Occasionally, an incident may still recall that old artisanal pride. One widow arranged to have her house walls painted white and was told that she might have to pay for a second coat of paint; she agreed, but when the second coat was on and she was presented with the bill, she said it was too expensive after all; the artisan promptly told his apprentice to bring a bucket of black paint and hurled it at the newly painted white walls—and left without a penny for his pains but with his pride intact.

Inculcating Love

Because artisans could pick and choose among possible apprentices, they could also treat those they hired with studied brutality or indifference. Not all, it seems, were so minded; but against those who were, there was no recourse. An apprentice who went whining about maltreatment to his parents might be sent straight back to the tyrant's lair. And for those village lads who sought employment in Athens, conditions were no better, especially as employers were under no pressure from kin or neighbors they might have shared with their apprentices' families. One boy who went to Athens to work as a baker's assistant in 1960 quit his job in disgust six years later when his employer refused him permission to return home for the funeral of his mother, who had unexpectedly died at the age of fifty-two. Employers definitely had the upper hand, and the only—economically risky—option open to apprentices was to vote with their feet.

Good apprentices were nevertheless not easy to find either—especially in the countryside, where artisanal skills were comparatively rare, most villagers being farmers and shepherds with specialized knowledge of their own. One former saddle-maker recalled how he had originally been recruited: his first master, a distant kinsman (a fourth or even more distant cousin, and not an agnate) of his father, had come searching for a likely lad in the villages of the Amari district where he worked. The saddle-maker made his choice from among the large brood of ten siblings. Because the saddle-maker quickly set his heart on recruiting this young man, the father was able to insist that the boy not be used as a *fameyos* (a live-in family servant, set to doing agricultural and household chores in addition to his tasks in the workplace) but be permitted to return home every night. This apprentice was very lucky; usually some level of domestic service was expected, and few were in a position to argue. Many fathers, too, relieved of the financial burden of keeping an able-bodied child at home, not only accepted this situation but condoned the plentiful use of corporal punishment when their sons misbehaved at work.

In some respects the situation is not vastly different today, although the masters' power is rarely shown through acts of serious physical violence. This is partly because there are relatively few young men interested in becoming apprenticed and partly because those who do opt for an artisanal career are much more fully protected from abuse both by the law and by a softening moral and political view of the appropriate use of authority. The artisans are still in a position to pick and choose, and many of them would ordinarily now prefer not to take on apprentices because of the attendant risks of exposure for not paying compulsory state insurance taxes. This simply makes what they have to offer all the more desirable.

Apprenticeship still serves the goal of helping children out of conditions of rural poverty, made even more burdensome today by the rising costs of living in rural communities that are no longer fully self-subsistent. "A father can't cope with the costs [of looking after his children] with the 500 kilos of oil he produces or with 500 kilos of cherries. So he goes after wages. And he says to me, 'Please, if you can, take my child to work for you. Give him as much as you can, [but] above all let him leave the village and "wake up" a bit more. In the town he'll need other kinds of things in any case, *more* things, and his intelligence should be developed in some way. And then he turns out to have a problem of slow speech, so perhaps by talking with people a bit he'll...'" Such pleas usually fall on reluctant ears. In this particular instance, however, considerations of kinship and friendship, and the possibility of performing a charitable act that would be socially well regarded, together worked their persuasive magic, earning the master a loyal—if none too bright—shop assistant to sell his products at the counter.

There is a curious ambivalence in the way apprentices express their attitudes to their work. It is an ambivalence that reproduces and reinforces the pattern of learning, whereby an affectation of deep boredom on the part of apprentices serves as a shield behind which they can observe and learn while resisting their masters' more importunate demands. It emerges in a series of apparent contradictions: between the generic expression of the ideal, that one should "love" one's work, and the specific expression of anger and resentment against the task in hand; between happy memories of past employers in general and criticism of—and sometimes quite startling insubordination against—the particular employer of the moment; and between generic admiration for the technical skills of the true artisan and specific complaints about the uninteresting nature of the labor that apprentices have to perform.

We can only understand such tensions, and dispose of the sense of paradox, by recognizing that the specific and the generic are balanced against each other in the process whereby every apprentice potentially becomes a potential master-artisan. This is the logic of the artisanal performance of self and craft, the play of inventive variation on conventional notions of self and style. But these tensions are also interesting for another reason: they reproduce similar apparent paradoxes in the larger society. Neighbors and kin are wonderful people, but one's own particular neighbors and kin exploit that expectation and so end up being worse than those with whom one has no relationship at all; Greece is the mother of European civilization but also the orientalized slave of the barbarian North; Greeks, and especially Rethemniots, set great store by the harmony by which they have traditionally lived but seem less capable of maintaining it than are those inferior northern creatures to whom they are beholden for their liberty and their economy. Finally, the idiom of affect is a key component of the interaction. Apprentices develop an indifferent mien toward their crafts, yet they are expected eventually to "love" their work, just as they may eventually transcend the gruff interaction that is the usual style of artisan-apprentice interaction and develop a relationship that is similarly characterized as "love"—manifested, in the rare cases where it is openly admitted, by the direct verbal instruction of the apprentice. When such an apprentice grows to full manhood and artisan status, he may in his turn—defying the conventional male wisdom—insist that meticulous explanation and careful instruction, rather than curtness and evasion, should characterize an artisan's dealings with apprentices because "the lad learns so he can help the shop." Such apparent pedagogical rationalism is itself, then, a claim to self-interested masculinity, but one that attempts to utilize both the symbolic capital of modernity and the economic logic associated with it; especially in its frank acknowledgment of the primacy of self-interest, it is not as radical a departure from local norms of agonistic social interaction as might initially appear.

In such a context, it would be all too easy to dismiss as false ideology the claims that, for example, an artisan's children, having decided that they did not want to continue their formal schooling and become bureaucrats or business clerks, came to evince pure "love" for their artisanal work. Doubtless there is, in many cases, an important element of self-deception; doubtless, too, such self-deception is also self-serving in a society where opportunities for advancement are not generous and where boastful acceptance of one's social place is preferable to the resignation of the obvious loser. Again we see how the Greek case frames and intensifies a key feature of the global hierarchy of value: tradition is at once a glorious heritage and a dispiriting weight on the back of the disadvantaged.

A pie-maker, for example, had this to say about his children's attitude to his profession: "If a child doesn't go ahead well and make progress learning 'letters,' so that he'll become something—a professor, a doctor, a teacher, whatever he will become I don't know—[if he doesn't succeed] in learning 'letters' and doesn't want to stay in the work [he has], [he could] go to another job if he wants to. *My* children love my work." Just as one's own wife, mother, or sister is sexually pure (but otherwise all women are suspect), and just as one's own first employer treated one with consideration (but all other employers are exploitative monsters), so one's own children become the emblem and repository of the pride one must take in labor that is otherwise considered demeaning or at least socially less than glorious.

Artisans frequently speak of their "love" for the work they perform, and this seems to be the clearest indication that they have broken free, not of their class identity, but—very much within that identity—of the dependent status of the apprentice. Now that the work is their own, they must love it, embrace it with the consuming passion called *meraki*—the total absorption and almost painful obsessions of the hobbyist, the artist, the artisan, or anyone engaged in a totally consuming activity.[23] Contingent economic necessity becomes a virtue claimed for a self represented, within the narrow local context, as having freedom of action and affect. A furniture-maker, explaining this emotion, claimed to have two guiding principles in his life: while the one is his craft, the other is provided by Christ—the emblematic figure, for many Cretans, of the heroic resistance, simplicity, and spontaneity that enable a man to stand up to the rapacity of the bureaucratic state and the aggression of the social world around him. A man who does not love his work cannot love himself; and he certainly cannot expect others to respect him for his independence. His affective relationship with his work nevertheless replicates the crypto-colonial condition of the country as a whole in the degree to which claims to independence, an independence grounded in commitment to collective tradition, can paradoxically only be made within a larger context of inescapable dependence.

Love for one's work is an attitude that artisans say is best cultivated at an early age. A garage mechanic told me that one young lad they hired at the age of about fourteen had particularly impressed him as "loving" the work, and added that his age was an important factor. The mechanic was especially impressed by the lad's ability to follow orders precisely in what even by local standards is an extraordinarily noisy environment. In focusing on the apprentice's tender age, the mechanic—an artisan working in an indisputably modern trade—reverts to a more traditionalist perspective, despite the fact that he was using it to justify a decidedly nontraditionalist willingness to instruct the boy in the details of their craft. Also unusual was his explicit discomfort with the ragging, conventional though that is in artisanal contexts, that he and others put the boy through.

The garage apprentice represents the extreme case of the school truant who somehow slipped through the educational authorities' net; he began working for a living while still just entering his teens. A jeweler complained that today boys would not usually begin working as apprentices at a sufficiently tender age to become habituated to the demanding bodily discipline of long and uninterrupted hours at the workbench. It is perhaps no coincidence that only school truants are likely to enter apprenticeships at an age even remotely comparable to what was normal at the beginning of the century. They are the ones who know that, in a time of increased general education, they will be at a relatively greater disadvantage later on, both socially and in the competition for jobs, and so their love for their work represents a social demonstration of investment in the only significant cultural and social capital at their disposal.

From resentment to "love," then, the attitudinal path of artisans reflects and follows their social emergence. It is this love of their work that Nenedakis chronicles when he recalls the saddle-maker who would tell his customers what they needed[24]—the customer certainly could *not* know as well as the artisan—and pride in work is tantamount to moral authority. It is an attitude closely tied to the local conventions of masculinity. Professional self-confidence serves as a bulwark against the corrosive doubts induced by a modernity of increasing complexity and ambiguity. The besieged traditionalist Cretan man will present it as flowing from an autonomous decision to perform the labor he loves. The garage mechanic's assistant perceives this clearly. As his employer affectionately remarked, "And you just have to get him once inside a car and you see that, when the car runs [properly], it fills him with satisfaction. He says, 'I like what I do because [*dhioti*][25] one day I'll do it too!'"

Yet it is equally clear that doubt remains—if not in each individual's reflections, then certainly in everyday talk. Greek peasants and workers often voice a strong desire to see their children settled in higher-status occupations. The pie-maker, for example, was waiting to see whether one of his sons would do well enough at school to merit the "sacrifice" *(thisia)* that the father would have to make, possibly to the point of sending the boy abroad for further study. If necessary, the father declared, "I will struggle" *(th' aghonisto)*—precisely the metaphor of social relations that so many observers have seen as the key to Greek social relations. Whether as artisans or as family heads, people have to work with the material that is available to them and then put an aggressively cheerful face on whatever eventuates. This is the proactive stance of people who, far from being fatalistic, continue to battle against the odds until they go down, since that struggle is the only thing capable of redeeming their social worth when all else fails. Declaring one's love for a low-status profession is as much a strategy for shoring up one's personal standing as it may be, in many cases, the expression of a genuine enthusiasm. Decrying the stupidity of those who "have letters" is another such device; envy does not generate praise.

While the possibility of escaping to a higher status is always present, then, the odds against achieving that goal are usually insuperable, and the feasible social battle for respect becomes more important than what for most is the unwinnable struggle for major educational advancement. Once that has become clear, the context of competition shifts to the workplace itself—to the contest between artisans but also to the struggle that apprentices are forced, within the narrower social confines of their profession, to undertake in order to achieve master status themselves. Here it is the hierarchy of master and apprentice that reproduces the larger class structure, as well as the relationship between marginal and central places and polities at all the levels I have mentioned. So we must now turn to the ways in which artisans both frustrate and train their apprentices, to see who survives this process and in what ways.

An Enveloping Silence

Artisans profess deep contempt for words—not only the words of the schoolroom but also those that betray the secrets of professional knowledge in their own workplaces. Rare indeed is the kind of artisan who openly advocates careful verbal instruction of the young. A common feature of craft workshops is thus the relative absence of speech of any kind beyond a curt command, an occasional grunt or expletive, and the suddenly gracious discourse that a telephone call from a customer or contractor may prompt.[26] A senior worker may curtly demand to know where a particular implement has gone; the response, however, is usually a brief gesture, perhaps a brief announcement that the tool has shown up, after which the apprentice brings the tool to the older man. There is no word of thanks here. Workshops are not silent places, but the dominant sounds are the repetitive sounds of productive physical labor: the crash of materials dropped on the ground, the whir and shrill of machine tools, the thud of hammers, the thump of presses, the snipping of scissors. Voices are rare: an occasional timid question, often followed by a snapped, elliptical instruction or a snarl of abuse and irritation.

Here there is little space for patient explanation or gentle praise. There are some differences in the sounds the various trades produce. Carpenters' and ironworkers' shops are dominated by the heavier sounds of machinery and occasional yells across the floor; in goldsmiths' shops the silences are punctuated by more delicate work noises, but the apprentices' sullen silence and the artisans' grim absorption in the work at hand are, if anything, more oppressive, although there may be a little amiable banter between a master goldsmith and an older apprentice clearly already in possession of advanced technical skills.

This controlled blend of taciturn interaction and the disciplined sound of work contrasts with the verbal bedlam of the crafts classroom of the state technical school. There, the teacher is besieged by importunate pupils cheekily demanding his immediate attention, his praise for their work, his instructions on how to proceed. These boys will for the most part never become craftsmen; their craft classes are a source of entertainment for them and frustration for the hapless teacher, who, faced with their unruly manners and unrelenting barrage of questions and insubordinate jokes, tries in vain to impose a modicum of order. These boys are learning, or have already learned, that in a society where the local values of self-regard and aggressive masculinity can be dressed up in the official values of democracy and free expression, no one can force them to learn anything or to keep their voices under control. Moreover, the craft class is of little practical interest to them; while some may be destined to become engineers or managers, their role in relation to manual labor will be to demand and consume its products, not to engage in it themselves. They are being prepared for white-collar jobs in which, especially in a culture in which a ready wit is highly prized and in which literacy is a skill to be displayed, their ability to maintain pride and social space will depend on the exercise of verbal skills.

The contrast between the craft class and the artisans' workshops is stark. Uniting what appear to be diametrically opposed styles of interaction, however, is a common and instantly recognizable feature: the agonistic tension between males. The difference is one of class—a difference that is reproduced hour by hour, day by day. It is expressed as an opposition between mental and manual labor. When one member of the artisan class, whose father had made enough money for the son to become a *rentier* but who had nevertheless remained a committed Marxist, alluded to that opposition in Marxist terms, his interlocutor—an artisan still—took offense and retorted, "Do you think I'm an idiot?" Yet the same upwardly mobile individual had taken advantage of his father's financial acumen, so that when another artisan asked if he would be interested in working as an apprentice for "pocket money," his father replied, "Doesn't he have a shop of his own, if he wants to work?" "Working," in this context, meant manual labor, and it is clear that father and son both took pride in having freed the son from the necessity of performing it. The father was more interested in the economic implications of this release and had little time for his son's intellectualism. The son, however, became almost notorious locally for his interest in talking about just about anything; as a highly erudite *rentier*, he no longer belonged to the class in whose interests he deployed and developed his formidable verbal skills.

An intellectual rarely engages in self-silencing; workers must often strategically do so. Their silence is not strategic in the political sense alone; it also marks a context of understanding that constitutes "an embodied telos too complex to be discussed in the narrower and simpler language of goals, tasks, and knowledge acquisition."[27] In Crete, moreover, the worker's silence is a mark of his continuing links with his rural origins. In rural communities, strong men glory in displays of both verbal dexterity (as in their inventive pleasure in merciless competitive verse duels) and expressive silence (as when they show a reserve that signals strength and continence). Indeed, the silence of the strong is part and parcel of their verbal agility: they know when to keep their mouths shut, when to convey power through restraint. In the mountain village where I studied reciprocal animal theft, shepherds admired especially those who did not rant and rage when they were insulted but simply took quiet, swift, and violent action. When one young man invited me to come on a raid and, after over two hours of chatting in a coffeehouse, made a gesture to me that we were about to leave, I responded by saying, in words, that indeed we should be off. He immediately relaxed back into the conversation, and we did not leave. When we finally walked out of the coffeehouse, I asked him what had happened. Testily, he explained that he had made a "significant gesture" *(noima)* to me and that I, instead, had "spoken." This apparently was a clear indication that I would be useless as a sheep thief—whether because I could not be trusted to keep silent if we were caught or because more generally loquacity signified a lack of self-control was never explained. What seems especially important here is that a term redolent of mental activity (compare the English word "noetic") is used of a gestural quality that is marked by the absence of talk: in some situations, especially those in which deep masculinity is at stake, speech is a womanly incontinence, a corruption of the warlike self-control of the tough man.

In the countryside, then, such strategic silence-making is part of men's verbal skill. A man who can turn a teasing verse with the best of them, but who does so only when he can come up with a really telling riposte (one that may bring about the silence of defeat in an opponent), may also be strong and silent in situations where only the truly strong can resist the temptation to erupt with a roar of rage. In the class-divided society of Rethemnos, where the educated elite still boasts of the town's fame for "letters" in Venetian times, silence has become an indicator of subordinate status. That does not mean, however, that it implies acquiescence in that status.

Indeed, it provides a means both of externalizing resentment (a sullen glare can speak volumes) and of containing knowledge that will give a young man advantages in the competitive world he is entering. Pierre Bourdieu has noted that verbality is at odds with working-class masculinity in France,[28] and this is also true for Greece. That similarity suggests a common code, in which, as formerly rural populations become absorbed into urban proletariats, men's knowledge of how to use silence self-protectively allows them to adapt to situations in which their amour propre is constantly undermined by the daily humiliations of working for others and having to display an appropriate sense of their reduced status. Their aggressive masculinity becomes at once the basis of their solidarity, especially in contrast to the supposedly effeminate world of the pen pushers,[29] and the mark of their inability to reach what in Greece is seen as a "European" form of sophistication. Paul Willis's analysis shows how that solidarity perpetuates and reinforces working-class identity; although the British boys he describes do display great verbal dexterity, it is of a rebellious kind, and their attitude to "ear'oles" is very close to Cretan workers' and peasants' resentment of "pen pushers"—which is itself a derogatory image they share with the boys Willis describes.[30] He attributes to the insidious workings of capitalism this process of willing adaptation to the relegation of self to the working class; I should add that it is the comprehensive reach of the global hierarchy of value that makes escape seem all but inconceivable, whether among British or French factory workers, among the deskilled shipyard fitters described by Joseph Blum,[31] or among the Cretan artisans we are discussing here.

Thus, for example, the problem with maintaining silence at work is that it allows those in charge to accuse their underlings of obduracy: cowed into speaking only rarely if at all, the apprentices stand condemned by the very silence into which they are forced. As their behavior becomes still more rebellious, they are confirmed in their role as members of the artisan class (their insubordination is, after all, encouraged and even applauded as a sign of real masculinity and ingenuity, just as Willis describes for English youths who become factory workers) and so, in consequence, they find themselves drawn ever more ineluctably into a subalternity from which escape is correspondingly difficult. In Willis's analysis, the capitalist system of education treats working-class boys as less well endowed mentally than those who go on to white-collar jobs, but they do not necessarily accept the implications of this ranking: "one of the things which keeps the capitalist system stable, and one of its complex wonders, is that an important section of the subordinate class does not accept the proffered reality of the steady diminution of their own capacities. Instead they reverse the valuation of the mental/manual gradient by which they are measured."[32] Being "good with one's hands" becomes a virtue, along with aggressive masculinity and the ability to control speech— to use it with clever and subversive cheek but only when the bosses are not listening. And so these boys willy-nilly play into the hands of the capitalists, for whom the maintenance of class hierarchy is essential.

The Power of and in Tradition

Willis's analysis is persuasive in part because of the fine ethnography with which he supports his argument. At the same time, it is important to recognize that the traps and inequalities he notes are not confined to classic class systems such as that of industrial northern Europe. The reproduction of artisanal craft culture in the European periphery refracts these dynamics in another way, by marginalizing precisely those people in whom the notion of tradition has been most heavily invested by the emergent nation-state. In France, to instance another contrast, Susan Terrio has illustrated the role of bourgeois nationalism in maintaining small-scale *chocolatiers* as the bearers of a tradition that reproduces the structural logic of colonialism: the artisanal class fashions "exotic" substances for bourgeois and aristocratic consumers.[33] One may also suspect, however, that with the decline in French global ambitions and fortunes comes a potential trap not unlike the yoking of Greekness to artisanship. In a world increasingly dominated by "audit culture" modes of assessing cultural and educational value,[34] and in which the English language has become the hallmark of a technological modernity, the pedestal of the *mission civilisatrice* may yet prove to be as much of a tethering post for French small-scale craftspeople as that of European ancestorhood already has for their Cretan counterparts.

At the outer edges of capitalism as it spread in the wake of the colonialism to which it lent its energy, this same logic produced a converse aesthetic by which, as in southern Africa or Latin America,[35] workers adopted (and not infrequently parodied) "European" taste in their clothing and other objects of daily use. All too often, however, they did so in ways that clearly marked them as naïve users. Those who dared to threaten the dominant aesthetic with outbursts of nativism, or who simply tried consciously to adapt European styles to their own local standards, simply found themselves trapped at the lower end of an already degrading scale.

What went for the consumption of goods also applied to manners and morals, which were similarly held accountable to an increasingly globalized standard. This is why I employ the term "global hierarchy of *value*." It makes no sense to distinguish here between ethics and aesthetics, or between manners and products. All are subject to an overarching valuation (in this form, the term already appears in Willis's writing) that embeds the Cretan artisans in the same determinisms as South African laborers wrenched from their tribal homelands by the apartheid system and as English working-class boys condemned by a supposedly meritocratic education system to celebrate their own marginalization. At stake here is what Bourdieu recognized as "cultural capital," although we should note the irony of this "capitalist" metaphor in the writings of a theorist who so resolutely attacked "economism" in social thought.[36] We cannot dispense with economism, if only because our own ways of acting and thinking are caught in the same logic; while for both Bourdieu and Willis education confirmed the enormous social benefits on those who could afford it in the first place, we should recognize that the current devaluation of academic knowledge in many sectors of the new world economy, especially in the English-speaking world, repeats the same process of marginalization, in the sense that those whose mental labor does not obviously contribute to the progress of the neoliberal project find their work accorded a low cash value—and therefore a low value, period.[37] If absent-minded humanities professors can no longer be productive, they will be banished to the back of the class—the economic class—and managers will take their place.

Certain things appeared, in the early days of capitalism, to represent all that was fine and wonderful about past ways of being, and these were wrapped in the logic of tradition, heritage, and historical commemoration. But now the trap that these designations represent has become far more blazingly apparent: the pedestal is properly unveiled and we see that it is, after all, a tethering post. This trap is perhaps nowhere more evident than in the creeping gentrification that expels workers and artisans from their homes at the same time as it labels these people as "traditional" or "ancient" and so dubs their former abodes, in the suggestive language of the real-estate business, as desirable residences—a few of them even decorated with the handiwork of the displaced artisans, although such items, which often use plastic, aluminum, and modern paints, are usually destroyed to make way for more deliberately produced forms of authenticity.[38]

As the artisans themselves become more and more marginal, their allegedly characteristic attitudes—a surliness that used to bespeak self-confidence and that today might still be considered amusing—will seem to "justify" their exclusion from the cultural mainstream. Less and less of their work will find its way into the category of "folk art," either because its "naïve" or "primitive" characteristics will be viewed instead as "mechanical reproduction" (as witness my own reaction to the Venizelos bookends) or because its functionality places it in direct competition with the standardized and more efficient products of the factory. And their own behavior will reproduce the "self-damnation" noted by Willis—but perhaps, because it is caught in a series of concentric cultural snares, in even more extreme form. They do not represent a "counterculture" in Willis's sense; the dominant value system tells them that they are the bearers of a glorious tradition, even while marginalizing them for that very reason.[39]

A Moral Economy of Manners

The situation is particularly dire for the artisans of Rethemnos because they inhabit a town that lives principally on tourism and thus not only is dependent on the capitalist system of service provision but is caught in the hierarchy of value that tourism itself perpetuates. These artisans, with the possible exception of the jeweler-goldsmiths, are poorly equipped to produce objects of aesthetic interest for the tourists' consumption. To make matters worse, the kind of tourism that Rethemnos attracts is of the cheap package-tour variety; local entrepreneurs complain bitterly about the tourists' failure to spend significant amounts of money in town. A few artisans exploit the situation as best they can; for example, a couple who specialize in making *filo* and *kataifi* pastry for sweetmeats sell little packages of these to tourists, who, in many cases, will probably not manage to use them, lacking the experience for which the construction of these complex desserts calls. This couple's evident charm and willingness to try to communicate, and their local stature as hardworking people whose children have benefited from advanced forms of education, have clearly worked in their favor. But they are hardly typical.

More common is the artisanal carpenter or construction worker who virtually never interacts with a tourist. People in this situation continue to engage in the brittle agonistics of what is seen as a traditional style of Greekness—a style whose very existence, for example, Greek students in the United States often deny or regard as irrelevant to their modern lives, so successfully has the new consumerism succeeded in, as it were, consuming them. Artisans train their apprentices in the old agonistic ways, even as they claim (since they, too, recognize the global hierarchy of value for what it is) that they are trying to undo these attitudes; the attitudes in question, while doubtless appropriate in the immediate context, ill prepare these unsuspecting youths for the polite world that will soon judge their every action, already populated as it is by young people who find such supposedly traditional ways of acting to be merely tiresome.

An ironworker's apprentice offers a fine illustration. This lad, ever resentful, would never, so his employer claimed, perform the easiest task right, even though he knew how to do it; his employer thought that this was simply evidence of a contrary character—quite the reverse of a lack of intelligence. The boy would also play small tricks on his employer, such as filling up his nearly empty coffee cup with water so it was extremely thin; on other occasions, he dropped a rusty metal object into the coffee he was ordered to bring for the older apprentice or added machine oil to the latter's coffee. His employer complained, "He tires me out!" After the boy consented, with no obvious reluctance, to let me videotape him at work, he soon began to duck out of sight every time I produced the camera. I eventually discovered that the master and the older apprentice had conspired to tell him that I was from the school truancy committee and that he would get into serious trouble if I ever managed to record him. This was a form of hazing (perhaps of the anthropologist as much as of the apprentice), designed to alert the apprentice to the tough realities out there in the real world and to train him in the importance of self-protection and avoidance. As a way of showing him that such distrust was appropriate even in the privacy of his workplace, it also underscored the very precarious conditions of his employment.

The boy was deeply sullen. On one occasion, when the master harangued him for being particularly unwilling to follow instructions, he appeared to acquiesce meekly in this dressing down, after which, as the master strode away, he turned to glare balefully at his back with a ferocity that for once he seemed more than willing to let me capture on video. The master complained to me that the lad was "heavy" (varis)—that is, not only that he did not speak but that his silences were, as we would say, laden. Normally, this is a term of praise for an adult man, although not in circles that pride themselves on a modicum of urbanity. This "heaviness" manifested itself as a refusal to communicate: "He doesn't give himself any freedom. He always wants to . . . be difficult. Not to . . . he doesn't speak, doesn't. . . . If I tell him to do something, he'll do whatever comes into his head, and if it gets into his head, he'll do it for fourteen generations. He's a difficult character, that is." And so, the master continued, "If I tell him, 'George, do this!' he'll do it even if he does it all wrong!" This is clearly a self-fulfilling prophecy: expectations of negative behavior generate that same behavior, and what is said (and done) to this one young apprentice is reproduced in most of the active workshops in town. Clearly, there are few incentives to act differently.

Note how the artisan blames uncommunicativeness on the personality of the young apprentice, whose obduracy he further attributes to a "soft" upbringing by an overindulgent mother—an upbringing that has produced what he called a "chocolate child" (sokolatopedho). When the apprentice went whining to his mother that the ironworker had kicked him out, it was necessary to explain that this was not the right description; the apprentice had simply not been able to bear his employer's well-chosen insults. The apprentice's cowardice at that moment is represented as the very antithesis of tough masculinity—the "liveliness," as it is often euphemistically called, of lads who do poorly in school precisely because they are not "breast-fed" (mamothrefta) and are therefore more suited to a life of struggle with their hands. Physical labor is in this sense the site of masculine self-realization. Whining to his mother was a mark of the lad's failure; by contrast, the sullen mien that he soon developed was not the mark of being a spoiled brat but a private space that allowed him to exercise a definitively masculine sense of autonomy.

That space is protected by not speaking—a silence that rejects others' right to command and control. But even speech itself can be a form of silence, or at least of deliberate noncommunication. For example, the master complains that he offers the apprentice the opportunity to come and work overtime, and that the apprentice accepts and then fails to show up. One might view this as simply a repetition of the pattern established by truancy from school or evidence that the child's mother was protecting him from the strains of working too hard. This pattern of making appointments one does not keep, however, is also recognizable, in the Greek context, as a way of avoiding unnecessary confrontation while maintaining a sense of independent action. In the end, the apprentice would not be able to avoid his master's irritation, but he would have won a temporary sense of acting for himself. In the final analysis, that sense would nevertheless turn out to be illusory, since his actions and his sullenness only served to confirm his master's low opinion of him and so would deprive him of those extra earnings that might otherwise, cumulatively and in the long term, have gained him a more sub-stantive measure of personal independence. In fact, the ironworker praised the boy's "one good point" as an ability not to answer back when scolded or cursed but to wait until the master's back was turned; since the master admitted to knowing that the minute he left the workshop the boy would start a voluble diatribe to the older apprentice, it seems safe to assume that the master was also aware of the boy's baleful reaction behind his back as well, or at least of the boy's smoldering resentment in general—which he saw as a great improvement over the boy's alternative of sheltering behind his mother's tender protectiveness. It is the boy's display of uncommunica-tive autonomy, which the master colluded in developing, that earned him the adjective "heavy"—a designation that, although offered as a criticism, carries strong connotations of manliness and adherence to traditional working-class idioms.

That this is collusion is clear from the fact that, his complaints duly delivered, the master stomped off, looking away from the field of action and refusing to oversee the apprentice's subsequent moves. Wearing a mask would be an admission of caution, perhaps even of fear, and, as such, a betrayal of the aggressive masculinity that the lad is clearly trying to develop. Silent, sullen, but also prepared to face bodily harm: these are the marks of a man who is truly "heavy." And his master's alternations of invective and indifference are the instruments of its cultivation—indeed, of its transmission, since we can assume that the master himself has passed through a very similar development in his social attitudes.

The contradiction between the master's ostensible complaints and the larger sense of "heaviness" as a working-class male attribute that he practi-cally encourages in his apprentice offers us an important clue to the ways in which masculinity is produced. It is a form of training for toughness, fear-lessness, and indifference to the slights of all except those one is prepared to acknowledge as moral equals. But it also entails the risk—risk is always central to men's lives here—of being put down as effeminate instead. We now turn to a consideration of what this implies.

Chapter Four

Engendered States

Engendering Power Relations

The relations of power between artisans and their apprentices must be read in the context of gender norms and practices in the wider Cretan society. These lads become stronger men through being treated, stereotypically, as the very reverse—as women. They learn to ignore discomfort and to master risk. Rather than evading risk, they embrace it, so that even if the consequences are disastrous for their immediate goals, they will at least not have to face accusations of cowardice. Men confronted with those rare women who demand to enter an artisanal trade may become particularly aggressive, as a way of testing what they see as a dubious commitment or an inappropriate gender role.

A leatherworker and shoemaker who had undertaken to arrange a special training school on behalf of a shoemakers' cooperative and NOSMBH, for example, was scathing when the two young women who had signed up, one of whom was a former literature student, complained that the building he had selected was unsuitable: "they wanted, so to speak, mosaic flooring and luxury in that space where we had arranged the cobblers' workshop so that instruction could be carried out. So I told them that such a space could not be found. And if it could, it would cost a lot of money. And the space would be the one we chose ourselves, for the purpose we wanted." In a short time, the whole venture foundered on this clash of expectations, which pitched modernity against tradition in the form of a conflict between genders. There may indeed have been a strong undercurrent of male fear about gendered competition, expressed as aggressive male doubts about female competence and the capacity for heroic suffering.[1]

One of the few women artisans in Rethemnos today, a leatherworker, found her forte at one of these seminars and proceeded to build up her business by employing much younger female trainees from a local school. The head-mistress cooperated, apparently because she believed that the leatherworker's workshop offered an educational opportunity that would also provide her students with a living. But this female artisan's case is exceptional; in its alliance with school authorities, moreover, it charts a course interestingly different from anything men have attempted. Women stand to gain much less from standing up to the state authorities and sneering at school learning than do men, for whom antiauthoritarian posturing represents less a choice than a social obligation.

Among the few female artisans and their apprentices still operating, relations are markedly different from those that subsist among men. Typically—and in contrast to her male counterpart—the female apprentice is a close kinswoman; she is encouraged to speak to her employer openly and with an affection one rarely encounters in the all-male workshops; and she does not represent a threat either socially or economically, either because she sees her labor as a stopgap arrangement before marrying or entering higher education or because she will be a valuable ally both in the continuation of the workshop and in the solidarity needed to survive in such an overwhelmingly male environment. This is consistent with the larger pattern of female sociability; while for men the coffeehouse can serve as a site of relative affability that cuts across lines of kin solidarity, it always remains a stage on which men must be prepared to defend themselves against insult, whereas women's gatherings, often confined to more private spaces, are less liable to break down in dispute.[2] Unlike her male counterpart, a female apprentice is likely to be related to her (female) employer, with whom the kinship link then serves to strengthen a shared commitment in the form of quiet but unmistakable affection and mutual support.

As for the few women who work for male employers, their skills have already ensured them a measure of what usually passes for respect but might be better interpreted as a form of exclusion. It would be too demeaning for an employer to mistreat his female workers, since his own manhood and sense of social decency would then be open to doubt. The polite consideration that men generally show their female employees and those of their friends, however, should not blind us to the strong encompassing sense of gender hierarchy, of which in fact it is a sign. It indicates that their female employees are weak, requiring male protection.

In short, women are excluded—and to some extent express pleasure in being excluded—from the heroic masculinity of the male artisans. Their own refusal to engage in the agonistic antics of male artisans and especially in their calculated roughness toward their apprentices locks them out of the heroic arena. They do not force their apprentices to steal their knowledge, and they do not try to keep those apprentices at a distance either by avoiding close kin or by the dour discouragement with which they treat them. In this regard, they offer a telling contrast with the male ethos, in which the acquisition of even the simplest technique becomes the object of a struggle over the possession of knowledge. At the furthest extreme of this heroic idiom of male pride stands the occasional artisan who boasts of never having been apprenticed at all—a man who has never accepted another's authority over him but has always relied on his own wits alone. He trumps his peers collectively by the simple device of virtually having purloined his expertise from them all while submitting to none.

In this context, men's belittling of younger and weaker males who work for them emerges as a form of symbolic feminization. It is clearly and explicitly understood as such. A rabbit-hutch maker described the apprentice's humiliation as "castration" (evnoukhismos) designed to induce "servility" (dhoulo-prepia), in the sense that those who fail to learn from it will never attain the respect that men consider the fragile but essential prerogative of their gender identity.[3] While this declaration follows a stereotype, it is important to remember that it is a stereotype entertained by local men (and women, although more critically); the play of variation in social performance and the bitter hurt that feminization represents for men accustomed to expectations of aggressive maleness would not bite very deep were there not a general recognition of the underlying conventions.[4] These gendered attitudes, moreover, are deeply ingrained; they are physically leached into the apprentices' habitual bodily stances. Jane K. Cowan has splendidly documented the ways in which bodies are gendered in everyday social interaction, of which dance forms then become highly dramatized sites for contesting what in older modes of analysis appeared to be static social value systems.[5] Cowan's work, like mine based in Greece, is particularly important for the way she shows how women come to incorporate, and sometimes to contest, male hegemony—the very model on which, although that is not her particular focus, the Greek nation-state (like so many others) has been crafted.

Following Cowan's example, I asked informants to view a series of video clips and to comment on them. Because my equipment was much smaller and easier to handle than hers had been a few years earlier, I was able to set up a systematic "visual questionnaire" with which I could elicit reactions from a substantial range of people. Unlike Cowan, I chose to do this outside the community where I had filmed the interactions, interviewing new sets of people in Khania and Iraklio instead. I wanted to see how people of differing age, gender, and occupational status evaluated the interactions, what they thought might have been said (the sound was suppressed on the clips), and what they thought about the learning process in particular.[6]

While most of the men who watched the videotaped interactions saw nothing amiss in the brusque treatment the artisans so clearly were meting out to their apprentices, the women (in a contrast that showed how hierarchies of gender and rank meshed with each other) almost all expressed sympathy for the apprentices. Many were particularly outraged that the masters did not tell the apprentices what to do—a telling contrast with the male assumption that this was normal and appropriate. It may be relevant to these reactions that a male Rethemniot said that his female assistant occasionally "did some stupidity"—a revealingly disdainful phrase—but would not confront her over these mistakes. He claimed that this stemmed from a deep reluctance on his part to discourage initiative. The same attitude, enacted toward a male apprentice, might have been interpreted by women as a refusal to impart knowledge. They would not necessarily have been right; this man also claimed that he allowed his female assistant to criticize the work of others in the workshop, including men.

The stereotypes are nevertheless deeply ingrained and do strongly influence people's perceptions of what is happening in the workplace. There is also some evidence to suggest that these perceptions are grounded in everyday experience. The only scene that did not lead most of the women who watched my video questionnaire to attribute gruffness to the older male was an interaction between father and son; the women's immediate identification of this scene as displaying a different kind of interaction was especially striking because the women had no knowledge of the relationship between the two people shown in the clip.

One of the women domesticated the issue of male mistreatment of apprentices by segueing into a detailed discussion of her garage owner husband's refusal to teach and explain carefully to his apprentices and about her own futile attempts to get him to change his ways and act more generously. She had a clear perception of how his practices were entrenched in notions of tradition: "I'd also like to say that there's this mentality that the apprentice should take from the boss on his own, to steal the work, as they say. Without the boss telling him scarcely anything. And I often tell my spouse that he should tell them certain things. But he reacts [negatively], because he says that, 'As I learned the work, by stealing it, so he [the apprentice] should learn it, because that, that's how I learned, that's how I started out'—and he follows that mentality." While she did not accuse her husband of brutality, and indeed claimed that he had excellent relations with his apprentices, her complaint about his lack of interest in teaching them the craft suggests that at some level she recognizes in his stand the perpetuation of the artisans' exclusion from the privileges of a dominant modernity.

The men, conversely, all seemed to feel that the artisans were disciplining the boys in an appropriate fashion, teaching them the virtues of self-sufficiency and autonomy; this attitude strongly recalls the childhood socialization that Renée Hirschon observed even among relatively affluent bourgeois Greeks.[7] These values were inculcated by getting the youth used to deception, which was normal even—or perhaps especially—among kin. The Irakliot viewers of the video clips thus confirmed a pattern of inculcation in suspicion and resentment that is certainly part of Rethemniot collective self-perception. One Rethemniot recalled how his own mother, worried about her son's absence in Athens for work, wrote that she was sick, simply as a ruse to get him to come back. One can read that incident as good training in deception, not unlike what happens to artisans' apprentices. But there is another aspect that is also germane here. Mothers are seen as dangerous to a boy's emerging masculinity. The ironworker complained that his apprentice's mother—recently divorced—was not in any state to impose serious discipline on her spoiled offspring: "They don't get tough with him at home, telling him, 'Look here, you, when you leave there'—as my father told *me!*—'when you leave your work, your boss, you will leave home as well! Then there's no home for you!'" In his own day, he insisted, an apprentice would never refuse his master's commands. Fathers did not protect their sons from their masters' sometimes violent discipline, and a master might occasionally ask for a father's permission—readily obtained—before taking a strap to a particularly rebellious youngster. One father, hearing that his son had been wasting time and had been caught smoking hashish in bad company, reputedly came to see the master and demanded, "Why didn't you give him a beating?"

Fathers and masters thus collude in generating a pivotal paradox: in a society where wife beating was not uncommon and women were seen as the objects of male contest,[8] they hope to turn the boys into tougher men by treating them as though these adolescent males were women. They feminize them in order to develop their masculinity: feminization provokes rebellion, which leads to sanctions that in turn produce new—and often subtler or more dissimulated—rebellion. Feminization and the development of manhood are thus linked less by an irresolvable paradox than by a sequence: the downward spiral that limits the development of independent personal power. By learning to dissimulate in order to avoid the humiliation of being feminized, apprentices trade a relative impunity for immediacy and effectiveness; in the concentric scheme of the encompassing society, too, the treatment they receive ensures that they will develop the laconic surliness that their masters had learned from earlier generations, so that they will become the living embodiments of picturesque crudeness, forever debarred from the symbolic resources of the powerful in exchange for being able to tyrannize a handful of cringing boys.

Their traditionality rests in part on their successful reproduction of this rude idiom of selfhood: they win tactical battles but lose the long-term war.[9] In the global hierarchy of value, they occupy a very low rung indeed, and there are few avenues of upward escape because the perceived social necessity of winning the tactical confrontations of the moments—such as affronts to personal dignity and aspersions on their manliness—automatically disqualifies them from the "civilizing process" that, in this European margin, corresponds, in the hands of the emergent and increasingly powerful bourgeoisie, to the *mission civilisatrice* of intrepid protocolonial explorers in exotic lands.[10]

Violent discipline—again as in the colonies—thus not only served the goal of maintaining immediate control, although this was certainly important, but also more or less guaranteed that insubordination would reproduce itself in subsequent generations, thereby perpetuating the marginalization of artisans and increasing it in the context of accelerated and expanded *embourgeoisement* during the second half of the twentieth century. The threat of a beating is as common as it is empty, so that young children, in learning how far they can try their parents' patience, get their first lessons in agonistic cunning. But while these adolescent apprentices are learning ever greater refinements in their insubordination, and take ever more audacious risks, the consequences of failure must be correspondingly more serious. This is entirely consistent with the suggestion that masters are actually pleased when their apprentices show a rebellious spirit; it is also consistent with the view, which often surfaces in the ethnographic literature,[11] that what matters is less the offense itself than getting caught or simply being thought guilty of it. Craft apprentices learn very quickly that hiding their own peccadilloes is something that they must be seen, paradoxically, to be able to do well.

That attitude is not consonant with modernist values. In the technical high school, where sixteen-year-old students take a class in "technology and production" for a mere five hours per week, a very different style of self-presentation prevails. Despite the principal's assertion of control—"I think we do not have discipline problems"—anarchy seems to reign. The students, male and female alike as well as together, are constantly calling out to their teacher in provocative ways, bursting into peals of undisciplined laughter at his helplessness in the face of their cheeky catcalls. They thus insistently draw attention to his inability to control them, showing that, for them, concealment is a mark of old-fashioned values to which they do not feel bound, whether through the constraints of gender or in any other way. This is not the sullen insubordination of the apprentices I have been discussing here but an outright challenge to authority that has more to do with modernist ideas about personal independence and individualism than with the sort of autonomy discussed by Hirschon and others, although there is some similarity between the two sets of attitudes.

Concealment of their insubordination is very far from these school students' minds, although they may be evasive in other ways. It is clear that many of the students in this classroom will grow into managerial modernists whose tasks will include the relegation of the artisans' products to the pedestal of "traditional artifacts" (as opposed to works of art) or to the tethering post of inadequately standardized products (as opposed to factory-made goods). The technical school students expect to escape the social confines of the working class, despite a pedagogy that is officially designed to encourage them "not to despise manual labor" (the principal's contemptuous phrase perhaps evoked the long fingernail that new bourgeois sometimes used to sport in order to flaunt their newly acquired status). They clearly intend to profit from the same global hierarchy of value that banishes the dwindling number of their uneducated age-mates to the margins of local society.

The relative indiscipline of the technical school students marks their escape from the constraints of manual labor. It also allows them freedom from gendered practices that condemn the artisanal class to the consequences of aggressive masculinity. In the technical school, girls and boys worked together, without apparent friction between the sexes. Gender was in any case not an overt factor in structuring the relationship between teacher and students; the absence of an explicit gendering of the classroom was itself a claim on modernity.

The situation of artisanal apprentices is very different. Not only is the master-apprentice relationship a transmission of unalloyed masculinity, but the exclusion of the world of women from most craft workshops marks a key moment in the socialization of young working-class Rethemniot men and gives a particular character to the discipline to which they are subjected. The statement that in the old days an apprentice would never dare disobey his master openly is clearly an idealization and represents a familiar pattern of structural nostalgia in Greek life.[12] But observations about the ways a mother might spoil her apprentice son reflect a social reality: women are categorically blamed, however unfair this may be in specific cases, for the weaknesses that male authority suffers and for the divisions that men, otherwise sociable, experience.[13] This, not surprisingly, is a type of event that I can only report by means of local people's accounts; intimate spaces are closely guarded from prying outsiders' ears and eyes. This defense of specific families' intimacy is especially salient here because it is the categorical or generic "house" (spiti), the realm of the female, that is blamed for the inadequacies that must now be disciplined in the workplace.

In particular, local people conventionally remark, a mother may be especially fierce in defense of a son who has been disciplined by the master because "a mother feels for her child more [than a father]" (i mana pio poli ponai to pedhi); female weakness becomes both an excuse for failure and yet also a source of greatly treasured affect, in a gendered argument that women are positioned never to win. Women may comment acerbically on male pretensions of power, pretensions to which they are themselves subject in the final analysis and that they heartily resent. Indeed, their resentment reproduces in the domain of gender that of apprentices toward their masters, just as the apprentices' powerlessness—especially in its constant air of frustrated insubordination—models class and cultural resentment overall.[14]

In the mythical stretches of the nostalgically recalled past, a father sent his sons to work in a space defined by a new and fictive version of kinship relations, a space where they were now "foster sons" to their new masters and thus had entered an expansion of the familiar world of home. This expansion represented the first stage in a young man's development of regional pride and national consciousness; familial affect was no longer an automatic or even normal accompaniment of the relationships he experienced on a daily basis, a change underscored by the absence of women, but discipline itself created the basis for a more mistrustful but still important kind of solidarity among those working together. Today, discipline has weakened in both the home and its extension, the workshop. But we can still see how the passage from family to workshop, from the control of a father defined by an infrangible link of blood to that of a man who "is putting at risk what he does, not what he is,"[15] moves the adolescent from the inescapable essentialisms of kinship to the altogether contingent and fragile conditions of employment and so uses the familiar patterns of kinship as a model for the unfamiliar but notionally concentric worlds that lie beyond.

Guy Lanoue's discussion of apprenticeship in central and southern Italy is particularly useful in showing how this transition works. In a family household, despite the obvious succession tensions that occasionally strain relations between fathers and sons, adjacent generations share an abiding interest in making sure that the household remains economically viable. When money alone is concerned, as in managing a shop or agency, men prefer their own sons to succeed them, and sons—or other close agnates—make the most trustworthy assistants, since they have no interest in undermining the success of the enterprise. A son who ends up displacing his father must also take responsibility for the father in old age. But artisans are engaged in the transmission of craft as well as—or sometimes instead of—financial stability. Their apprentices are most commonly not kin at all. This creates a tension: on the one hand, the master becomes more secretive and afraid that transmission of his skills might jeopardize his financial viability; on the other, the apprentice is brought into a wider network that builds larger relationships out of a model furnished by nuclear family ties.

Lanoue shows very clearly how the metaphorical character of a master artisan's being a father to "his" boys serves to underscore the fact that he is not, in fact, their father at all. For one thing, he may affiance one of them to one of his daughters; the situation of the apprentice who becomes the master's son-in-law would be unusual in Rethemnos, but ties of matrimonial and baptismal sponsorship are less rare and highlight the way in which apprentices begin to extend the construction of social ties beyond immediate kin and toward normatively less and less trustworthy others. From father to master is the first step, beyond which these young men work their way toward the network of social ties that will enable them to survive in a society where, they can safely assume, few will disinterestedly wish them well.

Misrecognizing Awareness

In this light, it is revealing that the ironworker described himself as a patient man who wanted to train his apprentice in personal skills that would serve him well in the real world of social relations outside the workplace. In this sense, he presented himself to me as the wise pedagogue who wished his apprentices nothing other than success and prosperity and a safe life amid the dangers of social life. But his contemptuous parody of the indulgent mother's voice—"Sit down, my poor tired child!"—showed that he clearly distinguished between his own role and that of a parent. Above all, it showed where this training was actually headed: toward developing a tough resilience, far removed from the tender care of an indulgent mother, so that the apprentice would acquire the confidence and social skill to face his peers. One of the Irakliot women who watched the video clip of this pair thought the master was saying, "I don't have time to bother with you now. I've got work now!" She described the boy, by contrast, as desperate for instruction (hardly the master's view of him!), attributing to him a beseeching desire to be instructed: "Will he give me any work to do with the iron? I'll manage whatever he gives me to do. Just let him have me try!"

The master's refusal to engage in conversation locks the apprentice into all the disadvantages of a palpably working-class mien. By effectively encouraging the boy's insubordination—although the master explicitly denied he was trying to do anything of the sort—he was certainly preparing him for the realities of social life, but perhaps not in the way that his idealizing rhetoric might have implied. In effect, he was helping the boy to develop a variety of low cunning that might make him an admirable partner in the management of a small artisanal business but that would debar him from polite society forever.

Indeed, the very denial of such pedagogical brutality, which is viewed negatively as unmodern in the terms of the global hierarchy of value, is in itself a piece of the puzzle. It suggests a strategy of facing the polite world in terms that conceal the very different reality to be found in the intimate spaces of family and workplace. This is a society in which mutual suspicion is generated and cultivated in the heart of the nuclear family but is disguised for external consumption. Ideologically, the family is united; pragmatically, it may be festering with insecurity. This duplex performance, the source of common Greek attitudes about not knowing what others really think or intend,[16] reproduces itself at all the encompassing levels of social life. Apprenticeship is one important arena in which young men learn to extend their social understanding beyond the home.

This refusal to acknowledge the brutalizing side of apprenticeship, a refusal that fits the pattern of duplex performance I am describing here, might be viewed as an example of what Bourdieu calls "misrecognition."[17] That term, however, reproduces the old "ideology as false consciousness" model, with all its attendant weaknesses. It is not clear that artisans are unaware of the advantages of refusing to acknowledge that they are exercising a particular form of discipline—one that, while it serves their own sense of control, also reproduces the attitudes that leave them socially weak members of their society and would do the same for their apprentices in turn. A man who has to earn a living may be less interested in long-term social mobility than in maintaining the limited power that he possesses in his own domain at a particular moment. Such patterns can be infinitely self-regenerating without necessitating any assumptions about a lack of self-awareness on the part of the actors. These are people who not only know that they have relatively few immediate choices but have learned to survive, both in the agonistic interactions with those of their social class and in the fight for recognition from those who exercise power over them—engineers, architects, and large contractors. Moreover, witnessing many of the interactions with the latter, apprentices learn how to play dumb (or at least be obsequious) while carefully observing. Some apprentices whose sullen slouch conveys utter boredom actually betray intense interest with their eyes, which thoughtfully follow their masters' every action. Masters must be aware of this; apprentices occasionally give themselves away by jumping a little too readily to anticipate what is clearly about to be a master's next command. One particularly wooden-looking lad, wearing the blankest of facial expressions, repeatedly managed to avoid glancing blows from a large piece of wood a more senior carpenter was casually swinging around as he inspected his own handiwork. Could it be that this skilled dissimulation is precisely the real lesson that masters want their apprentices to learn? Certainly it seems highly improbable that the apprentices might be unaware of their own devious self-management.

Reverting to a structuralist evocation of "unconscious models" may be as seriously misleading as the notion of misrecognition:[18] artisans seem to be very fully aware of the tight constraints on their range of possible social action, and that is consistent with an ability to theorize their social world. I suspect that the process of learning these sad facts of life begins in earnest with the frustrations of apprenticeship. Denial of any such consciousness is evidence of neither false consciousness nor bad faith. It is simply a key component of the techniques of living in a society where the unconstrained giving of free information—any information—is seen as squandering a scarce resource.

Thus, just as a child has to be trained not to blurt out family secrets to strangers,[19] the apprentice's first lesson is in the avoidance of speech. The first jobs the apprentice undertakes are of a kind that require no detailed instruction; they are boringly repetitive and hard on an active young body. A cobbler might have his novice apprentice spend each day pulling nails out of shoes awaiting repair; in earlier times, when most cobblers had several apprentices, the novices were expected to produce a whole kilo of used nails each day, hammering them back into shape on an anvil from opening time until at least midday. A tailor would have his apprentices work with needle and thimble on a rag until they could be trusted with the expensive cloth actually used in tailoring. Even in the relative comfort of a jeweler's shop, the apprentice is first, and for many months, made to process castings, at first working only on cheap materials that will never be sold. Hunched over the equipment for hours on end, repeating over and over a job that (as one master jeweler rather sternly remarked) requires "a lot of backside" (that is, sitting on one's bottom), he learns to slow down his movements, restrict his speech to what is absolutely necessary, and expect little praise and frequent grimaces of dissatisfaction and annoyance.

Even when it might serve the master's interests, speech in search of initiative is discouraged in apprentices. (Again there are striking parallels with what Lanoue reports from Italy.)[20] Initiative must come from within, from embodied knowledge rather than from verbalized communication. A baker's lad complained that when he and his mates ran out of dough and fillings, he would ask his boss what to do next. "'Didn't I tell you what to do? When you've finished, clean up,' he said, 'the walls, wherever they're dirty.' And I cleaned away the whole time. And as soon as I'd finished I would speak to him again [to ask for instructions], and then he'd give me a regular beating!" A former house painter explained that the one thing he would explicitly say to his apprentices was that he was not prepared to instruct them verbally. "Don't ask me anything, because I won't tell you how [it's done]," he would say. The apprentice was supposed to watch and observe, for example, the master's choice of paint color: "So you will learn how to 'steal' the work and it'll stay in your brain!"

This, however, was a benign mode, in which the artisan showed his pedagogical hand in order to encourage his apprentices to develop a sense of initiative. Others were considerably less gentle in their methods. A merchant who felt he had lifted himself out of a demeaning artisanal profession looked back at the way artisans treated their apprentices with barely disguised contempt, equating the absence of instruction with the frequent beating as two aspects of the same lack of polish: "He would beat you, for example, he'd beat you brutally [vanafsa], or he would not want to teach you the work. That is, the others [i.e., the other, older apprentices] would hide the work, knowing what they were learning, those others who were completely uneducated, because, completely lacking in encyclopedic knowledge or out of jealousy, they didn't want to show [how the work should be done]." A novice apprentice would often find himself trapped between the dour silence of the master and the jealousy of older apprentices who feared the excessive enthusiasm of the young interloper and would do everything in their power to exclude him.

But it was not only the older apprentices who zealously hugged the craft secrets to their secretive bodies. Often the master himself would be unwilling to impart any information at all. The motives for such secretiveness on the part of the master were not always clear. Sometimes he simply feared the potential future competition of a bright young lad, or sometimes he wanted to protect his interests from gossip; even the house painter kept the secrets of some colors to himself for fear that a chatterbox of an apprentice might reveal too much to a rival artisan. On other occasions, as I have indicated, an artisan may have been interested in developing the boy's initiative and resolve. For a good master craftsman, the real test of an apprentice was the latter's willingness to defy the master and ferret out the techniques and rhythms of work on his own. In the countryside, where a workshop often consisted of one artisan and a single apprentice, the master "didn't show you how to do something but wanted you to start off on your own, to take the initiative to do what was right and proper. And that, during the work, with certain hints, not with direct conversations, so he gave you the possibility of understanding, always in an indirect way, what was right."

Touch, Measurement, and Silence

It is certainly not the case that artisans are incapable of translating this pre-dominantly nonverbal mode of learning into verbal form. A builder, explaining how he always "stole" the techniques from his master, talked about how to break up stone in very specific terms: "But I learned the craft before he could tell me anything. Even with regard to breaking up stones; that is, if you hit a stone in the middle, it'll break up, it'll get really smashed to pieces. If you pay attention to a piece of the stone and hit it on the edge, only the protruding bit will break off. That, of course, he did not tell me. I saw it in practice. And I seized it." Words, useful in the attempt to generalize from experience, are no substitute for the tactility required of a truly proficient artisan in the course of the work itself; and when an apprentice finds that he has an apti-tude for the use of sight and touch in a particular craft, when he finds that this craft "inspires" him to acquire "huge amounts of knowledge," that is the craft (as the same builder explained to me) from which he will try to make his living.

Words are not entirely absent from all artisan-apprentice exchanges. Much depends on the attitude of an individual master, although even those who are more willing to impart their knowledge do so through a pedagogy that challenges the apprentices to greater ingenuity. A good master artisan might ask the apprentice searching questions, testing his developing knowl-edge by getting him to explain in the midst of the work what each move signified and why they were doing it, but even such an artisan would never himself provide explicit instruction as such. On the contrary, the imposition of silence deflects the apprentice from any incipient tendency to learn by straightforward means and teaches him that it can only be done—that any information at all can only be gained—by stealth and indirection. There is a close parallel here with the way in which the Italian apprentices described by Lanoue learn that shouted orders are often simply a way of wasting their time unless, on their own initiative, they perform unspecified tasks that can be done while dancing attendance on a peremptory master who in fact has absolutely no need of their presence at that moment but has simply called them to him as an exercise of authority.[21]

On the whole, most artisans do not give much latitude to their apprentices; as one person remarked, they do not give them generous "margins" within which to work—a comment that unconsciously (if inversely) echoes the "peripherality" that Lave and Wenger insist is in fact the appropriate context of artisanal learning. The person who offered this comment, and who was critical of the practices he saw around him, contrasted the ways in which artisans exploited their apprentices with what he called "an orthodox mode of learning." But this, too, is a curious inversion of what we might ordinarily understand by the term. "Orthodox," possibly intended here simply to invoke an image of pure learning, actually suggests an—also unconscious—echo of ecclesiastical models of monastic discipline, which included the fierce schooling of young pupils idealized by Chrysostom and perhaps reproduced in one Rethemniot jeweler's remark that learning the work required long hours of sitting still. Such rigid models as Chrysostom's are probably the historical antecedents of the ways in which artisans try to discipline young bodies. In their reliance on rote learning, however, these models also undermine the very idea of individualized creativity and thus the possibility of peripheral learning. They are in this sense much closer to the artisans' stern image of what happens in their workshops than they are either to the covert insubordination that actually takes place there or to the cheeky indiscipline of the modern schoolroom.[22]

In the larger workshops in town, moreover, it was the older apprentices who were supposed to speak to the novices if speech was absolutely necessary, but then only to growl, as one cobbler recalled, "You didn't do that right!" or "Fix it better!" In this way, the older apprentices, or *kalfadhes*, were able to maintain their authority over the novices (by curtly giving orders that showed their superior knowledge while refusing to offer any actual instruction) while accepting the ultimate authority of the master (by accepting the responsibility of transmitting it downward and thereby sparing the master the necessity of demeaning himself through speech with the novices). These older apprentices were, or so they hoped, on their way to achieving mastery of their craft and of themselves as appropriate embodiments of gruff masculinity.

Academics are liable to read silence as evidence of a lack of awareness, whether of self or of the surroundings. But this interpretation ignores the very different meaning that silence can have in a workshop where, aside from the fact that chatter is a distraction, both parties—the master and his apprentices—may have an interest, although not the same one, in maintaining a stony barrier against direct communication. (The older apprentices actually demonstrate awareness through their manipulation of the liminal zone between silence and speech, since it is a zone in which they can, if sufficiently skillful, stake out their ascendant authority and so show that they understand and have mastered the rules of the social game.) On the other hand, while silence may frustrate the young apprentice's attempts to learn, it also renders his thinking impenetrable to the master. And precisely because the apprentice's response will be a mark of his emergent social skill, it may also serve for the master as an index of the apprentice's success in doing things for himself. In that regard, even the older apprentices do not escape critical evaluation. The ironworker who had such a stormy relationship with his novice apprentice, for example, nevertheless seemed to think that the boy might eventually do very well, whereas he complained of feeling that his *kalfas* (senior apprentice) did not "love" the work, because "whatever we do I have to tell him myself; he has no leaning toward initiative." If we are to believe the master, he actually challenged the *kalfas*, saying that he had noticed the latter's disaffection, to which the *kalfas* had responded, "Yes, it's true that I don't like it. One of these days I'm going to quit."

It is the master who dislikes being forced to speak. Not only does speaking compel him to deal directly with his help but, in developing the latter's social and professional skills, initiative is the crucial factor. An apprentice's initiative saves the master time and therefore money, and it suggests a reliable partner in the making. The *kalfas*, often characterized as one who prevents younger apprentices from learning the trade, is always potentially also a failed master. He is someone who risks remaining forever close to the demeaning category of the "apprentice," someone who "does not have the capacity to develop into a master [*mastoras*] because of the mental deficiency he has"—a terrible indictment in a society where men are judged so harshly by their peers. Such a failed individual may indeed be "more to his master's liking" precisely because he poses no threat of serious competition. That is a social stigma that most Cretan men would do anything to avoid.

It is the fear of this failure (or realization that one is already accounted a failure) that surely reinforces the senior apprentices' displays of contempt or indifference toward their juniors: "The *kalfas* is the failure who doesn't have the vision to progress and have his own work and the rest of it." Such a person easily resents the precocious upstart who tries to succeed where he has already been condemned to failure in the eyes of their boss and the world, and who offers perhaps his last chance to prove (at least to himself) that he is aggressive and competitive. A young apprentice who demands verbal explanations may yet learn that this is not the way to get ahead; a *kalfas* who does so has clearly never learned the art of surreptitiously absorbing treasured knowledge and is therefore now unlikely ever to make a useful partner or ally. A young apprentice who asks a *kalfas* for direction is therefore opening himself up to having all the latter's failure heaped upon his own young head, especially when he does so in the form of a request for verbal instruction. Speech may be the mark of intelligence in the world of book learning, to which artisans proudly oppose their own universe of manual skill; it is the very opposite of the cunning, the *poniria*, through which a man can survive in an agonistic social world—a world in which dissembling, indirection, and the suggestive flicker of eye and hand convey volumes of social information too subtle to be effectively carried by words.

Even a more experienced employee may be forced to act in this way more than he expects, particularly if he comes from outside. Asked whether his Syrian apprentice was as good at the work as himself, a builder responded, with evident approval, that the young man was "worse than me!"—an expression that suggests admiration for a wayward character and its importance as the only viable basis for artisanal learning. When I asked whether a young apprentice had an appetite for his work, the approving answer was, "Yes, he's cunning [*poniros*]!" This is clearly high praise.[23]

Such attitudes are best learned early, but they may be very useful later on if one is forced to learn a new trade or in a new place. A pastrycook's assistant, for example, arriving in Rethemnos as a stranger, experienced entrenched hostility from most of his colleagues. Although he did not complain, he had to "steal with his eyes" just like a complete novice in order to learn how to make locally popular items; the others were not about to tell him their professional skills, since it was in their interest that this stranger should ultimately fail. They would have seen him as a formidable competitor, because they probably assumed not only that he possessed highly desirable skills of his own but also that what had induced him to leave home must have been the high wages, significantly above what they themselves could command, to which such imagined skills would presumably have entitled him. "I stole most [of the craft] by myself. The owners saw what was going on. I never complained about it." Presumably, the owners were waiting to see whether he would catch on—learning not only the secret techniques that the others were hiding from him but also the art of looking as though he did not really care even as he exploited the false sense of security that his silence created. Learn he did; and so he survived, bearing a heavy load of resentment but also glowing with self-confidence in his daily work.

The absence of speech is thus a mask or shield, and it provides the space for the actual learning to occur. That learning does not concern the craft alone. The hand and eye, said a builder, become accustomed to the work, and then "the brain is not absorbed." While confidence is both professionally and socially essential, it also relieves the artisan of the need to concentrate; indeed, as we have seen, concentration may actually undermine skill by producing too intent a focus on immediate ends. The menial tasks of carrying and bending that every novice artisan learns are the first to become routinized in this fashion; they constitute a "rhythm," as do such tasks as hearing the nails being pounded into a parquet floor and being able to tell whether the temperature produced by this action is rising to the point where the nails will become soft and start to bend.[24] If such complex tasks are harder to acquire than the simple fetch-and-carry variety, they are, by that token, all the more valuable forms of knowledge for the apprentice to assimilate. There is thus a part of the emergent artisan's mind that becomes free to wonder why it is that, just as he is becoming increasingly proficient at his work, he is also both debarred from more challenging work and becoming all the more skilled at dissembling and presenting a face of bored indifference to the world at the same time. If he is bright and observant, he will soon reckon that acquiring the craftiness of appearing none too bright or observant is part and parcel of the same process as learning how to craft objects of artisanal artistry. Both are expressions of a humble status that carries its own secretive pride.

There is another reason to avoid displays of verbal cleverness as much as possible. Speech interferes with perhaps the most important aspect of learning in an artisanal workshop: the analogical nature of the learning process itself. In Greek the word *analogha*, from which the English "analogy" is derived, does not distinguish between the twin meanings of "in proportion" and "analogously." In the most general sense, it is used to indicate a straightforward relationship of appropriate connection (as in "according to the circumstances"). This convergence of measurement, parallel form, and what is socially appropriate is highly significant, since it shows that, for speakers of Greek, there is no necessary conceptual distinction between fitting by size and fitting by shape or between what fits materially and what is "fitting" in a social sense. Perhaps "fitting" is indeed the best available translation of *analogha*. It comes across clearly in an artisan's quite casual remark that even on the commercial side imitation is the key to the way apprentices must learn: "Perhaps, let's say, if we go to the commercial level as well, an apprentice learns to see how commercial deals are made, so that he, too, learns how to behave analogously [*analogha*] in a similar [*analoyi*] situation." Here we see clearly the principle that work forms appropriate character. And while this speaker was cautioning against a too-ready assumption that artisans only use learning by imitation while apprentice merchants always require verbal instruction, a distinction in which many artisans certainly profess to have faith, we also see in this remark a realization that, as Lave and Wenger have noted, it is in learning rather than in the passive activity of being taught that apprentices come to learn the rules of the social game.

At one extreme, then, silence is the mark of a certain type of learning—learning that cannot be found in the schoolroom. The apprentice who remains silent, but unobtrusively watchful, has already learned the basic lesson. Those who are really aware of the nature of competition among artisans are aware, too, that speaking is a sign of excessive curiosity and perhaps of dangerous knowledge already gained: "I watched. But I did not speak. Because, if I spoke, I would have had to leave. I knew that I would [eventually] leave. Because whoever learned his secrets got into . . . I mean, he'd get what he needed after working there and then he'd have to leave—there was no middle-ground solution. And I preferred not to speak so I would learn more and leave when I wanted to, not when he wanted." This is the voice of one who learned the most important lesson of all: not only does the apprentice who talks too much disrupt the routines of the workshop and reveal his own potential weakness, but, if he lets too much information slip, he also reveals the very real danger of competition that he poses for his employer, who will then get rid of him as fast as possible. Playing dumb is the invisible mark of an intelligence that knows the arts of self-concealment.

Visible Secrecy

To be sure, the idea that apprentices do not learn from verbal instruction but are forced to "steal with their eyes" is not only an exaggeration but is far from unique to Crete. Nor is it confined to male interaction: Vanessa Maher, for example, notes that it is common among north Italian seamstresses.[25] In Japan, it is part of the accepted parlance of artisanal apprentices and their expected response to the austere conditions of many highly competitive trades.[26] But in a part of the world where reciprocal theft is still rampant in rural areas, where it has a high degree of normativity,[27] stealing with the eyes takes on a more explicitly masculine significance and conveys a sense of assured expertise and cunning. Theft is, after all, the ultimate expression of a competitive relationship. It continues long past apprenticehood; one artisan remarked that "my eye goes in and I steal ideas" whenever he saw attractively finished work in people's houses. Moreover, the ability to communicate without words is the basis for trust among strong men. That notion is perhaps most familiar from the "rule of silence" (omertà) to be found among mafiosi in Italy, but it is also deeply rooted in rural Cretan society—as its association with successful animal theft shows.

But theft is also associated with a form of secrecy that is highly visible. This is not as absurd as it sounds: when I was collecting narratives of animal theft in a Cretan village, for example, I found that shepherds would willingly come to my house there in order to record their wild tales, but that they would make a huge demonstration of appearing to come and go surreptitiously, perhaps hoping that these performances would be visible from the nearby main street. When I asked whether it would be appropriate to record lamenting at a funeral, I was told to place a discreetly small recorder in my pocket but to make sure that it was nevertheless partially visible, so that people would see and appreciate my efforts to be, ironically, secretive.[28] This is secrecy performed; and, as such, it is also the performance of a cultural competence. While for me it was positive, in that it enabled me to approach the social experience of the villagers more closely, for them, as for Rethemniot artisans, it confirms their culturally lowly slot in the global scheme of things.

The secretiveness of master artisans and apprentices' surreptitious "theft" of their knowledge are similarly performative and similarly limiting of their ability to function in arenas defined by ideologies of cosmopolitanism and sophistication. This aspect does not in itself have anything to do with the avoidance of speech as such: in a study of traditional Chinese medicine—in the transmission of which verbal instruction plays a central (if not always predictable) role—Elisabeth Hsu draws heavily but critically on Georg Simmel's understanding of the social basis of secrecy in order to show how master healers may engage in "a performative demonstration of possessing a secret that others did not have"; she somewhat cryptically remarks that such secrecy can be "a weapon of the weak."[29] While it may be grounded in the esoteric ritual practices of healers, that secrecy also apparently takes on political implications both between apprentices and their masters and between healers and the wider world.

In the context of the global hierarchy of value, the latter remark takes on clearer implications for the Cretan case, where silence may have the double significance of masculine reserve and a self-discipline, perhaps grounded in monastic models, that inspires trust and respect. Apprentices learn that a demonstrative ability to be secretive is an enormous asset in the short term: it shows them to be true men, it allows them to acquire esoteric craft knowledge, but above all it shows, by association with the idea that true artisans are those who can keep their secrets intact, that they are moving toward mastery of that knowledge. In that sense, more important than learning the craft is learning to maintain its secrets; and more important than maintaining its secrets is learning to demonstrate that this is exactly what one is doing. Such a tactic is unambiguously the kind of short-term device that James Scott calls a weapon of the weak and to which he attributes the quality of resistance. But, like all such weapons, it backfires in the longer term, here because it signals to others that the actor is dependent on such secrecy to maintain authority, which is consequently shown to have a very unstable shelf life—a classic feature of power in face-to-face societies but much devalued in the context of a global definition of modernity.[30]

Secrecy is also gendered through its association with domesticity. A revealing incident in my fieldwork shows how it can backfire. Markos, a merchant, was discussing with me the arrangements he had made to ensure that his two sons could avoid becoming wage laborers; he had set each one up with a shop, but the older son's wife then ended up working for the younger, so there was a measure of cooperation within the family. All this was a straightforward enough tale of social mobility, and Markos was clearly happy to relate it and have me write it down. Suddenly his wife, who had been silently following the conversation, exploded with unmistakable anger: she did not want me writing all that information about her sons, and she refused to believe that I would use it anonymously. Why should she trust me? In this community, she insisted, even a brother might do one harm, which was an extreme expression of suspicion toward kin that is nevertheless rampant in this community. Markos kept scoffing at her fears as women's stupidity and insisted that I continue writing down his remarks. This was an acutely uncomfortable situation for me; Markos himself clearly thought my ethical scruples about continuing the discussion were absurd.[31] His wife's anger was not—at least exclusively—a public performance of secrecy or a concern to safeguard the details of the family's income but revealed above all a deep concern that virtually any information could be used to damage a family's reputation: what the husband rather proudly regarded as his cleverness at setting his sons up in business might be construed instead as creating the dependence of one son on the other; and the older son's rise from an apprentice's pittance to self-sufficiency might be taken to reveal the working-class origins of one whose ambitions were now to stay unambiguously within the merchant class.

Fragility compounds fragility, the performance revealing more cracks in a façade of bourgeois achievement: a wife terrified of exposure, a husband unable to control her fury despite his highly gendered scoffing, an anxious desire to climb the social ladder that itself revealed how insecurely they all stood on the rungs that they had attained, and a society in which even the closest of kin might stand forever ready to knock them all off their social perches. Information is a precious commodity in such a setting; on this occasion, my own inquiries set off a variant of the usual suspicions about ethnographers, to the effect that either I was investigating local craft production on behalf of an American company for investment purposes or such a company would be able to use my data to that end. It is in this context of pervasive suspicion that we must also understand the angry anxieties of the shopkeeper's wife. The husband's airy display of insouciance—a gender-specific display that seemed intentionally contrasted with his wife's anxieties—might well have been a defensive strategy, a demonstrative but ambiguous form of secretiveness designed to deflect attention away from even more precarious aspects of their lives and so to inspire the confidence that is men's most reliable social capital. But for his wife this entailed too high a risk: any information at all, as she declared in a statement that had all the unchallengeable credibility of a proverbial assertion, could be grist to a potential enemy's mill.

Men, too, may be suspicious of the uses to which information will be put, but they will generally act as though they did not care. One former waiter, recounting the mean wage his maternal uncle had paid him at their village seaside restaurant, initially expressed great embarrassment that I would write down such an offensively low wage and relaxed only when I assured him that the information would remain anonymous. At that point, he could hardly have continued to show suspicion without incurring doubts about his self-confidence and hence his manhood (or perhaps his ability to understand what research was all about!). As far as I could judge, however, he did seem reassured at this juncture. His concern was presumably to avoid spreading revelations of unfairness at the very heart of his immediate group of kin—a normative strategy that has in fact long created the impression in ethnographic writing about Greece that families are always havens of pure domestic harmony.[32]

Rethemniots are very conscious of the fact that their community, while endowed with many of the features associated with bourgeois ideals of modernity, is still a small circle of people who often know each other well and observe each other's actions intently and not always benignly. This mixture of bourgeois aspirations and inescapable neighborliness is highly combustible. Housewives, for example, still sniff the air to assess their neighbors' economic state on the basis of how often the smell of meat can be detected.[33] Virtually anything can be used to assess another person's economic standing, personal stability, and moral worth. In this context, even the most trivial datum can take on the allure of a forbidden pleasure as well as the utility of a dangerous social weapon. A demonstrative capacity for discretion thus serves as a guarantee of social savoir faire. But there is an important distinction between the respective roles of men and women in this regard. Men occupy more public work spaces and more visible roles in daily politics. A man might thus display his concern to protect *others'* secrets, in contrast to a display of indifference about the fate of his own, while his wife must attend to the immediate business of protecting their domestic economy and may not be able to afford the luxury of appearing (as we would say) to give away the store. Indeed, her own reputation as a manager might suffer more from any hint of indiscretion regarding her own family than it would from gossip about others—a trait that is stereotypically attributed to women in this society almost as a matter of course, and that might even be appreciated as advancing her own family's interests by attacking those of other households.

Men must pay more attention to maintaining a reputation for discretion with regard to clients' affairs, and this becomes important in the several artisanal trades that necessarily entail learning clients' personal secrets. Perhaps most of all, goldsmith-jewelers are privy to an enormous range of highly personal information. One sternly told his apprentices: "You are to pay attention to one thing: what you see happening in this shop, and when various people come to the shop to buy, never going any further, you'll hear, you'll see, and you will not say anything about it. Because the goldsmith's work is like a doctor's. He sees, hears, learns about all sorts of things. Because it's about the [engagement and marriage] gifts, the marriage brokering, what with one thing and another, you must not speak about any of it." While the goldsmith's work does not afford the possibilities for displaying male physicality that one sees among ironworkers and carpenters, the need to impose a particularly rigorous silence not only makes good sense commercially, as it allows the goldsmith to build up a clientele of people who trust him to keep a secret, but also suggests the verbal continence (the avoidance of verbal promiscuity, as it were) that men claim marks them off from women.[34]

Speech thus represents a danger to the reputation of an artisan, while suppressing it implies tough masculinity, dependability, and self-reliance. No wonder, then, that artisans are reluctant to coach their apprentices verbally and see such instruction as an early sign of impending failure. If the apprentice will not learn silence, how will he learn the craft itself? And how can he ever be trusted not to spread craft secrets to rivals and not to broadcast sensitive gossip about valued customers? Silence is thus the first quality that an apprentice must learn. And it must not be mere silence; it must be palpable silence into the bargain—a silence that makes itself heard. This is more than the lack of verbality that one local boot-maker attributed to artisans' general lack of schooling; semiliterate Cretans are often highly verbal,[35] and their masculinity sometimes depends on demonstrating a clever control of language. The key, however, is control. In certain situations, of which interaction in the artisanal workshop is an excellent example, that control appears most clearly performed in a demonstrative reluctance to speak at all.

We can thus explain artisans' reluctance to speak with their apprentices in a more nuanced way than the usual focus on the fear of subsequent competition will allow. It is clear that the very refusal to impart knowledge directly forms a central plank of the pedagogical relationship: the apprentices learn that knowledge directly taught is neither reliable nor embodied, but they also learn that it displays the wrong mode of social relations. While academically learned knowledge may carry a higher social cachet, it provides a poor preparation for the socially competitive world in which artisans must live, and from which few envision realistic means of escaping. In general, artisans affect to despise the knowledge that comes from books and classes and avoid speaking to their apprentices. Their principled reticence thus demonstratively proclaims the importance of what is socially effective knowledge in its own right.

Chapter Five

Boredom and Stealth

Three Pedagogical Artisans

There are, to be sure, some exceptions to the harsh pedagogical pattern described in the last chapter, and these provide a point of departure for thinking about the relationship between artisanal pedagogy and the desire for modernity. Although it is hard to assess the degree to which they were simply reproducing a rhetoric of modernity in order to make a good impression, three artisans did in fact claim that they taught their apprentices very carefully. One of these, a floor-maker, elaborated a whole philosophy of pedagogy. A key emphasis for him lay on the need for school truants who apprenticed themselves to skilled artisans to acquire basic mathematical skills, not only as a shield against being cheated by unscrupulous clients but also as a basis for eventually becoming independent artisans in turn; he also tried to teach his apprentice the basics of good manners in dealing with clients at all times. Without those skills, he claimed, apprentices would be condemned to lifelong drudgery and economic dependence.

Perhaps because his own son, who gently explained many details to the slightly younger apprentice, not only was adept at the artisanal work but also was studying hard to achieve his ambition to become a teacher, the floor-maker was very much aware of the difference between the socially as well as pedagogically open-ended nature of formal schooling on the one hand and the sometimes deadening drudgery of craft apprenticeship on the other. He could afford to contemplate a future in which his son would reach a comfortable status as a teacher and have the means as well as the duty of maintaining the father in old age, while he could also bring a lively village lad into the floor-making business with the hope of thereby creating a new partnership and an eventual succession.

The second such artisan, a carpenter, claimed to be aware that any young lad who came to him as an apprentice would be looking to learn the trade: "the lad wants to learn; he doesn't come to get a wage—what's he going to do with it afterward? He comes to learn certain things, so to speak, and as much as possible I try to get him into the meaning of the work—its spirit, let's say. How a door is made, how you can measure a door, from the start." Note that here, too, measurement is considered important. A minimal degree of numeracy will allow a young artisan to survive in a world dominated by those who have completed their high-school education. This carpenter attributes the change in attitude he expresses here to the fact that today's apprentices are older than they used to be; this itself is a sign of the modernity to which he lays claim, as is the fact that he also emphasizes that the specific kind of instruction that had to be imparted verbally, and could not simply be learned by observation, concerned the sometimes very dangerous machines that an earlier generation had not known.

The floor-maker and the third artisan in this exceptional group were the successive employers of a boy who had come from the countryside at a very tender age to seek work. The floor-maker was patient but rarely spoke very much to the lad, although he insisted that he instructed him in the general terms of his philosophy and was certainly kind in the relatively few spoken exchanges in which I heard him engage with the boy. The boy's subsequent employer and my third artisanal pedagogue, a garage mechanic and thus a more obviously "modern" artisan, was so impressed with the lad's eagerness to learn as well as his helpfulness on the job—"How do we do this? How do we fix it?"—that he deliberately sought to cultivate his interest further. Far from displaying the usual impatience with verbal questions that infuriate so many other masters, he saw in them an eager adaptability that augured well for the boy's future in a "modern" trade—a trade that offered some hope of escaping from the lowly status with which the boy had entered it. The convergence of tolerance of the boy's insistent questioning with the exercise of a profession that proclaims its own modernity is not coincidental.

Promethean Tactics: Stealing the Artisans' Fire

For the most part, however, capable apprentices rapidly come to realize that the only way to acquire knowledge is by stealth.[1] What a European ideologue might represent as initiative, individualism, and career choice emerges as a necessity that inflects small movements of the body as much as large trajectories through time: "If you pay attention to a piece of the stone and hit it on the edge, only the protruding bit will break off. That, of course, he did not tell me. I saw it in practice. And I seized it." And the speaker elaborated with didactic speech—an interesting move, given that in his view this was presumably a mode of pedagogy to be used only with those of lesser practical understanding: "Let me explain something to you: a young person, who has a natural intelligence, does many kinds of job and learns many kinds of work— he learns many tasks, and then he ends up with the most...with the one that draws him. That is, a person with a brain acquires enormous knowledge. On his own!" We can hardly ignore the instructive irony of this man's verbal articulacy as I now introduce a further constriction of the communicative mode, this time moving from speech to writing.

When apprentices ask questions, they risk a reprimand or even physical punishment; but when they manage to work out the answers on their own, they may even be praised for their initiative. At least in the hinterland villages where some artisans (especially saddle-makers) still ply their trade, there is sometimes an explicit acknowledgment of the parallel with the reciprocal theft of sheep and goats among shepherds: "That is to say, I seized the craft by stealing it, as we say. As we say, now, *klepsia* when we talk about sheep.[2] That's how I got it, so to say: by stealth [*kleftondas*]."

In this way, again like shepherds, whose thefts serve to gain recognition for their manhood and alliances with their erstwhile foes, they move closer to the day when they may be invited into partnership as worthy allies and potentially dangerous competitors. A young man whose mother's brother was a butcher watched his uncle surreptitiously from behind a refrigerator. When the day was nearly done, the uncle would stride off from the shop, commanding his nephew to sweep the floor clean and lock up. This was the nephew's chance. He would gather up the scraps of meat that his uncle had scattered around the floor and practice cutting and slicing according to his secret observations.

This young man did not in fact enter the trade, being destined for other things (he eventually became a teacher of English!); but it is clear that, had he opted to stay in the butchering business, his skills would have been gained by peeping nervously from behind the refrigerator rather than as a result of any careful instruction his uncle might have offered him. Every time another young man, a plasterer's assistant, tried to imitate the technique of marking off the areas designated for plastering, his boss would send him off to fetch "mud" (basic plaster), ensuring that he would not be able to learn the technique because, the apprentice thought, his boss wanted "to have me as a laborer forever." A carpenter recalled how, as an apprentice, he would peer around his master or over the latter's head, but when the master caught him sidling up beside him, he would send him off to buy him a pack of cigarettes—a clear subordination of the apprentice to the master's whim, to his secrecy about his craft, and to the importance of adapting everything to the presence of the prominent everyday symbol and instrument of male sociability. This apprentice, like the butcher's lad, would wait for opportunities during the master's absence; once, wanting to copy a table for a friend, he looked at the work in progress while the master was absent and copied down the salient points on a piece of paper. He never let his master know of this surreptitious learning, still less of the literate means he used to garner it, but the master may well have been aware that something of the kind was going on. As some Rethemniots like to say, "Whoever is an abbot has also been a monk in his cell," a proverbial usage that serves to underscore the monastic overtones of artisanship, both in its implications of a disciplined life and in the echo of Chrysostom's recognition of the importance of dissimulation. The proverb resonates with intergenerational experience as well, since successful artisans would hardly have failed to remember their own youthful inculcation into artifice.

Generally speaking, the one situation in which a master will explain the techniques of the craft to his pupil is when that pupil is his own son. When I showed the video clips, many noticed that one particular master carpenter spoke to his assistant; what the viewers did not know was that this was indeed a father-son pair. A former tailor described his initiation into the trade at the hands of his father, who showed him how to sew and would occasionally tell him, "Stick the needle in like this!" But this man later became a clothing merchant; and in the mercantile trades, where absolute trust is essential because large amounts of cash often accumulate in the shops,[3] the only assistants likely to be found from outside the proprietor's nuclear family are, contrary to what happens in craft workshops, his close agnates—people who have an interest in his prosperity rather than in undermining it. (Merchants also seem more interested in keeping the firm within the clan, so those who have no male children are supposedly more likely to bequeath the business to a brother's, rather than to a sister's, son.)

As the tailor-turned-clothes-merchant said, a kinsperson who works in your shop "doesn't feel like an employee"—which is fine when all concerned share an interest in straight commercial profit, as in a clothing store, but can have disastrous consequences in a craft workshop, where it undermines discipline and provides opportunities to set up in competition. Older employees who may lack the capacity to develop an independent workshop are especially reluctant to let a new apprentice learn, "because they'd say, 'If he learns, he'll send me packing!'" Most of those kinsfolk the clothier employs in his store are students working their way through school; they have no ambitions in the business as such, and the owner can represent employing them as a form of mutual aid (*allilovoithia*) rather than as a form of wage labor. A baker recalled employing the children of relatives as a waste of time: these were not true apprentices but adolescents trying to make up for their parents' stingy allocation of pocket money and were more of a nuisance than a help.

There is a certain logic to the fact that agnates are more likely to show up as shop assistants than as craft apprentices. Stealing money from close agnates is far less lucrative, in the long run, than stealing craft knowledge, since one has less of an interest in setting up in competition with the owner than with keeping him as a friendly financial resource against a time of need. Even the clothier just mentioned, however, remembered that in the craft workshops masters were reluctant to explain techniques or share any knowledge at all. The apprentice, he remarked, "didn't just work in the shop. The guy might want to send me to the vineyard, to a vineyard to go and carry water and then to eat the food that he was cooking there. Or he'd send me to go and clean out the stable, to sweep up the donkey's mess, in that other house he had in the alley. Apprentices did many jobs, they didn't just do the work itself, and at the same time they learned the craft."

But learning was the apprentice's problem, not the master's, and this is another important lesson: "It is difficult for someone to show how a craft is done. You have to steal it on your own; they didn't show you, except when [the master] really liked you enough to show you the craft. So you are at it for many years. That is to say, the first two years would go by and you didn't know a thing; they didn't let you into the work at all." And the clothier dismissed the idea that masters might be testing their apprentices' initiative with a dismissive shrug: "Bah, they didn't want you to learn the craft so you wouldn't get [independent] work; [they wanted you] not to learn the craft so they would have you as their apprentice forever!" In a word, in this view employers lull their apprentices into the passivity that comes with endlessly boring routine. By so doing, however, they are also teaching the sharper apprentices that they must always look out for themselves, and they are drilling that lesson into them through sustained experiential pressure.

Battling with Boredom

The boring routines can easily discourage the less keen apprentices from pursuing craft knowledge with any tenacity. In fact, however, there is more to the production of boredom than simply the dulling of the apprentices' senses and sensibilities. For the sharper ones, boring routines have exactly the opposite effect: the boys learn to don a mask of boredom while actively probing their environment for new information. Men learn early to assume facial expressions that convey a conventional message.

Among such expressions, a common male habit of pursing the lips while nodding solemnly is, for example, an assurance of patriotic outrage; it almost always accompanies mention of the Turks and underscores assertions of a shared and certain knowledge of their predictable perfidy. In business relations, too, there are facial conventions that seem calculated to set the right tone. I particularly recall how one goldsmith with whom I was speaking would begin, every time a customer entered his shop, to make a slow, sensuous chewing motion with his lips before composing them in an unctuous smile of delight, after which he would swing his whole body into a welcoming posture and his voice into a roar of greeting. (Spontaneity is often performed, sharing much of the paradoxical quality of secrecy in this regard; it is hard for me to forget, for example, the tirelessly genial host who, with every raising of his wineglass in stentorian salutation, kept exhorting his increasingly jaded guests, "Be happy!") Rethemniots are well aware that such expressions of spontaneous enthusiasm may be contrived; the goldsmith, for example, was described to me as a "cold" man, which is certainly not what he wanted to convey, and it was hard to avoid the sense of being backstage at the theater when watching the careful assumption of an appropriate facial mask. A facial expression of bored detachment does not necessarily correspond to one's innermost thoughts; in a society where people say that those thoughts are always ultimately inaccessible to others, however, it may prompt all manner of guesswork. Apprentices' affectations of boredom are both highly conventional and an excellent preparation for the more genial displays of insouciance that come later, with eventual mastery of both craft and manners.

The condition of boredom is an especially difficult aspect of apprenticeship to describe. Even simply watching long hours of videotaped artisanal labor quickly gives one an all-too-direct encounter with the dreary ennui that apprentices must endure in a physically far more comprehensive and unending fashion. How can we describe the tedium of everyday drudgery without ourselves succumbing to its deadening effect?

Yet boredom, paradoxically, is a fascinating dimension of apprenticeship. It has two functions that appear to contradict each other but that in practice are mutually constitutive and provide the framework of that complicity—here are the seeds of Gramscian hegemony!—between the resentful apprentice and the angry, bullying artisan. On the one hand, boredom is a means of control, allowing the artisan to force his apprentices into routines that make it hard for them to be overtly insubordinate. On the other, it provides the shield of insouciant disengagement that will in fact prove to the world that one is skilled enough not to care about showing off, a mark of that self-confidence that inspires the confidence of clients, and at the same time it also provides a cover behind which the artful apprentice can observe his master and steal the latter's secrets.

The mask of boredom that covers the act of stealing the master's secrets is a kind of dissimulation that exhibits a refusal to become too dependent on the master, but the apprentice also knows full well that any other mien will get no encouragement and thus does not wish to put himself through the embarrassment of rejection or reprimand. Oddly enough, this stance recalls what was supposed to be the classic mien of the so-called aristocrats of the 1930s and earlier, who are said to have looked neither to the right nor to the left as they walked through the streets of the town. While theirs was an affectation of power, a display of the confidence that they were entitled to their arrogance, it was also a refusal to engage with potential rejection in a society marked by a staunchly egalitarian ethos. Theirs was a stance of hauteur or indifference rather than of boredom, but, like the latter, it made it possible to refusal potentially demeaning or humiliating engagement with others and so provided for the most envied citizens one of the props supporting the ever precarious outer walls of masculine pride and self-confidence.

In the artisanal workshops, boredom is an instrument both for the learning of such defensive tactics and for their conduct. A Cretan woman student who viewed my video questionnaire thought that she actually saw an apprentice carpenter's eyes engage with what was going on only when the senior assistant and the master were not watching; at the very least, her expectation that this would be the case is indicative of the overall attitude. But boredom is not just a distracting affectation. It is often real enough, to judge from reminiscences of apprenticeship, and is induced through tasks designed to humiliate the youthful body of the apprentice and discipline it to the acceptance of routine.

That is certainly what we see on the surface, and it is reflected in the vocabulary of work and bodily posture. The task of carrying water or plaster for one's employer, for example, is described with a verb, *kouvalao*, that, together with *skivo* (meaning both "bend" to a task and "bow" to those with greater power), conjures up the particular physical humiliations of the apprentice. There is no doubt that these actions, and the words used to denote them, are understood in such terms, which are sometimes made explicit: "I am the master, so to speak, you are the worker, let's put it that way. You carry [*kouvalas*] plaster [literally, "mud"]. That is, I do the building, you carry the plaster!" Resentment of the many tasks that were not obviously related to craft needs as such (even today, an apprentice may be expected to make the master's coffee or run to get his cigarettes) emerges frequently in the autobiographical reminiscences of older artisans. Even the more mechanical tasks associated with the craft are viewed as demeaning and as lacking in interest.

Not only do these various tasks—whether craft related or not—require no speech, but they also physically remove the curious eyes of the apprentice from the space where they could "steal" the craft ("What are you staring at instead of carting [*kouvalas*] bricks?"). But this banishment, for an alert apprentice, is a challenge. By imposing such tasks on the apprentice, the master increases the pressure on him to become still more devious in pursuit of practical knowledge. In the end, this can often mean that the apprentice has to depart in search of a new job, because otherwise his boss will generally keep him at the same routine tasks as at the beginning. As one former builder grumbled, this is destructive of the apprentice's ability to learn the whole range of tasks entailed in the craft: "Instead of learning, I *un*learned, because, if the master was going to teach me, he should have taken on a workman—to do the work I was doing so I could do something different." Whether or not his employer so intended, the apprentice thus learned a valuable lesson—a lesson, however, about the importance of asserting his own rights and interests.

The early stages of an apprentice's training are often taken up with the most mind-numbing routines. Even those imposed by relatively benign employers are often exhausting and uncompromisingly menial: class structure could easily be reproduced within the workshop. A tailor's most junior apprentice, for example, would go to the workshop an hour ahead of his master, "and I swept up, cleaned the equipment, put on the coal—we used irons that were heated with coal. I would make a fire under the iron and the coals would light up and the iron would get hot so that the older ones who came in later to work could iron." Even though this was gentle labor compared with that of a carpenter's or a builder's novice apprentice, it introduced the lad to a sense of the hierarchy that would forever govern his social relationships, even though he might expect to rise internally within that same system. Moreover, apprentices were routinely expected to serve as estate servants, an emasculating status that specifically required them to help with normatively female tasks such as those of the washerwoman (*plistra*) and the olive picker (*mazokhtra*). A former saddle-maker recalled the sense of resentment that came with this requirement: "I had this complaint, that he sent me to work in the olive trees, which wasn't manly work." Note again how the internal gender hierarchy seals the relegation of the artisanal class to a disadvantaged position in relation to members of the local elite, who disdain such aggressive male pride as backward and unmodern.

Even those who recalled their employers with an affection verging on the filial saw in this kind of work a direct and humiliating challenge to their masculine pride; specifically, they expressed resentment over the implication that they were always in danger of losing control over their sense of self. Gender hierarchy is clear, for example, in the challenge to his pride that the saddle-maker had to endure when, fully qualified and independent in his craft, he would nevertheless be mocked by those of higher status as "a donkey's dressmaker" *(ghaidhouromodhistra)*—a common description of his work that placed his social worth in the double jeopardy of feminization and being the servant of donkeys, the most common animal symbol of social worthlessness.[4] (Indeed, his father had not wanted him to enter so ill-regarded a trade: "You'll get involved with donkeys? Become a barber, become a tailor, become a cobbler!") An apprentice learns quickly that he will always have to expect and contest such aggressive ridicule. Men cannot afford to hesitate in the struggle for masculine status.

Other modes of induction were even more clearly devices for inculcating a sense of embodied and humiliating hierarchy, as in the practice of making every new recruit pass under the work-counter of a cobbler. Before the 1936 laws regulating child labor and bringing work relations under the direct social supervision of the Fascist state,[5] an artisan might lock all his apprentices into his shop each night, to control their behavior and conserve their energies for his own ends. Each Saturday, which was payday, a shoemaker who had many apprentices would make them sit in two groups, the *kalfadhes* in front and the novice artisans behind, and pay them one by one, in order to dramatize the hierarchy that bound them all. Artisans' life histories are full of the resentment they felt at the continual hazing, the roster of menial tasks, the brusque commands and physical abuse, and the silence that many initially experienced as oppressive and confining. The masters' displays of alternating temper and indifference seemed to encourage inaction, but inaction would bring down on the hapless apprentices a string of abusive epithets, of which "stupid" *(boudalas)* was especially common. Yet the last thing the apprentice was supposed to do was to allow his own body to surrender to the routines that were ostensibly imposed on it. The trick was to *seem* utterly uninterested and submissive, perhaps even truly dull-witted, while actually taking care to learn, biding one's time until one could spring the evidence of one's newly acquired skill on the unsuspecting employer—a potentially dramatic triumph.

To some extent, this remains true today. A young carpenter's apprentice may stand with his hands hanging by his side, "joyless," said one Irakliot woman who viewed my video questionnaire, and dissatisfied," while an iron-worker's apprentice appeared to another viewer as expressing *amikhania* (helpless perplexity), a term that suggests the absence of mechanical skills associated with machines (*mikhanes*) but also with the crafts that machines now threaten to uproot. Some apprentices are indeed as disengaged as they appear. Recalled one rurally based saddler: "I told his father, 'Take the lad away, because his brain doesn't take things in; he's not learning anything. Whatever he does, he takes on "monotonously" [*monotona*]. He won't learn even if he stays here for five years!' And he was with us for about a year and a half and he didn't know how to make a new saddle." Time does indeed tell: appearances may be deceptive, and an apprentice who has seemed utterly incompetent and then suddenly is revealed as smart and capable may be far more highly valued than one whose intelligence was clear from the start; he shows that he has learned not only the artisanal expertise that will be his professional capital but also the social expertise—the skill, above all, in dissembling—that will make it possible for him to use his skills and survive. This is social as much as material artifice.

Indeed, it is the art of surprise as we see it here that lies at the very core of what I have called "social poetics."[6] Just as a boy shepherd in the hill villages who seems unable to respond to an insult and then astonishes everyone by systematically depleting the flock of his nemesis makes his mark in the community by creatively exaggerating the role of the strong man, so the apprentice who has seemed utterly passive and then emerges as a skilled craftsman gains on several fronts. Not only has he mastered the craft itself, but he has shown that he is an agile social dissembler, a cunning fellow who can be trusted to keep a secret (this being the ultimate form of social continence), and a tough customer who can stoically endure ridicule in order to turn it triumphantly, and with interest, against his tormentors. Such a likely lad makes a good investment for the future; he can think for himself, and his body will not betray his opinions of the powerful, nor his tongue the secrets of his trade. His self-presentation is an endlessly creative display and exploration of this confident, self-controlled masculinity.

Training the Embodied Mind

If he is to arrive at this level of social proficiency, his body, while guarding the secrets it has learned, must also absorb them. Closely calibrated to the temporalities of learning and dissembling is the practical temporality (what Bourdieu calls the *tempo* of social interaction)[7] of bodily self-presentation. The pacing of production affects not only the crafting of objects but also the social reproduction of selves; well-produced objects reflect a self-confidence that must also be visible in bodily mien. While apprentices are initially subjected to the weighty burden of boredom, they must thus also use this time to learn attitudes of bodily insouciance that will in practice allow them to become, if they possess the necessary ability, relaxed, professional practitioners of their craft, artificers in every sense, and with every sense dedicated to artifice. The long-term appearance of boredom and disengagement may be reproduced in a fully socialized artisan as the nonchalant skill of one who does not need to think about what he is doing in order to do it successfully. It is not that he is indifferent; on the contrary, his nonchalance is the product of his *meraki*, his love for the craft, which is such that he neither cares about the jibes of others nor feels diminished by his own missteps; one artisan told me that my own enthusiasm for my research had revealed itself in my calling to make an appointment with him: "And if you write something stupid, it doesn't matter; it's *meraki;* [that means that] next time you'll make progress!"

The transition to such nonchalance is the critical step that is judged between an apprentice's initial arrival in the workshop and the final moment of deciding whether he is cut out for the work. A cobbler expressed this revealingly. He had suddenly been singled out for the excellence of his handiwork and "lowered his face" in embarrassment; he was later to hesitate to speak critically to his own assistant once he set up in business on his own because he was only nineteen and the assistant was thirty-two years old. Yet such bashfulness does not prevent him, at that precise moment of transition to full artisan status, from expressing his pride in terms that are fully in accordance with the local aesthetics of selfhood and with the years of painstakingly accumulated experience that lay behind his new status: "I'm telling you, people passed by in the street and stopped to watch me [work]. In the street, cobblers passing by—they used to watch me! Eh, I had that glory. What did I understand? I only understood this: that of course I never went short. I did what I could . . . , I managed to build a little house and I was not badly off, I struggled through life. . . . That's it. My satisfaction is that no one told me that my work wasn't good enough for him, or that 'you're useless,' at any point! At work I was the first to arrive and the last to leave."

We see revealed in these words the pride that a stance of modesty ("I lowered my face") both somewhat disingenuously conceals and at the same time artfully displays. The shoulder-shrugging tone of these remarks, the sense that after all one had just managed to do what every man worthy of the name should be able to do in providing a home for his family and struggling to make ends meet, expresses the economic aspect of that nonchalance with which Rethemniot artisans act out their performances of social success. It would be meaningless here to separate the aesthetic or the technical from the moral: all are fused in a claim to value pure and simple. Pride in technical reliability is indistinguishable from what we might regard as the separate issue of the aesthetic qualities of the objects produced, since a "beautiful" shoe is a well-made one that combines mastery over current fashion with reliability in use. It is thus a bluff, utilitarian, and technical evaluation, and it goes with a modest manner that represents a technique of the moral self. This is expressed in superlatives of self-effacement. These, by foregrounding the artisan's skill and dedication to appropriate norms of comportment, model in social form the technical industry of the true artisan: "I was the first to arrive and the last to leave." Fine artisanship requires fine character; fine character inspires trust in the quality of the work. In a boastful society, the truly adroit artisan must know how to be ostentatiously modest. Paradoxically, the limp slouch of the apprentice may thus be the harbinger of real competence, because it demonstrates an ability to absorb information and then use it without appearing to make any effort at all: "The eye must seize [on what it needs] in order to give orders to the hands and then to the brain, so that these can then make the things that [the eyes] have seen." Excessive eagerness may be the antithesis of social competence, and it undercuts the artisan's ability to hold the world's condescension and contempt at bay.

Artisans' apprentices thus learn a stance of disengagement that actually serves to showcase their skill. This is because their affectation of insouciance not only plays on a convention of false modesty as appropriate to truly proud men but creates the right conditions for the streamlining of bodily movement into a sense of action outside the artisan's conscious volition.[8] Cretan artisans, disdainful of what they see as the excessive literal-mindedness and fussiness of people who depend on the written word for a living, might be very surprised to see how well Rodney Needham's description of the writing process matches what they claim as peculiarly the mark of skilled manual labor, the ability to train the body to act on its own: "We may . . . become so detached from our apperceptions that the act of writing has a quasi-automatic quality—at least for as long as things are going well—and we may feel afterwards that the ideas thus expressed . . . had an autonomous origin in the very act of writing."[9] Or consider Giulio Angioni's comment that "one is only able to stammer about things that instead we know perfectly well how to do without even paying any attention to them—how to tie shoelaces in our sleep (but perhaps we all remember the effort of teaching children how to do it)."[10] When we juxtapose these passages with the frequency with which artisans speak of their unconscious absorption of technique and the seeming autonomy of their hands at work, long-established assumptions about the radical separation of mind from body seem particularly hard to sustain.

Yet this disruptive, Cartesian division of human experience is as much an article of faith with artisans as it is with intellectuals: neither side, it seems, wants much to do with the other. In Rethemnos, mind and body are not so much two aspects of the same humanity as the metonyms of two social classes, two ideologies, two realms of value linked only in their relative positions within a larger hierarchy that lauds the manual as long as it knows its place. Artisans, caught in this logic and forever tempted to exploit it for their own immediate self-satisfaction, take enormous pride in the manual tactility of their labor and sneer at the physical incompetence of those who work in offices and classrooms—precisely those who occupy "higher" positions in local society.[11] Theirs is a moral insubordination, analogous to that of sheep thieves in the hill villages, for whom the lowlanders and townsfolk are legitimate targets because of their presumed corruption and ill-gotten wealth. To labor with one's hands is a virtue that marks class identity and also sets the artisan off from the mechanical reproduction made possible by the advent of machinery. But here lies the trap: this difference also serves as a mark of the alleged backwardness that is the negative side, the tethering-post aspect, of tradition.

For many Greeks, manual work of any kind is associated with a particularly strong distaste for cooperation with others. A bronzesmith quoted a rural proverb—"let my threshing floor be small, but let it be my own"—that in the villages serves as the justification for avoiding any kind of reliance on others, and explained that he preferred not to have to worry about whether a partner was pulling his weight. Such worries increase with mechanization, which often brings consolidation of economic interests with it. He, by contrast, wanted to rely neither on machinery nor on the cooperation of others: "Because, I told you: I don't have machinery [*mikhanimata*]. My hands are my machinery. Do you see these hands of mine?" And then, displaying his calloused hands with enormous pride, he demanded rhetorically, "You'll ask me, 'Why don't you industrialize? Modernize?'" When he returned from a spell as a guest worker in Germany, he says, he saw how local people stabbed each other in the back. And so he preferred to remain reliant on the personal skills that had given him confidence early in life—a confidence that meant he would always opt for the masculine, traditionalist role of the man who worked with his hands, avoided too much talk or study, and stood economically on his own feet, and who consequently rejected the imported models of modernization as a matter of principle.

This, then, represents the limited choice of class identity and ideology, and it is literally embodied in the artisan's physical presence, metonymically captured as a pair of capable, calloused hands. The seamstresses of Turin described by Vanessa Maher learned, through the kind of surreptitious observation that is also the mark of the Rethemniot male apprentices, "the imitation of gestures and attitudes that would be essential to the future dressmaker, whose task it was to manipulate social appearances."[12] For Rethemniot artisans, however, such intimate involvement with the shaping of others' bodily appearance would for the most part be too obviously marked as a female concern (hairdressers are virtually the only female artisans who still often have apprentices in appreciable numbers), although barbers—a low-ranked artisanal profession in any case, because of the messy pollution of loose hair—are certainly involved in this process. An elderly barber boasted, "I've never cut anyone. My hands hold well. Still do. Because I abandoned wine, grappa, cigarettes, everything, so my hands wouldn't tremble!" The familiar but perishable symbols of masculinity are insignificant in comparison to the corporeal masculinity of those who maintain their physical skills and their economic independence, all the more so here because other artisans regard the barber's trade as defiling and unmanly. He knows this, especially because he began his professional life as a saddle-maker; but he also knows that his detractors may yet come to envy him for a skill that, with the kind of self-care that he describes here, can last for a relatively long time into old age.

Most male artisans' mastery is exercised in the shaping of inanimate objects, through which they express a sense of embodiment that is entirely their own and under their exclusive control. Nenedakis's story of the saddle-maker who told his customers how they should want his products made illustrates this perfectly. Acquiring the embodied capacity to perform manual labor without appearing to engage the mind is something that happens with time and experience, and it becomes the basis of the artisans' authority and confidence. It begins with imitation or with some kind of physical restraint; tailors' apprentices, for example, had their hands bound in such a way that they could use the thimble only in the sole correct position, until they learned to do it without the restraint. Eventually, the body would absorb even a complex set of routines and reproduce them without hesitation. A boot-maker boasted that in cutting the leather for seventy-four pairs of boots he had not made a single error, and he demonstrated how he could do the sensitive work literally with both eyes closed. A carpenter, speaking of the master who trained him, remarked, "He would take a chair and throw it away, as it wasn't burnished in the right way. At some point it got to me, too. . . . Then I would get upset [stenakhoriomouna] and would try harder, like, I'd try harder, and then I made it—I would make it perfectly. Until the point where most recently of all my hand would run along on its own. My hand would do the burnishing on its own, it didn't need. . . . I would be looking quite somewhere else, and I knew the sandpaper would go just where it wouldn't do any damage to the door [*sic*]." The notion of being "upset" in Greek is spatialized; the Greek term literally means "being put in a narrow space" and is associated with a range of forms of mental distress.[13] The apprentice is, as we would say, trying to "break out" and to "make a space for himself."

A good master provides the ideal model for achieving this, so that the apprentice is not aware of having imitated him until after the fact. A pastrycook recalled this early training in response to a question about whether the imitation was consciously achieved: "No, unconsciously. That way, in other words, his movements, everything he did, I have those things—without intending to imitate him—all those things, I copied them from that man. His movements, especially with the knife. How quickly the knife did its work." The master would select a knife from among the varied array on his workbench, throw it in the air from the hilt, and catch it by the blade even as he moved from one side of the bench to another. This gave the master a fluid continuity of movement. No form of spoken explanation accompanied this display of dexterity; the master was not openly eager to let his apprentice learn too much—always apparent is the fear "that a successor might appear"—and casual chat would have destroyed the production of bodily self-control that lies at the heart of successful artisanship and of male self-display. At the same time, the master's control of work rhythms meant that a good apprentice would also learn the crucial art of controlling his own impatience, which would equip him with a more formidable mastery than any verbal instruction could convey.

The contrasting case is that of impatient villagers who, having bought some tools and rented a shop in town, want someone to give them a quick-fix course by telling them all the moves. Their very desire to acquire the requisite knowledge in the form of abstract words and measures marks the distance between such johnnies-come-lately and true artisans. Nothing more clearly expresses the incompatibility of explicit verbal instruction with the inculcation of bodily rhythms in artisanal life. Even smoking cigarettes is, among much else, a "habit of the hand." "Like the *komboloi* [worry beads]!" replied an artisan who heard a journalist offer this comment on smoking. Both are ideal marks of male sociability, requiring no awkward moments of careful attention or painstaking skill but partaking of the masculine affectation of insouciant bodily self-confidence.

The cigarette represents the male world in many ways. As a source of health risk, it affords the chance of striking a devil-may-care pose. It features prominently, as I have just pointed out, in the bodily postures associated with masculinity. And it offers a measure of time that, being dramatically approximate, allows men to proclaim their disdain for the regimes of punctuality that go with being cowed by authority.

A popular story among artisans tells of a potter who let his apprentice open up the kiln by himself, only to discover that the pots were fragile and leaking; when the apprentice asked how long the pots really needed, the master replied, "Two hours." When the two hours were up and the apprentice wanted to open the kiln, the master invited the apprentice to smoke a cigarette with him and, when the apprentice demurred, replied, "It doesn't matter, it's high time now, you've grown up—smoke a cigarette!"[14] Only then, having shifted the sense of time from numerical calculation to a social measure of shared relaxation, did the master allow the apprentice to open the kiln—and the pots were sound. Said the apprentice, "These came out fine." And the master, allowing himself to verbalize the point for the first time (but still as a generic principle rather than in the form of direct instruction), responded, "You should know that everything happens in the time it needs" *(na kseris oti to kathe praghma yinete sto khrono pou khriazete)*. We see in this cautionary tale an explicit desire to deflect the production of artifacts away from temporal and verbal precision, with all the potential for obsessive attention to detail that this creates, and toward the absorption of appropriate work rhythms into a body trained into knowing displays of unhurried competence.

The apprentice thus learns the confidence that lets his "body hexis" take over. Speech—and indeed any activity that focuses too heavily on the form of physical action and makes for self-consciousness—undermines the confidence that master artisans instead try to inculcate by example: "At first he [the apprentice] thinks it's all difficult. That's why you give him the tools straight away and you tell him, so to speak, to be careful." The artisan should offer the apprentice specific guidance, usually by physically moving his hand rather than trying to explain in words. But where language does become important is in the naming of the tools; they are given human names in many workshops, thereby again producing the sense of craft as a form of social engagement. The language of such associations is far from abstract; it conflates selfhood with material. Thus, a hammer for breaking stone *(petra)* may be called "Peter" (Petros). Or an artisan may make up a "family" by giving variants of a single name according to the respective sizes of a set of matched tools (John, Johnnie, Big John). Such devices breed familiarity; and familiarity eventually should bring confidence.

Vision and Theft

That confidence is the key to what Cretans are prepared to recognize as manhood. Thomas Malaby recalls the mockery he suffered when he tried to help a coffeehouse proprietor serve coffee and was somewhat sarcastically reprimanded for being too attentive to his own movements, increasing rather than decreasing the risk that he would spill the coffee. One sees very similar exhibitions of insouciance in male dancers in Crete; their acrobatic leaps and upright posture require a demonstrative performance of disregard for what is happening when the feet touch the ground. In even riskier situations, men rage at their foes in the hope that others will separate them before blood is shed but also in the knowledge that this may not happen and that they will be obliged to see the violence through to its sometimes fatal conclusion. These are conventions—like the facial gesture that attends every condemnation of the Turks' role in international politics, for example—that only become remarkable when they are omitted. Present, they simply assert a right to take one's place in the company of men.

Men therefore avoid, as a matter of course, any use of their eyes that might signal anxiety about others' judgment of their competence or self-confidence. They avoid appearing to watch their own movements; they do watch others', as they both critically judge them and steal their embodied knowledge. They learn this double vision early; Irakliot viewers of my video materials noted, for example, that one apprentice used his eyes a great deal "and, I think, satisfactorily. The older person doesn't give him a nod for [instructions to help him with] learning. The lad uses both his eyes and his bodily posture to learn [see fig. 3]. But he gets no response. No reaction comes from the master." On the video, the boy's ocular activity was quite visible; I had noted it myself. In the workshop, however, it was much less noticeable, particularly as the boy remained, his body signaling resentful boredom, largely behind the older craftsman and thus out of his gaze. Curiosity must itself be protected from the threat of others' curiosity.

There is another aspect of this attitude to vision-related postures that may well be more than coincidental. The eye is the prime instrument of observation—a dangerous weapon in this agonistic society. To see is always potentially to steal; to stare is to invite more lasting forms of evil down on the heads of those one is watching so intently. While other organs may register information (as when one checks cooking odors to assess the frequency of neighbors' meat consumption), it is the eye that notes the largest range of useful data of this sort: "Money cannot fail to be apparent. Only money can't hide. When at this moment you see that—what do you know?—this year he has gotten [evghale][15] a BMW, for example, and next year he builds a house, doesn't he have money?" The convention of bemoaning one's poverty is irrelevant; everyone does it—especially, perhaps, those who have wealth or other sources of happiness they would rather hide from the ocular malice of their neighbors.

(a)

(b)

Figure 3 Two apprentices at work. (*a*) The eyes of this carpenter's apprentice demonstrate closer attention to the work than his slack posture seems to indicate. (*b*) The auto repair shop apprentice is encouraged in his interest, and he reciprocates with a body posture that openly confirms the absorption that his eyes also convey.

The role of the eyes in "stealing" craft knowledge partakes of some of this tension in the sense that artisans fear the transfer of information, even as they encourage such crafty duplicity by blocking off other avenues—notably explicit verbal instruction. Verbal instruction conveys a sense of exactitude that does not sit well either with the cultivated nonchalance that I have been describing or with the "ethos of imprecision" that governs informal commercial exchanges among friends or neighbors—an attitude that treats too close attention to weight and price as antisocial and grasping.[16]

Bodily and social skills here converge, and may do so for women as much as for men: the affectation of relaxed posture goes with the approximation we would associate with "eyeballing" produce as a prelude to pricing it. An artisanal baker, asked by a customer for 1,400 grams of her product in a manner that implied that no inaccuracy would be tolerated, explained to me that she had watched his eyes, which were clearly measuring with a socially unacceptable degree of precision. Her own eyes had taken in this information, but *she* was not going to engage in such pedantry—her own eyes not only could recognize the customer's pettiness at a scornful glance but were also, unlike the customer's, skilled at assessing weight without any artificial aids. Her very casual, fleeting glance at the scale announced to all and sundry that trust rather than profit was the capital in which she wished to deal. It is also true that, by her own admission, she deliberately would underestimate the weight as she was about to place the goods on the scale, so that she could then, having made a point of removing the excess pastry, charge a higher price per unit of real weight than she usually charged her more familiar and accommodating customers, whom she often casually treated to a little extra pastry as a matter of course. Such pragmatic manipulations of the sense of social obligation are generically understood to be normal, and it is only their magnification in the exploitation of kinship that sometimes occasions real anger. The baker knew just how far she could push her customers; and she pushed them just that far.

As we see in this example, eyes that can assess the weight and value of produce in a socially benign fashion can also probe the secrets of others' conditions and attitudes. Of all those curious eyes, some, credited with the supernatural power of inflicting harm, are both the index and the instrument of a particularly noxious—if supposedly involuntary—form of jealousy. The allegedly involuntary nature of the evil eye, as this phenomenon is usually called, shows that it is less a matter of individual character (although its bearers are reviled as morally flawed and antisocial) than it is a mark of the degree to which society as a whole is pervaded by the corrosive force of jealousy—a feature of the generically fallen condition of humanity in general, Greeks in particular, and local people most of all.[17]

Greeks attribute the power of casting the evil eye to an excessive form of attention, whether concealed as deep jealousy or manifested as excessive admiration. Those who seem too tautly focused on any object or person are suspected of harboring malice, but they also lay themselves open to highly damaging charges of antisocial attitudes. Greek men, in particular, are clearly uncomfortable with any too-obvious grasping for control, political or conceptual. In a highly competitive society where the actual stakes are quite small, such jockeying for authority must be done subtly, through hints and indirect displays of a mastery that does not look too carefully deployed.[18] The common rhetorical disavowals of self-interest in which these men engage illustrate the same principle at work. It matters not a whit that probably no one actually believes such posturings of innocence and modesty; what matters is that others are uncomfortable with those who fail to follow the convention.[19] The eye, as the organ of a covert theft of others' knowledge, must not be too obviously an instrument of calculation—although everyone knows that this is precisely what it is: apprentices "steal with their eyes," but while trying to look as if they were totally uninterested. Anxiety to acquire new knowledge is hardly the mark of self-confident manhood; bodily action, especially of the eyes and hands, must reflect the complete absence of that "excessive attention" that betrays concern. Serving coffee with a flourish, casually pulling a pot from the kiln at the precise moment at which it is at its best, tossing sharp tools through the air without dropping them or slowing production: skills such as these are at one and the same time the instrument and the expression of practical knowledge.

Malaby, moreover, found in the highly educative moment when his coffeehouse proprietor friend told him to be more relaxed about carrying trays of coffee precisely the kind of seemingly trivial and commonplace social action in which an anthropologist should recognize key social values in action. He thereby gained an understanding of the nature of risk for Cretan men in general, in which their acquisition of bodily poise is related to the affectation of insouciance that the highly agonistic idiom of their social life requires. The stylish performer is one who, by appearing to disregard the possibility of failure, is in fact much less likely to suffer it.[20] The risk is real because an agonistic society rarely shows much mercy in moments of failure: there *is* the risk of failure, and there *are* those who will seek to profit from one's discomfiture. Hence the apprentice carpenter's "upset" when he failed to sand the wood in just the right way: he knows his master is watching and judging, feels the threat of failure as a constriction of his psychological and social space, and knows that success depends on overcoming the fear of failure that is, at the same time, the source of the artisan's power over him. Releasing the body from its dependence on an overanxious mind permits the release of the young male's sense of self from the dominance that is exercised partly to bring about precisely this effect.

The nonchalant pose also speaks to a larger disregard. Kalymnian sponge divers, at least until the 1960s, deliberately spurned diving equipment that might have protected them from the "bends" (a paralysis induced by a too-rapid return to the surface), seeing in it a threat to their masculinity because it indicated an excessive concern with protecting the body from risk.[21] A similar attitude today informs Greek male drivers' refusal to wear safety belts, a phenomenon that a columnist for a very conservative Athens newspaper castigated as directly comparable to "Saudi Arabia, Pakistan, etc."—and thus, he implies, antithetical to European values, at which in this regard even the Turks do better![22] This author explicitly recognizes the stance as that of the "heavy" masculinity that "doesn't take much lying down" (note the adjective "heavy," which we have already encountered applied to the recalcitrant apprentice of the ironworker). These attitudes are cast in a negative light even (as the case of the ironworker's apprentice nicely demonstrates) by artisans who are also engaged in passing them on, encased in an aura of constricting inevitability, to the next generation.

The price of demonstrative masculinity within the global hierarchy of value is thus a high one: the more appreciated such braggadocio is as a sign of personal self-confidence and local pride, the more it excludes its bearers from European modernity. On the same day that Greek drivers were being compared unfavorably with "Saudi Arabia, Pakistan, etc.," another columnist, writing in a more liberal Athens newspaper, lamented the fatalism of Greeks who would gawp at a traffic accident but who could not organize a swift and effective response to help the victims.[23] Fatalism, an image of passivity that sits unconvincingly with what we know of Greek social attitudes,[24] also featured significantly in local explanations of the failure of cooperative business ventures; here, the display of insouciance required for social consumption excluded the possibility of precautionary measures, whether against the physical risks of accident or against the social risks that too aggressive a mode of self-display can entail.

A man who bears himself with caution, who wears a seat belt while driving (and especially one who does so for fear of the police), a sponge diver who wears special equipment to protect him from the bends, a man who patiently bears the insults of his business partner in the interests of maintaining a profitable relationship—such a man may fit well with the new Europe; but he fits very poorly with the received values of his home island. Here, however, we are back to the duck-rabbit aspects of the Cretans' predicament: what counts for masculine pride in the local context can appear instead as its very antithesis, cowardly resignation to the inevitable, in the context of a modernist vision of social efficiency and omniscience. Or, to put this in another way, modernist affectations of precision and prediction are, in the final analysis, a way of trying to control uncertainty or at least—since this is what is socially salient—trying to look capable of controlling it.

Embracing the aleatory aspects of life is also, as Malaby emphasizes, a socially good way for a man to do business.[25] It shows that he is able to master chance rather than let it dominate him; and the risks attendant on modern financing are surely no less threatening to these small-town entrepreneurs than those associated with animal theft or an angry confrontation in the highland villages. "The element of chance," declared one Rethemniot in a presumably unconscious echo of Max Weber that equates the defiance of chance with a specifically Greek masculinity,[26] "is being emasculated [*eksovelizete to tikheo*]," and he criticized as a "wholly oriental mentality" the attitude of saying, "Let's open a shop and God will provide." Here a local person has internalized the orientalist critique of Greek culture, which he represents as becoming fatalistic even as it retains the stigma of uncontrollable jealousy: "People say, 'As others are working, so to speak, let us be working, too.'" Thus, what capitalists would view as the benign proliferation of businesses and the assumption that the weak will go to the wall, he views instead as a crass competitiveness that is more destructive than productive, and that reflects an increasing inattention to standards of craftsmanship and of personal idiosyncrasy. This is a refusal of the aleatory, a parodic construal of modernity as necessarily defined by durable security in the form of a simple accounting of profit.[27]

For the old-style artisan recalled by this astute local critic of modernity, the stylish self-confidence of local masculinity sits ill with the deliberate self-awareness and reliance on explicit logic and instruction—the attempt to routinize certainty—that are the alleged hallmarks of modern production. For the committed modernist, by contrast, the older mode must yield to an efficient productivity according to principles deemed capable of transcending local constraints; yet social critics, like the author of the *Eleftherotypia* article just cited, remain ironically unconvinced that Greek attitudes to social and political responsibility will be transformed by the modernist project of achieving "transcendence."[28] Locally, too, people both have internalized the dominant binarisms between East and West, tradition and modernity, *Gemeinschaft* and *Gesellschaft*, the aleatory and the efficient (it is along the axes of these binarisms that the global hierarchy of value operates) and yet, at the same time, are excruciatingly aware that their own ability to climb onto the modernist project is limited and not always what they want. Could it be that this is not because modernity has eliminated risk but because it has enlarged its scope while also offering more comprehensive, complex, and inaccessible means of harnessing risk?

Aggressive masculinity creates this sense of frustrating paradox within the global hierarchy of value because the very features required to maintain an authoritatively traditional masculinity limit access to external power. Older attempts to explain the prevalence of male aggression in rural Mediterranean societies included the functionalist notion that it served to displace the humiliations that men suffered at the hands of bureaucrats in authoritarian state systems.[29] Whatever the virtue of such explanations in respect of particular cases, at the collective level they do not adequately account for relations of cause and effect; bureaucrats promote their own teleology, arguing—as did the colonels during the Greek military dictatorship of 1967–1974—that so aggressive and quarrelsome a people requires strong control from above, which reverses the functionalist argument. There is also nothing uniquely Mediterranean or rural about this; nineteenth-century Britain, for example, saw working-class struggles riven from within by male recalcitrance in the face of women's calls for equal pay and full recognition, while in the following century at least one major artisanal industry, printing, was the scene of a similar belittling of women's abilities and rights.[30] It makes more sense to recognize that in Greece (as in most countries today) citizens and bureaucrats share a good deal of cultural ground; their relationship is not simply the domination of one cultural world by another, and no one-way explanation of the relationship between them can suffice. In confrontations between government and people, each side essentializes the other; they understand each other perfectly because they are involved in the same negotiation of blame and responsibility, and we should not confuse these attempts at self-justification (on the essentialist grounds that the citizens are unruly or that the bureaucrats are self-interested) with an analytically persuasive explanation of the situation as a whole.

Functionalist explanations satisfy an academic aesthetic of neatness and closure, and they also often coincide with reasons of state, but they do not account for the quandaries of embodied experience. What we have observed here is an ongoing tension between the will to stabilize small increments of power and the realization that the tactical guile needed to achieve that end can also entrap its users. Appearing indifferent to these constraints is itself a rhetoric of power building, occasionally effective in an immediate confrontation but in the long term—sometimes in consequence of too many such confrontations—usually evanescent. It is an embodied rhetoric that requires many years of inculcation to master, and to be mastered by it at the same time.

Artisans' ongoing efforts to instill insubordination into the bodies of their own apprentices do not preclude awareness of the constraints that are thereby reproduced; those artisans who deny that they are engaging in any such process are not so much "misrecognizing" it as proactively recasting its meaning in a way that does not make them the dupes of their own victimization. In narrating the general pattern, they may even betray their conscious expectation that their apprentices not only will, but should, deliberately develop the habit of learning by stealth,[31] ostensibly at the masters' expense: "I'll tell you how to do it once or twice. But then, to learn the craft, you should watch, steal the craft!" They are co-opting the most cunning and the toughest of their apprentices in alliance against what they perceive as a frustrating world of people who demean the one thing—tradition—that constitutes the basis of their authority.

The more the state's presence pervades their lives, the more the agonistic relationship of master and apprentice appears to resist the impending collapse of the institution of apprenticeship itself. In this way they are operating much like the besieged Cameroonian elite described by Nicolas Argenti; as part of an ongoing struggle to maintain its own authority, the palace co-opts the most insubordinate of the carvers who do not accept the discipline and authority of palace-approved apprenticeship.[32] The Greek state, similarly, has had to struggle to maintain its authority over a rebellious island that nonetheless represents the extreme incarnation of the national spirit of freedom, and over men who embody that spirit in their daily actions. The master artisans in their workshops, bullying and hectoring their apprentices, are reproducing patterns of contest and co-optation that link their daily interactions to the dynamics of international power relations. Beset by much the same sense of an always potentially humiliating ambiguity in their claim to represent authenticity and tradition, they try to inculcate into their apprentices the passionate appetite for insubordination that is the social realization of that claim.

Encroaching Disenchantments

In this field of agonistic relations, the possession of self-confidence is both a treasured resource and a challenge to all comers. The older artisans could project self-confidence in their daily mien because they lived in a society where it stood out as an exceptional quality—albeit one to which all aspired—against the backdrop of unceasing, tense competition over minimal resources. They developed bodily styles that also produced—and were reproduced in—recognizably individual work. A stonemason from a nearby village expressed this clearly: "With us, everything that is made, every job, you've got to be right there on top of it [i.e., making your mark on it as a person], so that the design will be different, a different appearance. Even if it's just a hearth, we have no prefabricated forms for the hearth so that the placement of the top will be standardized [*standar*]. But I can say that every hearth is worked differently, and each hearth of ours is not the same as any other, even one made by us."

Plagiarism of an artisan's style was then understood as a betrayal of professional pride. This view has remained as an ideal and in turn has become one key to the ideological claims made by official promoters of local handicrafts that Cretan artisans are the truest of Europeans in their constant refusal to copy others. But modernity and the advent of mechanical reproduction have posed enormous new challenges to both local practice and official ideology.

With the advent of machinery, even something as simple as making a buttonhole for a jacket (which "needed some skill," as a former tailor told me) virtually disappeared. Standardization became the norm in many trades and served to project the modernist project Max Weber called "routinization" into the workplace: it is the routinization of practices, whether in terms of efficiency or as an aesthetic principle. As the former tailor remarked, the emergence of industrial standards meant a working idiom that "doesn't need much skill." In this regard, he echoes a frequently voiced romantic nostalgia, thereby also intimating how much social theory follows this convention of everyday speech in seeking lost Edens.[33] Meanwhile, some artisans complain, standardization even invades the traditionalism of their crafts: now that the few apprentices they are able to find come to them at a relatively late age, these young men do not have the time, and are no longer sufficiently impressionable, to do more than learn how to make a few standardized items. Artisanship, too, has surrendered to the reductive logic of the factory, but without acquiring its efficiency and speed. If the local artisans did not manage to rise to this level of standardization, however, it was not, I suggest, because they were incapable of it, but because they were ill-equipped to take the actually much larger risks of venturing into a highly competitive, increasingly globalized market of mass-produced goods and preferred instead the security of picturesque unpredictability. The striking frequency of their diatribes against standardization, outbursts that at times seem almost to parrot official praise of the endless inventiveness of the small artisan, suggests as much.

In the newly disenchanted world of mass production, mathematical precision keeps costs down and makes artistry redundant at best, a source of disorder at worst. The stakes are higher and must be managed in new ways.

As a result, the cultivation of insubordinate initiative is reversed and becomes instead the streamlining of the working person as a cog in a huge machine: this is the essence of deskilling. In this setting, too, the self-regard of the flamboyant waiter or the creative carpenter is transformed from an ability to dominate the social context into a form of antisocial eccentricity, which can be redeemed only by being placed on the pedestal of "tradition" and associated with an admirable crustiness that effectively keeps the artisan out of any real control over his own destiny. He has become dependent on others' condescending admiration and amusement, responses that can easily turn to anger when he steps too far out of line. Skills are lost; even those who in an earlier time simply loitered in front of the artisans' workshops without experiencing the pain of apprenticeship now set up on their own as cobblers and in other crafts, but their work is as shoddy as their knowledge is shallow. Mass production today undermines the artisan from one side, incompetent imitation for an ignorant clientele from the other; and his irritable complaints only serve to shroud him in an ever more crepuscular gloom.

Chapter Six

Associative States

Forming Associations

Insubordination, "stealing with the eyes," is part of the older process of learning how to be a good artisan not only technically but also, and above all, socially. Learning in context, rather than teaching-dependent transmission, is the predominant idiom in the settings in which apprenticeship occurs, as Lave and Wenger note.[1] It is the emergent young artisan's ability to snatch opportunity from an ever-threatening destitution that really matters here. The apprentice is learning to learn; and the knowledge is not exclusively, or even primarily, of a technical variety that could easily be reduced to verbal formulae. Above all, it is knowledge about how to survive in an often hostile and risk-fraught environment.

Employers—who surely remember their own boyhood years—almost certainly realize that it is when they turn their backs that the apprentices are really able to develop new skills. This is a system in which the weak fall by the wayside, while the proud and conniving are those with the best chances of survival. Those who must depend on verbal instruction are inculcated into another mode of life; they are, in a word, emasculated. It is they who trade the school of life for a life of school. In the words of an artisan from a nearby village: "What I'll show the lads is not books. It's the putting of whatever's in a book into practice that counts. If the kids don't learn to put what they find in a book into practice, the lad is a blank blackboard, a parroter of others, he has certain bits of knowledge that he can never adapt to practice. But if he can adapt the smallest theorem, the smallest law of nature, to life, then he's succeeded." Artisans are those who realize abstract knowledge through their craft, which is testimony to their manhood as independent actors and shapers of the material world. Men who enter the bureaucracy, by contrast, abjure their manhood forever by willingly accepting the role of employees—those who serve *under* others *(ipallili)*—and will never leave behind them any tangible evidence of personal creativity.

Artisans are notorious for their resistance to any form of control, either over their bodies or over their art. They especially enjoy those (usually brief) periods of economic upswing when they can afford to demonstrate their independence by turning unwanted business away: "You went, arranged to do a job, were paid, then decided to avoid the job and not do it, and you ran the price up by one unit for each unit already priced, you doubled the price, so as not to tell him, 'I can't fix it because I have [other] work to do.' So you told him, 'If you want me to fix this thing'—a table, or whatever—'I need ten thousand,' whereas the real value of the varnishing was five thousand, okay? But he still told you, 'Here you are!'" And perhaps then, if the artisan succumbed to the lure of profit, the high pay might compensate for a loss in dignity or serve to restore it.

The artisan had set his own terms and been taken into partnership on those terms. The construction worker whose fine masculine body cannot be subjected to the muck of the building site expresses another version of the same idea; in times of prosperity, the artisan comes into his own because he can afford to spurn those who will not afford him due recognition. This is where the artisan is to the merchant and bureaucrat what the shepherd is to the peasant: the strength and skill of his body, rather than his dexterity with words, release him from dependence on the structures of petty power. He despises those who are unable to release themselves from such humiliation. What the cobbler's apprentice once accepted as a temporary and metaphorical bodily embarrassment when he was forced to crawl under the counter, the bureaucrat and the shop assistant are forced to accept as a lifelong condition of existence. The early humiliation of being forced into artisanal work by failure at school can thus be transformed into pride at having escaped the greater humiliation of unceasing subordination within the bureaucracy. Thus it is that the demeaning ritual of making the novice pass under the counter became, with maturity and reputation, his metaphorical claim to a skill that only those who have served as true apprentices can ever possess.[2]

Some families even claimed to see going into a trade as a superior lifestyle to that of the educated. A shoemaker recalled how his older brother found him an apprentice's berth: "He tells him, 'Look here, I'll bring him along, for a tryout. He can do one week, and in that week if it turns out that he doesn't have the head for it, let's take him back and send him to "letters" [i.e., school]; I'll take him back.' And he says, 'Fine, bring him to me.' Ten days later I went there. I stayed for a week, following the whole line so to speak.

And he says, 'He's an ace [*tsakali*, literally "jackal"],' my boss tells him." And so the boy entered a trade in which he could take pride, never knowing what level of success he might have achieved had he remained in school.

Even those who completed school and did not in fact fail may nevertheless have been deliberately avoiding the risk of failure at precisely that point: "I finished high school; I didn't want to become an employee, so I [just] didn't take exams to get into some school of higher education." In this context, the conventional reverence for the world of letters is turned on its head, so that bookish learning becomes a sign of weakness and of social and moral failure. But there is a hegemonic trap in this illusion of escape and freedom. The artisans must produce their work within a system in which those who hold power have a very different view of the artisans' pride. They see it as the self-confirming obduracy of the ignorant and uncultured, who, supposedly lacking the wit to rise above their present condition, can rely only on brute strength to maintain their place, while expressing jealousy—for so the powerful must interpret it—of those who wield power while seated in comfortable office chairs.

Yet masculinity is not only a matter of bodily strength; it is also, crucially, about possessing the dexterity, both manual and social, that ensures survival in a world where absolute trust, while desirable, easily succumbs to the competitiveness of everyday life. Those apprentices who never master basic skills—either because they lack the manual agility or because they are too slow to pick up new knowledge on the fly—are thus condemned to work for others. Some who might otherwise have the qualities that might enable them to escape these conditions nevertheless lack the role models that might have lit the way. A boy from an orphanage, where no real father could toughen him up for the competitive rigors of real life, had learned little of the basic mathematical skills needed to develop initiative in the floor-making business where he worked. As a result, unable to rise above the level of an assistant to that of a master, he faced a life of enduring subordination: "For a lifetime he will be a wage earner." Better by far, then, to show some initiative as an artisan's apprentice: then there is at least the possibility of independence or of forming an association on more or less equal terms. Many a small artisanal workshop is run by an aging master and his younger ex-apprentice, now raised to the status of equal economic and managerial partner.

Artisans especially fear that a disgruntled apprentice may set up in business independently. It is not uncommon for an erstwhile employer to try to sabotage such attempts. One specialty baker, trained to manufacture a product that could be produced by factory methods but would then be greatly inferior, broke away from his employer mostly, it seems, because the employer's wife made his life miserable with her constant demands for ever greater effort; men protect at least a semblance of male solidarity by blaming a female presence for most such rifts. Whatever the actual causes of the split, the apprentice had by this point successfully appropriated the master's craft and had added a few technical advantages of his own. When he discovered from a kinsman that his former employer was siphoning off orders from an out-of-town customer, he went to the place where he knew the customer's driver parked his truck and stood on a nearby wall where he would be seen. "And as soon as the driver saw me, he said, 'Dimitris, I've found out [what happened], so don't say anything and I'll take care of this business.' And the next day they send a letter from the [customer's] workshop [to tell the former employer] that the [pastry] that you are sending us isn't the same [as before]. Because Plakas wanted very good [pastry]. I made it in twenty- by fifty-centimeter strips, which didn't exist then—but I'd made a little counter and cut it on that counter, and it came out all the same size. My [former] boss didn't know, and so the way he produced and cut it was all different sizes, some small, some big." In this way, the former employer learned that his perfidy had been unmasked, and he retreated from the contest. Later the younger baker went and spoke directly with his customer, who agreed to a higher price because he liked the regular size and high quality of the product so much, and this enabled the baker to keep producing; within a short while he had driven his former boss out of business and, in consequence, out of town. The apprentice had observed and then surpassed his master, not only in his skill at the craft but also in patient cunning—"the good thing was, I had patience," as he remarked—and in his ability to manage the embodied, gestural discretion that marks successful entrepreneurial manhood and management as much as does the ability to know when to negotiate verbally. "From the customers I knew from working there ten years, I heard their complaints . . . and I knew where to hit him!" It is precisely this kind of well-informed competition that some artisans try to squelch by co-opting their best apprentices as partners.

Given their background of distrust and festering rivalry, however, these artisanal partnerships are notoriously unstable. A few last as little as a couple of years, and virtually none survive for long into the succeeding generation. The usual explanation offered for this weakness is, again, a defense of male solidarity. Men blame the mutual jealousy of the partners' wives. This is exactly the same explanation for failure as that given for the inability of brothers to form enduring joint households.[3] Some claim that partnerships between brothers-in-law are somewhat more stable than those formed by brothers, because a partner whose sister is married to the other man feels a moral obligation to safeguard her interests and so himself has a greater interest in maintaining a positive relationship with his brother-in-law. Even this situation, however, is open to exploitation. In most partnerships the antagonisms are entirely predictable; it is as though the partners and their wives feel socially pressured to conform to the stereotype of the situation.

Jealousy among the wives supposedly takes the form of distrust over matters that may be financial, familial, or both; one wife complains that another's husband is taking a disproportionate number of Sundays off work, for example. Some wives, I was told, accuse each other's husbands of embezzlement or worse. Rifts of this sort seem to be more frequent when men marry after the creation of a partnership; if they are already married, they presumably know what they are getting into. In either situation suspicion, once aroused, can virtually never be dissipated. One partnership collapsed when, around 1980, the wife of one of two unrelated partners demanded to know why her husband was paying 2,000 drachmas more than the other man in taxes; if they were making equal amounts of money, they should have paid equal taxes, but the fact that the other man was paying less tax seemed to her to indicate some shady dealings in the background. In general, men charge women with financial greed that overcomes considerations of social or moral obligation, even attributing the prevalence of corruption and influence peddling to the demands of civil servants' wives for more money so that they can compete with each other socially.

Wives may also exploit local solidarity themselves by attacking non-Rethemniot employees. In some trades, such as pastry-making, those who come from outside expect to earn more than those already employed in the shop; it is the other employees' wives who then try to stir up their husbands' jealousy, or so the men complain. They become jealous of each other as well: "My wife, let's say, dresses well, she's all primped up, and she goes down to the market to do her shopping and all the rest of it, and meanwhile you're [i.e., another man] telling your wife to be frugal because there's not enough money: 'How are we going to manage?' And she sees my wife, let's say, and blows on the fire. And she starts sticking a fork into you [se pirouniazi]: 'You fool, what's going on here? Here they are robbing you, and you haven't noticed!' And that's where the quarreling starts."

This, at least, is how the men describe the process; again, all is hearsay, because people take good care to conceal such domestic strife from others—from local neighbors and competitors as zealously as from the visiting anthropologist. The image of the manipulative wife provides men with a collective excuse for their frequent failures to achieve solidarity: it is the wives, as outsiders (and all the more so when agnatic kinship is emphasized, as is the case in western Crete), who allegedly corrupt the social Eden.[4] Men may also claim that they only quarrel because their wives are difficult at home. A man who listens to his wife too much, they claim, cannot maintain clear judgment— "because a woman, in particular when she moves around in the outside world, doesn't work, can't see, she can't judge what's going on in the *piatsa*. Not the *piatsa*, not the market. Nothing at all, in fact." But we should remember that male sociability, while highly affable in relatively innocuous contexts such as the coffeehouse,[5] is rarely placid or fixed.

Men are thus careful, when they want a partnership to last, to keep their wives out of business matters as much as possible. This suits their masculine pride, but it may deprive them of services that they themselves are unable to provide, especially when the wives are better educated than the husbands. The overriding concern is always presented as the avoidance of any potential for conflict. A food producer and merchant described how he drew on his observations as a young apprentice when later, as a married man, he had to consider the risk to his long-standing business partnership: "When they get mixed up in things, women can make trouble. I worked hard, I washed a lot of plates, I washed even more metal trays, and, whenever there was some disagreement, some problem between partners, the wives were the cause. I attribute it [the instability of partnerships, about which I had asked him] to that as well. My own wife was for a while involved in the shop, but how? As the accountant. My wife is an accountant, she has a degree in accounting, and she kept our books. But as for coming into the shop [in person], never! For about five years she kept our books. Then she gave birth, bore two children, and I told my brother and cousin [the other partners], 'We'll give our books to an accountant, because my wife can't cope, she has two small children, she can't keep the books, and she'll make some mistake and we'll pay the tax people a fine. . . .' And we found another accountant."

Note how the speaker both takes pride in his wife's elevated educational status and yet blocks its use by simultaneously emphasizing her domestic obligations and his own concern for his family and his partners. A mistake by his wife could, he reasons, raise destructive suspicions about her motives. In this society no male is likely to object very strenuously when others suggest that his wife might be capable of error: better that than that she be accused of embezzling the partnership's money. Even the accusation that she forced her husband to concentrate on other business ventures on the side can be harmful enough when the result is a serious imbalance in working hours. As women are focused more on the management of the individual household economy than on long-term company profit making, a distinction that men zealously maintain, such charges can sound dangerously persuasive. They are dangerous because, while women may be skeptical, it is the men who are at risk of ending up in a bitter fight. In these quarrels, as men invoke the traditionalizing morality of family solidarity, they secure their wives' complicity in being excluded from the management of the men's work spaces. There is a revealing parallel with the pattern whereby artisans' professional and personal traditionalism, reproduced in daily practice and inculcated anew in every generation, constantly reinforces their political, social, and economic marginality. Indeed, the exclusion of women from male-controlled spaces of work and leisure is part and parcel of that same, persistent idiom of self-confirming traditionalism.

The Contours of Collapse

It is a traditionalism that also defines partnerships as inherently unstable. They are subject to pressures analogous to the division of property among brothers, not only because of allegations that partners' wives are jealous of each other, but also because, when the sons of two partners quarrel, each may claim that his father contributed a higher proportion of the capital originally invested in the enterprise. There may also be a component of sexual jealousy in the categorical predictions of collapse that are a convention of discussions about the problems of partnership. An old tale has it that an artisan bet his apprentice that if the latter could sew faster than the artisan's wife, the artisan would let the lad have his wife—and when they started to sew, the wife kept urging the apprentice to win! Given the frequency with which partnerships begin as artisan-apprentice relations, this story suggests one potential basis for real tension, although I never heard an actual case of the collapse of a partnership because of sexual rivalry. Allegedly, bourgeois women in the pre–World War II era were much more jealous of their servant girls, who were known as "slaves" and suspected of flirting with their mistresses' husbands,[6] than any man was of a boy apprentice's potential as the seducer of his wife. But the story may also be a metaphor, couched in the language of masculinity, for other kinds of suspicion.

Such suspicion is most commonly of a professional variety. Partnerships are grounded in precisely the kind of professional rivalry, or in the tension between a master's productivity and an apprentice's willful slacking, that they are supposed to remove. An apprentice who has successfully "stolen" his master's craft secrets is brought into partnership in order to prevent him from setting up a rival business, yet that possibility never entirely disappears and remains a potent threat at any moment when tempers rise. Even when artisan and apprentice are kin, it is suspicion that leads the former to offer the latter a partnership—"so he won't steal from him," as I was told of one man who made a partner of his sister's son and erstwhile apprentice. The presumption of an untrustworthiness that must be circumvented in a close kinsman is not unusual. In accordance with the same logic, an apprentice might be brought into partnership in order to give him a motive for not slacking at work, a specific form of "stealing": being a shareholder provides strong incentives for shouldering one's share of the productive labor. But that very assumption is also a starting point for the most corrosive of suspicions; as one partner (again sometimes allegedly incited by his wife) begins to doubt the other's industry and commitment, tensions quickly flare up and consume the companionship of the workplace.

Here, sometimes, a tie of kinship between partners may help to stabilize matters for a while and may even be invoked as the explanation for an unusually long-lasting association, although the consequences of an eventual dissolution must prove correspondingly more embarrassing for those concerned. But this is a world where men rarely hesitate to call each other "worthless" (*atimo*) to their faces, and where even a restaurateur—whose establishment should ideally be a place of social goodwill—insults his employees as a matter of course and consequently leaves them little choice but to walk out on him in retaliation. Where two men create a partnership and thus must also accept equality with each other, the slightest hint of discord can quickly send the whole relationship spinning noisily out of control. Then the ties of kinship are more of a liability than an advantage. Rethemniots see the inability to sustain a partnership, not as a serious personal flaw, but rather as the kind of weakness that characterizes local culture, Cretans and more comprehensively Greeks at large, and even human beings in general; they attribute it to generic historical and cosmological causes that respectively led to the fall of Byzantium to the Turks and to the fall of humankind at large to the allure of sensual temptation. Recognizing this inherent collective problem, some simply avoid partnerships with kin: "Because, at some point, he will do you in and you will do him in," and the kin group stands exposed to ridicule. In these terms, no one has a claim on the moral high ground.

In some special cases, the erosion of trust may nevertheless be a slow process. A butcher took his son and then his sister's husband and their two sons into partnership, and the business initially flourished because, one of the younger partners maintained, "it was a family circle and there was the respect of the younger ones for their elders." With five partners, the business also benefited from a wide network of acquaintances. Business flourished, and the partners bought and began to operate their own pig farm. This was when the inevitable happened. After working together at both the pig farm and the butcher's shop, they began to divide up the tasks that they had initially shouldered collectively, with the result that some began to feel that they were working harder than others. In addition, one of the younger partners ended up working almost exclusively at the pig farm: "Eh, when I set out at seven-thirty or eight in the morning and went to the unit [the pig farm] and came back at around one in the middle of the day, well, what was I to do at the shop? Then in the afternoons I went back up there. All right, so, for the little bit of time left over, I came back down to the shop, but I wasn't really in the swim of things in the shop; I was always off over there." Meanwhile, the older partners were beginning to lose interest and eventually retired, one of his cousins was in the army, and the remaining cousin could no longer manage on his own. Finally, the partner who was looking after the pig farm bought a hotel and incurred substantial debts that could be relieved only by selling the shop; and the entire, long-lived partnership died.

In this case, the relationships among the partners apparently did not become particularly bitter, but the same strains that in other situations produced a total rift were at work. We can observe here a variety of developmental cycle in the history of each partnership, from its genesis as a single-family affair to a more complex cooperative effort, and thence to eventual implosion and collapse.[7] The unreliable glue provided by kinship and even by genuine affect cannot withstand the pressures of economic competition where, in the final analysis, a man is responsible for the prosperity of his own nuclear household and where the kind of official support for partnership that might provide incentives for greater stability is lacking. The very forces that encourage the emergence of partnerships—the expansion of labor, the creation of larger networks of potential customers, and the greater efficiency of production that come with these collective arrangements—also increase the range of issues on which jealousy can gnaw.

Even among merchants, who pride themselves on being more modern in outlook than artisans, provocations for ending a partnership are frequent. The acquisition of a second shop by a merchant partnership of two brothers may create too alluring a temptation. A property so easily divided will not often remain intact for long: one brother demands that the partners split the shops between them and that he be left to go it alone. Siblinghood is certainly no guarantee of stability; in one partnership, a pie shop originally started by two third cousins (and members of the same clan), a decision was made to include the younger brother of one of the partners: "Then we saw that we were getting very tired and I had the brother with whom I worked at that bakery in Athens, and I say to my partner, Mikhalis, say I, 'Let's take Vassilis on board, either as an employee [*ipallilos*] or by making him a partner.' Says he, 'Good idea, partner, so we won't have any reason to quarrel about whether you are giving him a little or a lot, so we won't have such affairs!' And we made him a partner. He put in his share of the money [i.e., working capital] and came in as a partner." For a long while, everything went smoothly, but we should not forget that the very possibility that the original partners might have taken the brother on as an "employee"—a degrading term for Cretan men, who seem very conscious of its literal meaning as "one who works *under* [someone else]"—could easily have rankled.

Even here, such a good beginning could not deliver on its promise. Some years later, with the very same justification ("we were very tired"), these men partially dismantled the partnership: "We agreed that one would take on the [savory] cheese pies and the *boughatses* [sweet cheese pies] and open a separate shop, and the other two would stay on making pizza." The two brothers ended up with the cheese pies and the separate shop. The choice was resolved by tossing a coin—a device startlingly reminiscent of the casting of lots by which property is often divided among coheirs in the Greek countryside in order to reduce tension among siblings and deflect possible resentment over the outcome against the hand of fate instead. Greek villagers actually expect that tension will be especially high among close kin, leading to a higher risk of discord and even violence.[8] In this instance, the speaker attributed the stability of the brothers' working relationship to the fact that they had served as employees together and had learned to trust each other: "That means we didn't say, 'How many pieces did you sell—where's the money?'" The cousin remained an independent operator, although—whether because no anger was ever expressed or because all those concerned understood the dangers of exposing the clan's collective standing to the ridicule that discord often brings—there is no outward hint of tension or discord between the former partners.

Small flickers of pride (such as the sense that the other partner is not pulling his weight) can ignite the fires of mutual enmity, and few craft associations can long survive the bitter quarrels that ensue. In one specialist carpentry partnership, the former apprentice became addicted to drugs; under suspicion in a series of burglaries, he began ignoring his responsibilities to the firm and blaming customers for refusing to pay their debts. The senior partner told him that if he had received such complaints, it would be his responsibility to approach the defaulting customers in the appropriate way, since handling customers with discretion and tact was an important part of their work: they were constantly in customers' houses and could be asked to do various extra odd jobs that a high-handed but well-heeled customer might demand more or less as a right. The younger man, miserably entangled in his own troubles, had no appetite for such fine points of business diplomacy, on which success especially depended in the tight and personalistic economy of Rethemnos, and eventually the partnership collapsed.

That partnership was at least grounded in an apparently deep friendship and took a relatively long time to fall apart. Few, however, have the patience the senior partner showed—at least in his own account—in trying to help his associate overcome his personal difficulties. More commonly, partners are ready to quarrel almost as soon as they set up in business together. A too-trusting disposition, once betrayed, will get a partner mocked in the larger society, in which malicious third parties are also often standing by with destructive gossip designed to drive the associates apart. Just as alliances based on reciprocal animal theft contain a corrosive residue of mutual distrust, so that a single act of disloyalty can lead to complete breakdown, and just as marriage negotiations between mutually hostile households entail enormous social risk,[9] so craft partnerships are subject to the gnawing doubts engendered by their genesis in the fear of competition.

The parallel between such partnerships and marriage alliances is explicitly recognized. But unlike marriages, which are also alliances between households and even clans, work cooperatives are not held together by sacrament. They are even more unstable, in this regard resembling the alliances of animal thieves rather than those of affines. Indeed, as we have already seen, local observers view their eventual collapse as in part the result of a "fatalistic" orientation; if there is ultimately no hope of maintaining such fragile arrangements, men are certainly not going to risk their masculine pride by acquiescing in any degree of compromise. On the contrary, an expectation of deep mutual suspicion provides the grounds for the highly destructive rhetoric of recrimination that constantly batters the very possibility of trust. A tailor attributed the instability of most cooperative craft businesses (he was proud to note that his was one of the few exceptions, having lasted a quarter of a century) to the conventional expectation that the partners "will start to steal from each other." One merchant who had tried to run a business jointly with his brother described the backbiting with which, as he noted, in a "small community" like Rethemnos others attempt to turn the brothers against each other by describing one to the other as lazy and dishonest; he compared the partnership itself to a "marriage brokerage" (*proksenio*) that these "pimps" (*roufiani*) were forever out to spoil.

The machinations of malicious neighbors take hold because the fear of competition from those one has trained is grounded in everyday experience, and perhaps also because the fear of looking like a trusting fool takes precedence over the desire to believe in one's partners' honesty. Trust is possible to a limited degree. A restaurateur, for example, claimed that he was able to feed schoolboys and workmen on a credit basis because "Rethemniots are the best people. The most honorable [*timii*] and honest [*dombratzidhes*], as we say,[10] that is, sincere. Sincere people. If he comes by and says, 'Dimitris, I'll pay tomorrow,' he will pay tomorrow!" But this is a generalization based, first of all, on a limited kind of credit *(vereses)* the failure of which would quickly embarrass the defaulter much more grievously than the restaurateur, who would simply cut off credit and let it be known why he was doing so; second, it must be read in the context of a conversation in which the restaurateur was relying on the idiom of the disclaimer ("it's not because we are in Rethimno right now"), reproducing the conventional protestations of personal honesty at the level of a collective local sensibility.

Such frequent disclaimers, personal and collective alike, undermine their own credibility: people protest too much, especially given Rethemniots' unflattering self-stereotype as people who habitually stab each other in the back. But that encompassing aggressiveness is, in fact, just what the disclaimers are all about. They are not meant to persuade so much as to challenge others to match them in displays of agonistic self-promotion thinly disguised as modesty. Here is a master pie-maker's personal version of that rhetoric: "I may have suffered, I may have been worn out, I may . . . I never thought, first of all, that we are a monopoly in Rethimno on pizza, cheese pies, sweet cheese pies, and all that stuff; I never thought—and I think that this helped us in our professional career—that now that I have money in my pocket—look, money in my pocket, my pocket's filled up with money—I never thought to use inferior cheese, to make smaller cheese pies, to adulterate them. We never thought of doing that."

While this self-promoting posturing suggests deliberate social management in itself, it also frankly reflects practical strategizing on the artisan's part: being known for inferior products is particularly dangerous in a small and closely knit society such as that of Rethemnos. It is worth noting, however, that the pie-maker's declarations of total honesty came hard on the heels of an equally disingenuous insistence that he had always enjoyed perfectly harmonious relations with his business partners, a brother and a distant agnatic cousin. The point of all these rhetorical displays, then, seems less to convince others that the speaker is better than they are than to show that one at least understands the nature of others' doubts and suspicions and to express a readiness to rebuff them at every turn. They are a boastful dare, a snarl of defiance against the expected calumnies that are themselves an integral part of everyday competition. Here, too, we may sense the ever-present fear of the "pimps," who may, as in every aspect of Rethemniot life,[11] come from among one's most familiar neighbors, friends, and even—or especially—kinsfolk. The important thing, as a realtor put it, is to "be proud to say, humbly and with elegance, that I am not ashamed when I go to the marketplace,[12] because no one will call me a scoundrel, no one will call me a fraud." In other words, whatever others thought, they would not dare to use such words of a man who was in a position to insist that they show him respect.

Needless to say, no artisan ever expresses any aspersions against his own probity. One man revealingly declared, "I personally have never thought of robbing my partner. Now, what my partner is thinking, what he's doing, I don't know. I can't exclude that possibility [that he is planning to rob me]. I can't exclude certain possibilities. Of course, I want to believe that it won't happen." But if it does, he implies, the speaker will already, with these words, have proactively made sure that everyone knows that he was not a trusting fool or a fatalist[13]—just an honest man trying to give the other fellow a break but prepared for the worst nonetheless. After all, as every Greek knows, you can't tell what another person is thinking.[14] You just have to act as though you could and keep trying to guess. The worst-case scenario will probably turn out to be the right one, because in truth people expect to be able to judge others on the basis of what they know about their own intentions and motives, which are equally opaque, and equally guessable, to those others. The artisan who wondered about his partner's honesty went on to say that the advantage of a partner was that one could go to one's home village for a day or two without worrying, whereas a simple employee (or apprentice) might stab one in the back immediately. But this comforting claim overlooks the crucial point that today's employee might well be tomorrow's partner—because that may be the only way to co-opt him, at least for a while.

Corrosive Competition

Constant competition is part of everyday life. The cunning that apprentices learn is all about competition. Builders' apprentices soon discover, for example, that if, having learned a few basic skills, they can then hire themselves out to rival artisans, they can more easily dictate terms to an employer trying to get them back under his control: they claim they have now achieved the status of "junior master" (*mastoraki*) themselves and that they therefore expect a much higher wage if they are to return. They may themselves be the sons of artisans and have inflated ideas about the wages they can command; a coffin-maker's son, a boy in his midteens, asked a floor-maker for two and a half times the wage that the latter was prepared to pay him while he was acquiring the rudiments of the craft, because, having watched his father take in that amount for an hour's work, and perhaps unwilling to see that floor-making could be much more intricate and complex than coffin-making, he felt entitled to comparable remuneration. (The floor-maker, on the other hand, was proud of the kind of knowledge that he could impart and felt that the boy should not have asked for any money at all, so good was the instruction he would receive: "from morning until evening, for eight hours I'd be talking to him; for eight hours I'd not close my mouth"—a very unusual claim for an artisan in Rethemnos.) Some apprentices raise the ante by taking on piecework *(meremetia)* in one of the relatively few areas of skill that they have genuinely mastered; the more entrepreneurial building contractors may be willing to employ them on this basis as a quick solution to immediate construction needs, and in the process the apprentices again acquire a great deal of bargaining power with any erstwhile employer who is anxious to get them back under his immediate control. This clearly illustrates how the new economic conditions have undermined the social aspects of apprenticeship as well as the careful acquisition of skill.

Cooperative partnerships are partly a strategy intended to establish precisely the kind of control that will relieve artisans of their dependence on such increasingly transient and professionally unengaged forms of labor. They are conceived in somewhat conspiratorial terms in relation to other people, especially rival artisans and former employers; a tailor called his unusually long-lasting partnership a "ganging together" *(sispirosi)*. Professionally, too, aggressive competition is part and parcel of an outlook that makes the male artisan's self at once the touchstone of distinction and the essence that others see in his products.

Steal such an artisan's trade secrets, and you steal his selfhood. The apprentice also "steals," at least metaphorically, and this is a source of great tension between him and his master; but the theft is a socially legitimate act that complicates the hierarchy of relationships negotiated in the intimate space of the workshop. Paradoxically, the development of the apprentice's skills through imitation is also the basis for his eventual liberation from a control to which he has more or less voluntarily submitted and enhances the master's reputation as the metaphorical father of an extensive line of well-trained artisans.[15] Quite the reverse applies to poaching by the artisan's commercial rival, an indiscreetly public provocation and immediate commercial threat for which there is no such trade-off. A cobbler was particularly scathing about the crassness of those who did not submit themselves to a lengthy apprenticeship but sought to make fast money by imitating others' products. To him, as to so many others, quick copying was a denial of what artisanship was about.

He expressed concern, less about the ethics or aesthetics of plagiarism, than about the spiritual cheapness that imitation displayed. He especially showed contempt for those who placed income above principle: "I'm not interested in having an income to live on! Because if I just live on my income, I am nothing! Just a person who will be wandering hither and thither spending his money. I am interested in having an ontological presence [*mia ondotita*], a personality, and one that comes from my work itself. Because usually it's your work that gives you your value [*aksia*] as well." He also attacked official attempts to encourage the kind of work that he regarded as plagiarism.

State officials, charged with encouraging initiative in small businesses, were delighted with one low-level bureaucrat who had learned at one of their own seminars to reproduce handmade leather goods "with a pair of scissors, with a razor blade, and with a punch," and who had then gone on to provide "wonderful seminars" of his own. Apparently, he had copied the work of the artisan who recounted this tale to me; the latter, who scornfully dismissed the possibility that such a man could produce work of a professional quality, was convinced that these seminars were simply a ruse so that the officials in question could show that they were working productively. The development of a true artisan cannot be hurried; and the production of an artisan's selfhood cannot be achieved by bureaucratic means, which in any case encourage crass imitation rather than the creative distinctiveness that is the mark of the true artisan.[16]

If selfhood is expressed through the production of objects, ideas about the relations among selves will presumably be reflected in ideas about originality, stylistic debt, and the force of convention. The distinctiveness of what an artisan produces perpetuates the performance of his selfhood, projecting it above crass commercialism. Artisans disparage the rush, regardless of quality, to open more and more shops and ateliers as "(hyper)professionalism," which they attribute to people who have sold a piece of land in order to buy a shop space in town and have jumped into the market without bothering to acquire the necessary skills or aesthetic devotion. This is a pose of disdain for mere money. Ironically, however, it is the distinctiveness of these artisans' products that provides their competitive edge in the market—an advantage as fragile, as fraught with risk, as grossly inflated by the frenetic pumping of capitalism, as the masculine self-performance that materializes that distinctiveness as personal style in the social arena. The temptations and pressures are such that an apprentice can buy a set of tools and call himself a master artisan; but the old hands are ready with their instant contempt. "In the old days, thirty years ago, a lad didn't have the possibility of buying tools and saying, 'I am becoming a master!'" Modernity has allegedly cheapened the coin of both artisanal skill and male selfhood by fueling the sense of competition with an excess of cash; and it is, one jeweler insisted, the lack of skill rather than the proliferation of rival businesses that drives the incompetent into bankruptcy.

The ability to make distinctive products is thus a claim on individuality as well as on professional success, closely linked to the devil-may-care performance of masculinity. It is opposed to the possessive individualism of property owning that so irks artisans when banks refuse their loan requests on the grounds that artisans usually have no real estate to offer as collateral. In general, banks and state agencies will waive such quantitative requirements only under political pressure from a political patron—another reason for which artisans end up expressing great contempt for bankers and politicians alike. Within the global hierarchy of value, artisans' sole true capital is their skill—intangible, evanescent, and irreducible to the bureaucratic criterion of measurability. The banks' policy denies them even a toehold on the ladder of economic self-improvement leading to the acquisition of property, confirming the message of their feckless disregard for risk: their traditional mode of being, in life as in craft, is both the evidence of their failure to achieve modernity and the fundamental justification for keeping them out of it.

Yet they are far from lacking in calculation. The leatherworker, for example, admits that he can no longer produce the elaborate workmanship that marked his first attempts; told by an Italian master artisan that he had put too much work into these items, that they would not prove economically viable, he now says he does not have the "patience" *(ipomoni)* for such complex artisanry. He has recalibrated his sense of patience, which for artisans is a bodily virtue associated with continual learning by trial and error, to a more reasonable degree of complexity that acknowledges the economic reality of Rethemnos (as opposed to an Italian city), as well as, perhaps, to what another artisan recognized as the gradual dulling of the enthusiasm that sustains this patience.

In the same way, while emphasizing the central role of aesthetic and technical pleasure, he also acknowledges the importance of training the apprentice's eye to measure the best way of cutting a piece of leather so as to waste the smallest amount; unlike metalworkers, who can simply melt and reuse their mistakes, leatherworkers—like carpenters—cannot afford to make serious slips. Thus, it is not the case that they do not calculate. On the contrary, they are extremely careful in their assessments. These, however, do not involve acts of precise measurement with a ruler but the riskier technique of judging by sight—a poised skill for which "stealing with the eyes" is clearly, as the leatherworker acknowledged, the ideal training, since it reduces dependence on mechanical means and places the entire burden of judgment on the embodied skill of the emergent artisan. His financial viability further depends, not only on acquiring this skill and applying it consistently, but on inspiring in his customers the confidence expressed in the sure movements it generates.

Moreover, the distinctiveness of what such skilled artisans produce is also a means of protecting the very economic self-interest that the rhetoric of art-before-money masks: the same artisan who expressed such disdain for monetary considerations also pointed out that the only workshops based on quick-fix knowledge acquisition and rote production that survived for any length of time were nuclear-family concerns, in which the availability of unpaid working hands somewhat compensated for the poor quality and unoriginality of the products and for the apparent lack of self-confidence that the producers brought to their enterprise.

These family-based solutions are insecure and often short-lived business arrangements even by local standards. They offer weak competition for those artisans whose work is respected. The latter have clung jealously to their skills and their standing, partly by making imitation as difficult as possible. Yet this individuality is not an unalloyed good: these artisans' tenacity in clinging to their secrets enhances their personal standing, but it also removes them from the forms of exchange and imitation that confer an aura of bourgeois modernity. Their suspicious view of the world makes them old-fashioned; it marks them as eccentrics in a homogenizing age. Yet its roots lie precisely in the social conditions that make such an attitude sensible in the immediate local context. Masters' reluctance to teach their apprentices is often explained in terms of the likelihood that the latter will rapidly set up competitive businesses. "There, if you're smart, you should steal with your eye from your boss what he shouldn't, and won't, show you. Because it's not in his interest to show you!" Stealing the master's professional secrets is a way of destroying not only his economic base but also his distinctiveness as an artisan and, with it, the core of his social self—a self locked into its "traditional" identity by the secretiveness, uncommunicativeness, and displays of self-assured masculinity with which he operates.

There is, logically, an intrinsic relationship between the fear of competition and the desire to create partnerships. This is not unlike the ambivalence that shepherds experience when their sons first start to challenge their authority and set up independent flocks.[17] Apprentices are impatient to set up independently; masters, whose work ethic includes a heavy emphasis on the patience needed to absorb skills in the body, may appeal to just this principle— "it's not yet time [for you to learn that]!"—as a ruse to keep apprentices both ignorant and under the masters' control. An apprentice, faced with such a situation, "will be forced to leave." One carpenter, for example, recounted how his master had sought to keep him on with the status of an apprentice even after he had thoroughly absorbed the craft: "He proposed to me that I should work for him that way again. But I told him, 'Thanassis, I can't do it, either [what I am asking for] will happen or I'll open my own shop.' I was there and he had brought me up, so I had a more obstinate mind." Here the threat of becoming an independent operator proved sufficient to persuade the older man into accepting a partnership on more or less equal terms, leaving the erstwhile apprentice to succeed him as the owner of the business after the passage of a few years. This carpenter is also acknowledging that what enabled him to put such pressure on his employer was a relationship not unlike that between father and son ("he had brought me up"), a relationship between a "foster son" and his boss that allowed the former to stand up to the latter's power.

Festering Fosterage

It is this capacity to reproduce filial demands on the employer that also allows older artisans, reciprocating at the level of reminiscence, to deny that their own employers had ever treated them with the physical severity that they attribute to the category of employers as a whole—much as an actual son will affectionately recall his father's relative indulgence even while invoking the strictness of his father's generation as a justification for his own relatively muted manifestations of paternal authority. On the other hand, a foster son could be asked to perform tasks that a son might perform willingly but an unrelated person would resent: "The apprentice did all the jobs; that is, he could do anything from being a servant in the house to being a worker in the workshop. That's the meaning for which an apprentice [parayos] is an apprentice—that is, like his son [yos], an apprentice [parayos]." One carpenter, recalling that *his* master had trained him by explaining and showing him how to perform various tasks rather than just forcing him to learn on the sly, commented, "He couldn't *not* show me [how to do the tasks], since the responsibility was his, not mine!"

This paternal image may not correspond to the reality experienced by most apprentices (and it conjures up all the uncertainty about affect and support that fosterage implies). It is nevertheless an image that they often invoke when, grown to manhood, they recall their own relations with their respective masters. A floor-maker, recognizing the role that a now elderly carpenter had played in forming the skills of many younger artisans, commented, "That man is our father because he is now eighty-five years old." The younger men all address this father figure as *mastora*—in this instance a term of respect that reflects glory on them all as the disciples of a particularly successful master, albeit one that locks them all in an aura of backward traditionalism. In similar fashion, the phrase commonly used of a well-trained artisan ("he passed under the bench" of a particular master) encapsulates a historical memory of the cobblers' humiliating initiation ritual; the very idea of manual skill contains symbolically demeaning implications. In modern Greek usage, *paideia* has become the formal mode of education, in which corporal discipline has all but disappeared; but we should not forget that the cognate verb *pedhevo* still means "tease, torment." The historically proximate model may be monastic—one thinks of Chrysostom again—but the goal is less that of passively accepting the mortification of the flesh in anticipation of a spiritual afterlife than it is a deliberate roughening of psychological calluses in anticipation of a thoroughly agonistic here and now.

These days, the term *afendiko*, "boss," is more commonly used for a master, but it may be ironically reversed when the master wants to belittle an apprentice's displays of independence, just as a man may ruefully call himself *parayos* in the context of acknowledging his wife's control of the domestic purse strings. The term *parayos* itself has not lost its negative implications even with the decline of the institution that it represents, because the prejudice against fosterage is still very powerful and so the term retains implications of the bogus claims to affection that are attributed to an unnatural—that is, purely social—bond.

The father-son relationship in a family is ideally one of hierarchy leavened with deep affect. In some trades, notably the jewelry business, it provides the only possible channel for the transmission of secrets that can be learned nowhere else. Said one goldsmith, "I went to the Goldsmiths' School up in Athens, [part of] the Ministry of Labor, but the secrets that my father taught me at work cannot be learned, Mr. Michael—not at school, nor [anywhere]!" This, the lived experience of those who work with their fathers, is also the ideal model for the relationship between a master and an unrelated apprentice. Transformed into a professional relationship in the remembered workshop, the hierarchy and the respect it entails often live on, idealized and purified, in the nostalgic tales artisans tell of their apprenticeship years.

The affect thus recalled, however, is often suppressed or even completely absent in both the memories and the present-day experience of the workshop. In this sense, the role of a son is altogether different from that of an unrelated apprentice—another reason for avoiding that area of disturbingly ambiguous sentiment represented by the hiring of agnates as apprentices. A son can exercise a degree of authority over even those unrelated apprentices who are his seniors; one former tailor, having expatiated at some length on the uncultured brutality of older apprentices toward newcomers, recalled that his father's single *kalfas* treated him well: "Well, he loved me because I, of course, was the son of his boss." This was not only a special instance of the principle that one's own boss always seems to have been better than others' employers. It was also a rich comment on the instrumental "love" that is, in the local view, the only kind one can expect from nonagnates, especially when even one's own kin can routinely be expected to exploit the convention that their affections are *not* motivated and therefore *should* be exorbitantly rewarded with favors![18]

Assumptions about the interested motivations of apprentices toward their masters' sons are consistent with the metaphor of an adoptive relationship between master and apprentice.[19] A foster son is always at the mercy of one who can claim the tie of blood, and the principle of a solidarity based in common blood is theoretically extendable to the whole range of agnatic kin. While apprentices rarely work for agnates, and artisans even try to avoid hiring their agnates at all, artisans create in miniature what is virtually an alternative clan: a zone of professional solidarity and intergenerational discipline. The clanlike ethos makes the employment of agnates redundant. But there are also striking differences that set this arrangement off from normative father-son relationships: it is much closer to the fosterage after which it is named, in the sense that apprentices are brought in on sufferance but feared for that eventual stab in the back that no truly filial son would ever attempt; they, in turn, have every reason to fear the anger of their masters' actual sons.[20]

This fundamental distrust among people working in close and ceaseless bodily proximity may largely account for the instability of partnerships between masters and their former apprentices. Because it begins in a relationship of fundamental inequality, moreover, this kind of arrangement is liable to more than the usual degree of jockeying for authority and advantage, which is also exacerbated by the constant awareness—sometimes expressed as a very dim view of human decency—that very small economic differences can make the difference between survival and ruin. This awareness constantly undermines the will to cooperate on equal terms.

There are additional, material reasons for which starting up in competition with erstwhile employers is always a temptation for young and newly skilled artisans: in particular, the simple equipment most of them use does not cost much, so the overheads for a new departure are small, even by local standards. Some apprentices do have an interest in staying with masters who are their kin; a baker, for example, recalled that his maternal uncle was the only master baker who could afford to take him on, as the police were checking on uninsured workers (baking was a so-called protected profession [*katokhi-romeno epangelma*], meaning that insurance rules for workers were especially strict), and a master craftsman would rarely be willing to risk breaking the law except under family pressure. In such a situation, the necessarily high degree of mutual trust involved derived from the obligations associated with kin solidarity.

Where kinship is absent, other devices may be brought into play. One way in which artisans sometimes seek to control their apprentices is by offering to serve as the baptismal sponsors for the apprentices' children. It is very difficult for an apprentice or junior partner to refuse such an offer, which conveys implications of hierarchy and indebtedness that the junior may resent but can reject only at considerable peril: material peril because he is refusing the closest thing he can get to a guarantee of job security; social, because he will be viewed in the larger society as a disrespectful ingrate and may find it hard to find alternative employment. The junior partner can rarely do much more than avoid any display of excessive eagerness, which would only increase the depth of his perceived dependence: "He says to me, 'Shall I baptize your child?' Say I, 'Well, it's no skin off my nose [*dhe me niazi*],[21] since that's what *you* want,' and so . . . he baptized my son."

One sees here something of the Hegelian master-slave dialectic: the master is quite dependent on the apprentice's remaining with him and seeks to dominate him by means of a ritual tie that is egalitarian in religious terms but is understood to have social implications of obligation and consequently also of inequality. Normatively, in fact, the baptismal sponsor is understood to be morally superior to the child's parents, so that the junior partner has only one option short of refusing: he can undercut the master's assumption of symbolic power only by agreeing as though he was the one doing the favor. By being placed in a position of being unable to refuse what was both an honor and a moral responsibility, the employee found himself shackled all the more inextricably to his boss.

Even so, the baptismal tie was not always sufficient to maintain that relationship. One artisan had allowed his sister to baptize his employer's child, which was itself an unusual reversal of the expected relationship between the two families; but he eventually became so incensed at the employer's constant swearing that he quit. As a member of the morally "higher" family from a religious perspective, he could implicitly chide his boss for failing to uphold the ethical standards that superior status demanded; this is the rhetoric whereby Greeks often criticize both priests and bureaucrats, arguing that their greater responsibility makes their derelictions all the more reprehensible. In this case, the employer was palpably perturbed; such a savage blow to his standing could not easily be concealed, because his employee had so clearly seized the moral high ground. He therefore sent "mediators to bring me back. He even went to my brother and told him, 'Tell him to come [back]!'" But all the boss's efforts went for naught, although whether this was really because of his angry demeanor is not entirely clear: "I wanted to learn better work." The agile apprentice is always alert to the chance of learning something new, and even the nominal obligations created by the baptismal tie could not offset that hunger for the knowledge that older artisans concealed with such jealousy.

The baptismal tie does normally offer some assurance of trustworthiness, especially in businesses that are both artisanal and involve a rapid turnover at the cash till. A pie-maker who was in partnership with his brother, for example, explained: "So, given that you're going to take on a lad you don't know, [you don't know] what family he comes from and just what he is, we preferred to take on my brother's godson [*vaptisimio*]." This hire worked out so well that the lad returned after doing his military service and today "he's learned ninety percent of the work."

The pie-maker claimed that he never hid any of the technical aspects from his staff but pointed out that this apprentice had spent perhaps as little as one year at school and so would have to learn by experience at every step along the way. In this case, a baptismal relationship provided a more intimate and nurturing framework for working together; since the pie-maker's business required a relatively high degree of trust in money matters as well, both sides had an interest in maintaining that framework for as long and with as much mutual affection as possible.

The other lad working in the shop is a member of the partners' clan but is at the closest a fifth cousin, and the pie-maker who talked with me about these arrangements emphasized that this lad, who was retarded and, "if you'll permit the phrase, a bit uncultivated," was mostly given the job of selling pies in the shop—simple work that required the sort of financial trustworthiness one might expect from a clan-mate who was also none too bright. This was a classic example of the excuse made for employing agnates: that it was a form of solidarity. "Yes, he got things mixed up, so I got him a price list and I would tell him, 'one cheese pie, one hundred and fifty [drachmas]; two cheese pies, three hundred; three cheese pies, four hundred and fifty.' I made him this list, okay, and he gradually got to manage it. The lad managed it, we wanted to keep him since he was a poor kid; that is to say, we helped the kid and his family." And he added, in response to my asking specifically about the agnatic relationship, that he helped the boy "as a fellow villager, through knowing his father, and as a clan[-mate]." Such acts of charity are the only more or less risk-free ways of employing agnates; a lad like this had nowhere else to go and would certainly never achieve the level of partner. The brother's godson was presumably another matter entirely, but he, too, had good reason to stay loyally with the business. These exceptions to the rule of avoiding the employment of clan-mates are in fact demonstrations of the principle that underlies the rule: clan solidarity in the face of an often mocking and hostile social environment. Father and son, or a pair of unmarried brothers, are exceptions that in effect do not count, because these are pairs that would be expected to sustain their solidarity under virtually all circumstances: they share a common interest, and any discord between them poses the risk of total humiliation and ruin.

Indeed, categorically a son cannot be an apprentice, since the latter is a "foster son"; here the "real" link of blood is accorded absolute priority. And when a man takes on the training of a brother, this is also excluded from the realm of apprenticeship by the cautionary phrase *"but they were brothers"* and by the symbolism of "sleeping in one house, eating from one plate." Partnerships based on these pairs are thus relatively stable, since they are in principle not based on an initial rivalry, although the eventual emergence of mutual jealousy or rivalry is a serious threat in the longer term.

Trust and Ambition

It is not always the junior person who causes a partnership to break up; some young artisans see these arrangements as highly desirable means of establishing a professional reputation and clientele. The impetus for a breakup may indeed sometimes come from the senior partner's restless ambitions. One carpenter took particular pride in the fact that his erstwhile master, having trained him and eventually taken him into partnership, deserted the new arrangement in search of other opportunities, only to return after three and a half years because—in the speaker's view—the people with whom he had tried to work were unable to attract custom. This carpenter narrated a story of gradual habituation: his master was a difficult person, but the speaker was the one apprentice with whom he had been able to reach a degree of mutual tolerance, so the master took him into partnership and, having walked out on their working relationship, came back in the hope—eventually realized—of re-creating their partnership. For all the intervening time, the master never visited his former apprentice, who still attributes the lack of contact to the self-absorption of one who remembers his former power. But circumstances may reverse that hierarchy. The former master now addresses the younger man as "master" (*mastora*) with a pitiful humility that the latter ironically recalls: "Then he started dropping by here: 'How's it going, master? How's the work?'" Then comes the brazenly direct question that signals the new balance of power: "'Where are you [working?]' I ask." And the other man admits that he has been working with other, less competent partners and has consequently paid a heavy price.

Self-regard is the key term here. It is this defiant stance that defines the masculinity to which most of the apprentices apparently aspire and on which they also blame the arrogance of their seniors. Exceptionally, a woman may invoke the same principle. One female artisan claimed that her vindictive response to an apprentice who cheated her of large sums of money was an expression of *eghoismos* and that she acted in this way "because I am a Rethemniot woman!" Such unusual female invocations of the principle confirm its significance: in a situation where a woman in a normatively male role confronted an employee acting like a male rogue, she felt entitled to play out this conflation of masculine and local identity to the full. Through hard work and success, she had established the moral authority necessary to do so on her own account, a stand that would have been unthinkable, for example, in the much more rigidly gender-segregated mountain communities. On the other hand, her revenge took the form of legal action, which for many men is contrary to the essence of manhood. Also, she insisted that her work was artistic rather than a craft, again a stand that contrasts tellingly with male claims to a more practical sensibility.[22]

Something analogous to this gender inversion also happens when a master serves as the baptismal sponsor for a child from the apprentice's family. In the more usual situation where it is the employer who serves as sponsor, however, self-regard sets a limit to the servility that agreeing to the boss's offer of baptismal sponsorship might otherwise create. This clarifies the role of self-regard in the creation of partnerships. These are risky enterprises, since everyone knows they are unstable; yet refusal to engage in them can also be a risk, that of seeming too timid. If men who are considered to be afraid of taking risks are unlikely to succeed in this society, it is because self-regard makes it impossible for men to display any uncertainty about their bodies or their persons: any physical sign of hesitation or excessive concern can be fatal to a young man's standing. By the same token, a show of reluctance to accept an employer's offer of baptismal sponsorship enlarges one's reputation for independence of spirit and action alike.

Devil-may-care affectations, or simply the assumption of a willful indifference, are central to the performance of Rethemniot manhood. They are the clearest signs that a youth is "heavy": he will mature into a man to reckon with, even though (or especially because) he is an obnoxious brat at the moment. We see a clear anticipation of that development in the infuriated ironworker's backhanded praise of his recalcitrant apprentice. Apprentices learn early that it is better to seem indolent or uninterested than to demonstrate too much anxiety about learning the craft.[23] Affectations of unconcern are rife in this society: we have already seen the casual indifference that a young man shows in response to his senior's request to baptize his child. Moreover, people generally do not show much overt interest in the fortunes of others because this is seen as the sign of possessing the evil eye; yet everyone knows that everyone else is, in fact, intensely curious about all the other members of the society. People dismiss the very idea of guessing what others' motives might be; yet it is precisely this guessing game about motives that occupies an enormous amount of their time and energy. Affecting a complete lack of interest avoids provoking the ire of those who might resent any sign of inquisitiveness and at the same time allows a young man to show that he is completely unimpressed by another's authority. He has mastered the "instrumental nonchalance," to use Malaby's term, that one must display toward the techniques of his master's craft.

Self-regard nevertheless lies at the heart of the tensions that the birth of a partnership can rapidly bring into view. Some partnerships do work well, and their advantages are obvious to all: "On the one hand, expenses are reduced, and the cost of rent. The rent! Eh! You save [the expense of hiring] a worker; you save on one worker. Because when we have work, the two partners will sit and work. Just two hours longer! Three hours longer! There are two of us; you don't get bored by working on your own. You have company, and you chat. And you work. When you're on your own, you [get up and] leave. A worker will sit there for eight hours—then *he will leave!* He's not interested!"

There is also a dimension of ideological purity to partnership, which, although a business arrangement, is conceived in terms of "socialism." The same term, *sineterismos*, serves for both "collectives" and business partnerships. Any sense that business partnerships represent a local form of collectivism, however, quickly falls afoul of the self-perception that many Rethemniots entertain as individualists who do not easily tame their spirits to a common goal. One bakery partnership in a nearby village even collapsed because the senior partner wanted to use the holiday bonuses that are a legally required part of every salary to pay their collective dues to the local trade union! Most Rethemniots seem to think that cooperatives are an "Anglo-Saxon" or "European" institution that requires a level of honesty they are either incapable of achieving or too fixated on short-term gain to want to achieve.

Even artisans who make it into the merchant class often fall prey to the depth of suspicion that makes cooperation difficult. One such man assured me that Greeks in general were thieves and too interested in making a quick profit to be able to sustain a partnership. He related a series of examples in which large cooperatives had been formed, ostensibly for reasons of cost-efficiency but in reality (so he insisted) because, having sold shares in the cooperative, the partners could then help each other to profit from acting as suppliers to the company: "and all of them together become one big thief!"

At the level of the small-scale business in which he was personally engaged, a man he deeply trusted betrayed him in the same way. One function of their business was as a foreign currency exchange for tourists, who were content to receive the official rate and rarely demanded a formal receipt. For every ten lots of money he changed, the partner changed seven from money out of his own pocket, keeping the commission; of course, as my aggrieved friend observed, the partner was only stealing from himself, because he would have received half the properly registered profits anyway. So my friend told a Swiss customer to change some money at the partner's office, saying that he and the partner were not on speaking terms and not revealing that they were in fact in business together. The next day, my friend caught his partner's brother changing some money in a local bank and, no doubt having access to some pliable clerk, was able to view the cash and recognized it instantly since he had written down the numbers. This, he said, was clear evidence that the Greeks were not fit to run cooperative ventures of any sort.

Interestingly enough, he offered his justification for this view, as he himself put it, "fatalistically" (*mirolatrika*), and he described the Greeks as "miserable wretches" (*kakomiridhes*, a term that implies that they are the victims of fate rather than of their own willful wickedness). Here we see clearly expressed the ideology through which the elite maintains among its followers the view that Greeks are better off without such arrangements, for which they are not ready; he explicitly praised the conservative prime minister, Constantine Mitsotakis, for his attempts to abolish cooperatives of all sorts. He has absorbed the demeaning view that Greeks are fatalists, or at least that he would be justified in feeling resigned and fatalistic about their proclivities. We can read these remarks as an expression of submission to the logic whereby Greeks in general, and working-class Cretans in particular, are kept in place. The speaker, an outspoken communist, has internalized an argument that serves the interests of the political right wing (as his praise of Mitsotakis confirms) and perhaps of outside interests as well. While cooperative ventures (including partnerships) are generally viewed as praiseworthy in principle, people seem to accept the premise that they are foreign to Greek character and experience: national character is destiny embodied—and, as destinies go, it is, as we would appropriately say in English, an unfortunate one.

This is directly related to the social attitude that is thought both to inform and to erode cooperation among male artisans. Like the notion of partnership itself, *eghoismos* is a double standard. It can mean the competitive spirit that leads men (in particular) to compete in establishing their superiority as artisans and merchants, in which case it emerges as the context for a local germination of capitalist enterprise, as when it leads to a sudden proliferation of coffeehouses in some of the highland villages. But it can also mean the divisive touchiness that undermines any attempt to set up a stable business in the first place. While in its positive form *eghoismos* can mean a spirited defense of home and kin, its tendency to break down into the very opposite of such solidarity forms part of the artisans' self-deprecating rhetoric and serves as an instrument of their co-optation into the global hierarchy of value.

Fellow apprentices, schooled together in the arts of allying against a powerful employer, may offer the best prospect of long-term cooperation; even here, however, a tailor was moved to comment on what an impressive fact it was that for a quarter of a century he and his partner, erstwhile apprentices to the same master, were able to work together without the slightest sign of discord. Kin, ideally those whom one trusts, become instead quite the opposite. Precisely because the ideology of kin solidarity affords the best opportunities for manipulation, kin constitute the principal category of coworkers to be avoided: their self-regard will drive them to try to take over the business or to complain unceasingly. And this sad state of affairs, remarked one cobbler (in an apparently unconscious replay of earlier scholarly discourses about "amoral familism"),[24] is due to the backwardness of the Greeks. Once again we see how a Greek observer may become complicit in a process by which the global hierarchy of value demeans him. Another man, a restaurateur, saw the instability of partnerships as the consequence of a low level of education in the country, a state of affairs to which he also attributed the absence of a "work ethic."[25] Here, too, we see the self-deprecating comparison that marks co-optation by this hierarchy.[26]

What did the restaurateur mean? Interestingly enough, having railed at "shit Marxism" as the evil corrupter of his employees' minds, he—with seeming inconsistency—insisted that their lack of an appropriate work ethic was somehow typically Greek. But at the same time, in a further reversal of his logic, he argued that it was because Greeks lacked the traditionalist's passion for fine work that they always failed to make a success of partnerships: "Yes, it [the profession of restaurateur] fulfills me. And I constantly try to improve it. The other guy, however, the one who wants to become my partner, comes above all else because he sees that this shop has succeeded and he sees it in commercial terms, he sees it as a [source of] profit. 'Let's go ahead, let's say, and I'll put in some money and earn a profit.' His philosophy is one thing, mine quite another!" As a restaurateur, the speaker was a merchant rather than an artisan in his own right, yet his rhetoric invokes the artisanal ideal of "love" for the practice of the trade. At the same time, to his would-be partner he represents the artisanal proclivity for traditionalism as the foe of economic progress. That attitude is also to be seen in the artisans' resentment of the shortcuts to which some managerial contractors—notably construction company owners—drive them for the sake of relatively small but frequently repeated economies.

Such disagreements sometimes lead artisans to quarrel with contractors in ways that ultimately serve to confirm the general impression that artisans are both backward and wayward. They may also fall afoul of government agencies capable of giving them a significant amount of work, usually again because they do not easily accept the nonnegotiable character of the labor for which they are asked to contract: one ironworker was convinced that for five years he had not received any commissions from the historic conservation office (already notorious for generally not employing local artisans) because he had quarreled with its staff. Artisans are also sometimes forced into petty ruses that, while exhibiting their solidarity in the face of exploitation, also leave them open to charges of dishonesty or pettiness. For example, an artisanal producer of specialty doughs supplied one of the big hotels; when the managers started ordering the cheaper commercial product instead, the hotel pastrycook, a friend of the artisanal supplier, made sure that the commercial product kept breaking into small pieces, ruining the appearance of the finished pastries served to the hotel's clients.

It is thus the artisans, who in this respect are contrasted with merchants, whose atomistic conduct of social relations—whether as quarrelsomeness or as professional and ideological solidarity—becomes a matter for comment. Their demonstrative individualism, hallmark of their artistic excellence, easily appears instead as the incriminating evidence of their supposed backwardness. Here is the duck-rabbit of the pedestal that serves as a tethering post: what locks these people into the global hierarchy of value is the assumption that their Greekness depends on their doing what most effectively ruins their chances of achieving modernity, both in their social conduct and in their professional practices.

This is why the predicament of these marginal people offers an unusually clear window onto the operation and dynamics of the global hierarchy of value. By the same token, the "collective" aspect of a partnership, often categorically viewed as socialist in inspiration and therefore inimical to (and threatened by) the capitalist and individualist readings of *eghoismos*, can also be transformed into the model of a dynamic moneymaking partnership in which that same competitiveness is all to the good. It can also be read as "modern" *because* it is a "socialist" ideal; in that case, it becomes the object of some of the more vitriolic rhetoric produced by conservative officials and politicians—those who perhaps have the greatest stake in maintaining Greece's beholden global status. In either case, it is an oppressive liability.

Chapter Seven

Artisans in the State and the Nation

Exhibiting Tradition

Every year, the crafts fair organized by NOSMBH not only displays the range of what officialdom deems Cretan tradition to be but also reveals some of the mechanisms whereby state officials are able to reinforce their own position within the global hierarchy of value. Not only do we see a clearly demarcated range of aesthetic and thematic possibilities, but the extent to which cooperative artisanship is politically permissible stands clearly revealed.

The opening of the event regularly involves prominent local politicians. In 1992 and 1993 a conservative (New Democracy) government was in power in Athens, headed by the Cretan politician Constantine Mitsotakis; the guest of honor was the minister of the interior, a scion of one of the mountain villages of the district of which Rethemnos is the capital. While some of what follows here is more pronounced than what we would expect to find under the more left-wing governments that have since come to power, the convergence of a conservative leadership in Athens, a significant representation of Crete in that leadership, and the absorption of Greece into the European Union created ideal conditions for tracking the operation and effects of neoliberal economics in the local scene.

The 1992 fair was opened by the minister of the interior. Speeches were also made by the local Orthodox bishop and by the head of the Rethemnos office of NOSMBH, as well as by the head of the local chamber of commerce. The more obviously political speeches produced a message of startling clarity: that the destiny of Greece was to enter Europe irrevocably and decisively; that this destiny rested on the Greeks' originary contribution to the rise of European civilization; and that European civilization, represented locally by the handicraft traditions of Crete, was one of individualism and creativity and, as such, to be contrasted with the mass productions of certain Eastern countries such as Japan and "Formosa." As an illustration of cultural fundamentalism, this combined message would have been hard to surpass.[1]

One of the local speakers, moreover, granted me an interview, in the course of which he very explicitly elaborated some further implications of this value system. This man was a stalwart of the local New Democracy party, and his comments revealed a close connection between his political affiliation and his cultural ideology. In particular, he contrasted the situation of the very country whose Europeanness he had been so energetically lauding with those of countries where unionization and cooperative ventures had become commonplace. Greece, he said, lacked a widespread bourgeois tradition, and the Greeks themselves had little aptitude for cooperation. Thus, he reasoned, the authorities would have to take a hand and develop artisanal crafts in their own way. The NOSMBH office was especially to be praised, in his view, for its efforts in sustaining a program of engaging artisans in teaching a new generation—without interference even when what was taught was "erroneous" because it was not really "traditional."

A bedrock of authenticity underlay this vision, but it was authenticity that a self-declared bourgeoisie was clearly expected to take the leading role in defining and maintaining. It was an authenticity marked by the absence of standardization, an absence guaranteed by NOSMBH's energetic defense of tradition against corruption. The only effect of the "erroneous" methods now being taught would be a slowing down of production. Moreover, he argued, Cretan artisans do not deal with their apprentices from a position of power, as (he asserted) happens in France. Greece (and here he was at pains to emphasize that he was no chauvinist!)[2] is not an industrial country; rather, its wealth lies in its long and rich tradition. Crete, he added, was even more traditional than the rest of the country.

The global hierarchy of value lies exposed here in full array. The bourgeoisie is to lead the nation to its European apotheosis, determining along the way which elements of traditional culture are to be considered contributions to that march of cultural progress and which are to be treated as impediments to it. The individualism of the Cretan artisans produces work that resists standardization and thus avoids the crass plagiarism attributed to industrialized Asian countries. That individualism is also what works against the modernity of cooperative ventures, the tutelage of which must, once again, rest in the hand of a qualified and highly educated bourgeoisie.

Thus, it is the bourgeoisie who will lead the country back to its inevitable European destiny, to which the quaint habits of the countryside and the insubordination and efficiency of the urban artisanal class are equally irrelevant except as historic points of departure. A few supposedly erroneous methods would be tolerated in the charitable interests of creating a self-sustaining community of artisans (the decorative setting of glass bottle bases into walls was mentioned)[3] but these would mainly serve to show how deeply the artisans actually depended on knowledgeable leadership; that leadership intended, I was told, to create an archive of acceptable traditional motifs at the NOSMBH office. In Crete such efforts were expected to bear fruit because the bureaucrats regarded the island as home to a deeper form of tradition than any other region of Greece and therefore as more likely to respond to such tutelage.

This is unambiguously a modernist project. It frames tradition, not as something to imitate (perhaps ironically, as postmodern architects might imitate it), but as something to incorporate, enumerate, and discipline; and here, in the farthest margin of Greece and of Europe, the depth of traditionality represents special opportunities and challenges for cultural, as well as political, management. The operation of hegemony is clearly visible: those who dare challenge the notional domination of "Europe" risk marginalizing themselves ever more inextricably. It is not that they have remained outside the process of "inventing tradition." To the contrary, they attempt to contribute to it; images of the Cretan former prime minister and liberal hero Eleftherios Venizelos that appear on the wooden paper-holder were not part of an earlier repertoire of motifs, yet so strong is this man's association with ideals of Cretan identity that his distinctively twentieth-century visage—glasses and all—has already become an almost obligatory motif of local aesthetics. The problem is precisely that the artisans are highly inventive (as well as, on occasion, imitative), and their inventions play into the official view that their culture is now so fragile that it needs rescuing from its bearers' own incompetence and ignorance.

The Unity of the Clan

Much the same can be said of the artisans' social values, especially those linked to the aggressive performance of masculinity. I have already mentioned the peculiar status of agnatic kinship in Rethemnos. This has specific consequences for work relationships in general and for the forms and practices of apprenticeship in particular. Although many denied such a bias, Rethemniots were often particularly concerned to have good relations with their agnatic kin—much more so than with those linked to them through female relatives. When I lectured on apprenticeship at the local campus of the University of Crete, during the discussion one man affirmed the centrality of agnatic relationships to the institution of apprenticeship, recalling that an apprentice of his acquaintance had been so outraged by the master's constant swearing at the boy's clan that he declared, "Listen, boss—go ahead and curse my mother, curse my father, but my clan do not curse!"

Rethemniots see agnates as sharing "blood"; other kin, while important, were not in this sense consubstantial kin. Apprentices, classified as virtual foster sons, could be maltreated with relative impunity because the feminizing implications of hazing unrelated apprentices did not threaten the masculine solidarity of the clan. But the discrimination between agnates and others had more damaging consequences in the larger world of national values. It made Rethemniots look a great deal less "modern" than the nation-state, even though this discourse underlies the entire ideology of Greek identity. When the modern Greek nation-state came into being, the nation itself was conceived as a "patriline."[4] But the state rapidly moved to co-opt other prerogatives of local power, overlaying them, in what is a classic European pattern, with the complex intersections of cognatic kinship and so discouraging internecine strife and taking the power of punishment out of the hands of feuding clans. This is part of the overall process that Norbert Elias saw as "civilizing." For Cretans, with a stronger sense of agnatic kinship than is common elsewhere in Greece, the denial of the primacy of agnatic links was complex and sometimes painful in the context of the larger European ethos. As Rethemniots in particular became increasingly bourgeois and with growing fastidiousness sought to put a conceptual and social barrier between themselves and the animal-stealing swashbucklers of the hinterland hill villages, they identified agnatic kinship as a mark of Cain—of a violence originating, so they came to assume, in the deleterious effects of Turkish culture and controllable only through the policing powers of the state. Nowhere do we see more dramatically illustrated the extent to which a group of Greeks could internalize the orientalist fictions as a mark of their own degradation than in this narrative about the Turkishness of a kinship mode that their apologists *also* used, in other contexts, to demonstrate their essential connectedness with their ancient forebears.[5]

As a result, agnatic kinship became a part of that zone of cultural intimacy to be concealed from potentially unfriendly outsiders. Thus, despite the Rethemniots' denial of any preference for supporting their patrikin in municipal elections, in practice that was precisely what they did. Why was this an issue? The answer is, I suggest, to be found in village life and in official ideology. In many villages, where blood feuds are still in motion, patrilineal kinship is a strong determinant of loyalty. During times of relative calm, on the other hand, villagers like to emphasize that all kin are kin, regardless of the type of link involved. When feuds or other forms of violence are at stake, men emphasize their solidarity by using group terms such as *fara* or *soi* (both meaning "clan"). In times of peace, they generally opt instead for the individuating labels of a cognatic terminology that makes no distinction between uterine and agnatic kin: an uncle is an uncle, and that is all that matters. Peacefulness, moreover, is not only part of the local vision of urbanity in general, and Rethemniot urbanity in particular,[6] but belongs unequivocally to the prevalent ideological sense of what makes Greeks European and unlike their allegedly bellicose neighbors on the other side of the Aegean Sea. Both in the villages and in Rethemnos, there is a *generic* attachment to agnatic groups; when people reconstruct their genealogies, however, they do not display a notably greater ability to remember the identities or names of agnatic kin than of others.

In Rethemnos, by contrast with village usage (where the state's *mission civilisatrice* is more openly resisted), cognatic kinship seems to dominate conversation about family relationships and marriage arrangements. The group terms for "clan" and its subsidiary components almost never appeared, although the common question "Which ones are you from [*apo pious ise*]?" is unequivocally understood to mean a group defined by its common surname. (Indeed, the importance of understanding *implicit* meanings is key to the cultural intimacies entailed in the language of kinship, as of so much else.)[7] The general reluctance to name the agnatic clan as such, however, suggests the Rethemniot self-image of peaceful coexistence and disdain for masculine braggadocio (although there were certainly men who exhibited the latter in generous measure). One eccentric, an ambitious poet and novelist whose self-promotion mostly seemed to consist in getting his books privately published and who generally seemed disinclined to get into fights outside his own heated imagination, nonetheless harped on the bodily stance (*kormostasia*) that he associated with masculine pride, deriding what he saw as its absence in other men. He also argued strongly that a true man should respect his own body and avoid subjecting it to the humiliations of physical labor that is neither clean nor independent, as in construction work: "if . . . you have a wonderful body which a woman enjoys during the night, and you give her as much pleasure as she gives you, you don't accept next morning [having] to throw it into the muck." True masculinity cannot abide subjection to others' control: true Cretan men should always be ready for a fight. Yet even this man rarely talked about his agnatic clan and in fact took pride—something one would rarely encounter in a rural setting—-in voting for a party opposed to that supported by the brother whose mercantile activities meanwhile provided both with financial support; he showed his masculinity by standing up for his personal ideas rather than by endorsing clan solidarity. Boasting of one's agnates was unacceptable, even for him, and indeed it would have circumscribed his ability to distinguish himself electorally from his own brother.

Yet clearly some Rethemniots were in fact extremely conscious of their agnatic identities in practice. They would vote for a patrilateral third cousin rather than for a matrilateral first cousin. They would rally to candidates who bore their respective surnames, often ignoring political ideology in the process. The one thing they would not do was to admit that this was what they were doing. Conversely, they would rarely admit that they specifically avoided hiring agnates as apprentices—the opposite of what one would expect in a society, such as many parts of China,[8] for example, where agnatic solidarity is a virtue so openly espoused that on occasion one would find it embarrassing to hire anyone *except* agnates.

Agnatic solidarity is arguably a marginal phenomenon in today's Greece. Just as the politicians who opened the NOSMBH exhibition sneered at non-European conformism, however, so too some Greek scholars who espouse a Eurocentric view of their society and see entry into the European Union as the fulfillment of national destiny and character also regard the peculiarities of rural society as irrelevant to this vision.[9] Indeed, Rethemniot embarrassment about admitting to supporting agnates in elections speaks to the curious ambivalence Cretans in general entertain about the strong patrilineality to be found in many parts of their island and will help us understand the avoidance of hiring agnates in the workplace. On the one hand, an emphasis on agnatic loyalties fits well with their vaunting of masculine virtues. On the other, the entire complex of masculine values sits poorly with their chivalric image of what European civilization is all about and with the official view just described. Such is the ideological conflict at the heart of local identity within the Greek national polity. Obligations to patrikin had to be met: hence the voting patterns. But overt recognition of this principle was tantamount to accepting the taint of Turkishness, so closely are the agonistic male values in question seen as "un-European."

Such a formulation is historically inaccurate: some ancient Greek populations certainly entertained agnatic models of kinship, while in the Balkans the Muslim populations have sometimes turned out to be less interested in agnatic ties than have other groups.[10] Given a powerful sense that cognatic kinship is the European norm, however, the historiography of Greek kinship has been reformulated in the popular imagination to suit the dominant ideology, much as the Venetian occupation of Crete has been reimagined as a roseate time of cultural liberty when it seems to have been a period of cruel religious and cultural repression from which local Greeks sought relief in the arrival of the Ottoman forces.[11] Agnation is locally understood as a mark of the barbarity—and hence of the "un-Greekness"—within. The dominant ideology, itself firmly embedded in the global hierarchy of value, has deeply permeated local self-perceptions.

Yet if proof were needed that agnatic relations have played an important role in Rethemnos, the occurrence of occasional vendettas provides it. A butcher sent his young nephew—his sister's son and, as such, not a member of his own clan—to run an errand on a bicycle, and the boy was hit and killed by a car. Immediately, the boy's patrikin began threatening to kill the butcher and his sons, who avoided any place where they might have come into contact with their accusers (including the funeral of the dead boy), as though the uncle had been directly responsible for the death—which, in the logic of the agnatically structured vendetta as it still occurs in the hill villages of the hinterland, he was.[12] While Rethemniots profess to view such vindictive responses as barbaric (and in fact neither the butcher nor any of his proximate agnatic kin were ever actually killed as a result of this feud), the rhetoric of urbanity conceals a very pervasive attachment to agnatic loyalties that is especially apparent during elections and may sometimes flare up dramatically in the wake of some traumatic event.[13] Thus, we must interpret the refusal to attribute any significance at all to agnatic principles as a defense of cultural intimacy: in the global hierarchy of value, forms of kinship that are associated with systemic violence are viewed with even greater disapproval (in contrast to the local insistence on their moral importance) than are such supposed incivilities as political corruption and especially nepotism.

Rethemniots quote a proverb—*Me ton edhiko sou fae, pie, ghlendize, ali-siverisi min ekhis*, "With your own kinsperson eat, drink, and be merry, [just] don't do business!"—to "explain" why they are reluctant to take on kin as apprentices (and also, occasionally, to explain the difficulties of running any kind of family business requiring partnership among kin). Such a pattern of avoidance may superficially seem to fly in the face of Rethemniot (and generally Greek) claims to place kinship loyalty above all other considerations. But Rethemniots in fact openly admit that kin are a source of problems. In a familiar use of hyperbole,[14] they not infrequently insist that kin are the *worst* people to deal with. It is precisely because kin can invoke normative ties of obligation and solidarity that they can force one to act against one's own interests in order to serve theirs. Social relations are one matter; business relationships, where serious economic concerns are at stake, are quite another.

In this context, the avoidance of hiring patrikin as apprentices is especially striking. Rethemniots insist that it is not a good idea to hire one's own kin whatever the precise nature of the relationship; some claim that one should even avoid hiring people who are kin to each other even when they are not related to the employer in this way, so great is the risk that they will either quarrel or gossip. Being under another's command is a trying condition at the best of times; being under the command of a clan-mate tests the bonds of agnatic solidarity to breaking point, and even the authority of a uterine uncle can pose real problems in a nominally egalitarian context of kinship. These avoidances are all about the protection of zones of social intimacy against the prying of local outsiders. When questioned, however, Rethemniots usually deny that there is a specific bias against hiring members of one's own agnatic group. That denial is a way of protecting the local community from collective public embarrassment in the eyes of non-Rethemniot outsiders. Avoiding any recognition of the evasion itself (and more generally of the significance of agnatic kinship) serves the encompassing and concentric goal of protecting the collective *cultural* intimacy of town, island, and nation against charges of Turkishness and primitivity.

But there is a further complication. Within the intimate spaces of Rethemnos itself, the importance one accords one's own agnates is seen as more or less natural. In that context, however, the dynamic of embarrassment is logically reversed: what has to be explained there is not the high significance given to agnatic relationships but, on the contrary, the fact that tensions do exist between agnates—and especially that they are so prevalent that one would prefer not to risk exposing such tensions by hiring agnatic kin at all.

Internally, men deal with this problem by turning it into a gender issue. As in so many other dimensions of this masculine perspective, it is women who bear the brunt of the blame for the breakdowns that occur within agnatic relationships. It is the wives, in particular, who are said to support their own kin, to the exclusion of their husbands' agnates, and so to trigger bitter disputes. A jeweler remarked that this happens "because the family in Crete is matriarchal." Such a statement, which ironically inverts the persistence of powerfully male-centered power structures, draws on a scholarly idiom that owes much to Friedrich Engels and the topos of primitive matriarchy that has been a staple theme of left-wing Greek nationalism in search of ancient roots.[15] It allows men to be good neoclassical nationalists at the same time as they absolve their gender from responsibility for its own squabbling. But it is also a convenient generalization that resembles, once again, the notion of Original Sin in the religious sphere or the taint of Turkish occupation in the political, in its provision of a collective moral alibi for the perceived social weaknesses to which all men are prone. And it fits perfectly with the standard explanations for the breakdown of partnerships.

Rethemniots are so uncomfortable with the idea of working for their own kin *in general* that they usually offer excuses for doing so—commonly, and suggestively, to the effect that the speaker's exceptional merit as an artisan in the making was sufficient to supersede all other considerations. This is especially ingenious because it allows one to praise one's own kin group without appearing to do so for any other reason than praising a particularly good artisan: "No, look here, I went there because he had . . . he wanted some staff, and then since I was a boy I'd been a good worker, as they say, I *worked!* I didn't want to go and be paid by the guy, so to speak, and not to earn the money I was getting. I wanted to work that bit extra, like. That is to say, I deserved what I was getting." We also hear in these words a common rhetorical claim to masculine pride. It, too, is deployed here in defense of working for kin, a situation that is otherwise potentially as embarrassing for an employee as it is for an employer. Today, hiring uninsured minors for dangerous work such as construction exposes employers to the risk of prosecution, and this makes them slightly less reluctant than previously to hire kin or ritual kin (the latter category potentially comprising not only those who have baptized one's children or served as one's wedding sponsors, or for whom one has performed these offices, but extensions of these primary ties through ordinary kinship as well). They implicitly excuse themselves for violating a social norm in this way by appearing to succumb to the pressures of moral "obligation": the obligation to kin and ritual kin becomes, suddenly and conveniently, more pressing than unspoken social norms of avoidance.

Masculine pride is heavily invested in the performance of social obligation. Failure to perform according to one's obligations is the antithesis of social acceptability. But there is a complex link between obligation and distrust; even in something as trivial as gift giving, which is not gendered, the remark that "you've placed me under an obligation" carries a slightly reproachful tone, while merchants who sell basic equipment and other products to food producers such as pastrycooks say that "you are ashamed" (*drepese*) not to buy some of their finished specialties during the holiday season in reciprocity. The minor obligations thus created generate a low murmur of reciprocal moral pressure that can always be broken off when one loses interest in a particular business relationship. Not so with kin, with whom the sense of mutual engagement is categorical and, at least nominally, unbreakable—a source of never-ending irritation.

Close kin are perennially suspected of exploiting one's sense of obligation, a perspective that easily leads to avoidance and coolness. Ordinary acts of expense sharing, for example, always have the potential to become the source of petty but potentially disruptive disputes among the closest of kin. A man who constructed a tomb for his still-living father received from the latter a sum of money equivalent to his eight siblings' shares of the expense of this work; the ninth part was his own contribution. He insisted that he did not care if his father chose not to ask one or another of the siblings for that individual's full share: that was between the two of them. But he did not accept the possibility that he himself might not be paid in full, either directly by each sibling or by his father; nor did he expect to evade contributing his own share to the full expense. "Each one [of us]," he proclaimed, "should take on his obligations."

The concept of obligation—which is viewed as particularly binding on those who are close kin to each other—has been central to analyses of Greek society, where it serves as the moral basis of appropriate action within the more intimate spaces of social life.[16] It provides an ethical alibi for actions that people otherwise recognize as socially risky and consequently as a possible source of embarrassment. Obligation is thus an effective excuse for hiring kin as apprentices and assistants; it is also an excuse for working harder for kin than one might for an unrelated employer, in a society where nonkin are normative rivals. A boy who went to work for his mother's brother, a butcher, lived in the latter's house and claims now that he felt a deep sense of obligation to work well: "He obliged me to—no, it's not that he obliged me to do it, [but] I wanted to work [hard] because I had to work since I felt an obligation toward him." The uncle refused to acknowledge any special bond, avoiding, for example, the use of the address "nephew" (anipsie) that would have been usual in this relationship, perhaps in order to protect himself from any of the pressures that hiring a kinsman so easily bring in their train.

In Greek as in English, the grammatical structure of the nephew's declaration that he "felt an obligation" reveals the ambiguity of social bonds grounded in such a concept. The speaker knows that his uncle exercised a degree of power over him, in part thanks to the kinship that also nevertheless gave him a degree of safety from abuse even if it did not carry any special privileges. He presents this, however, as his own, autonomous embrace of a moral commitment. That commitment and the reciprocal bond that it implied neither prevented his uncle from treating him as a menial from whom the techniques of the trade could be withheld with impunity nor inhibited the nephew from secretly acquiring those techniques by "stealing with his eyes." Indeed, the nephew later remembered the uncle as a man whose eghoismos led him to deny the nephew access to any technical knowledge at all, although—again in a shift that makes perfect sense in light of the relationships we have been examining here—when the nephew's secretly acquired skill began to reveal itself, the uncle also praised him as one whose "eye cuts [i.e., observes with precision]."

Similarly, a carpenter had his nephew as an apprentice and was very angry when the young man, who had secretly copied his work, moved to an unrelated master in the hope of learning the trade more fully. The boy's mother asked him why he would go to an unrelated person instead of an uncle "who loves you and will look after you." The uncle, offended by the lad's desertion, scoffed when the boy finally opened his own workshop, dismissing him as unskilled. But when he saw the quality of work the young man was able to produce, he asked him in some astonishment where he had learned such skill. The youth replied, "That's my secret!" He never did tell his uncle how he had surreptitiously copied the latter's work; artifice compounds artifice and becomes especially problematic when it conflicts with the sense of obligation that the family had earlier tried to exploit in urging him to go back to work for his uncle.

Obligation in this sense is clearly a complex matter. A parent who tries to get his kinsman to take his son as an apprentice starts playing on the pressures of obligation and so places the artisan in a quandary: does he recognize the more personal obligation he has toward the boy's father as his kinsman and give in, or does he instead recognize a larger obligation to the kin group as a whole and gently edge out of the situation in order to avoid the risk of an embarrassing internecine fight? These are dilemmas that it is rarely easy to resolve, because satisfying the one moral obligation leaves one open to charges of having ignored the other. A builder recounted how he solved the problem, on at least one occasion, by finding an apprentice's position with another builder for his young kinsman: "I say to him, 'Master Pavlos, take a young nephew of mine on the job and make sure you help him to learn!' And indeed he went there, they took him on the job as an assistant there, he [the master] had him close by, and in two years he made a master mold-fitter out of him, those guys who pour concrete into molds. And he ended up a master artisan, and now he works on construction and builds houses!"

This was an ingenious way of discharging both obligations, the specific one to his kinsman and the generic one to the agnatic group. It is worth noting that this builder was quite explicit about the particular avoidance of hiring agnates: he contrasted his action in this case with his willingness to take on another and equally closely related nephew, but one from a different clan, as an apprentice to himself. And he made a point of emphasizing that he always inquired after the agnatic nephew's progress, much as a father might: "I didn't take him on, I sent him to a master who was a friend of mine, but I asked continually; we meet every day in the coffeehouse. I'd ask him, 'Master Pavlos, how's the boy doing?' He'd reply, 'He obeys [akoui].'[17] He made a master artisan out of him! Whereas he was my nephew in the first degree, and I didn't take him on!"

Kin will sometimes bring a great deal of pressure on an artisan to take on a son as an apprentice. These blandishments are hard to refuse. So strong is the sense that employing kin is to court disaster, however, that artisans sometimes display enormous ingenuity in avoiding that situation. Aside from the possibility of finding the lad a different berth and continuing to show an appropriately avuncular interest, as in the instance I have just recounted, the artisan must find a self-deprecating excuse for persuading these insistent kinsmen to look elsewhere. One device is to point them in the direction of new and exciting jobs of a technological nature—first with watchmakers, then radio repair shops, and now to garages and electronic repair firms. By describing his own work as too menial for such a bright young lad, the artisan can strategically present himself as a good and loyal kinsman while protecting himself against those who may only be interested in exploiting the relationship.

Parenthetically, it is worth observing that fobbing the young kinsman off onto a technological apprenticeship fits the logic of the situation in more than one way. Aside from the affectation of concern for advancing his young kinsman's interests that it affords the reluctant artisan, it also appeals to the lad because it offers an intensified arena for the learning and exercise of the cunning at which all forms of apprenticeship aim—as in the case of the apprentice who, confronted with an apparently malfunctioning radio, realized that the only problem was that the batteries had died but told the customer that he had replaced a damaged transistor; or who found that a watch had stopped simply because a hair had become tangled up inside and removed it with a quick puff of breath. "The lad has learned an undemanding job he'll truly keep for many years!" It is a job that even offers the comforts normally associated with being a bureaucrat, but with all the social intimacy that goes with being an artisan among his fellows and a reputation for being a crafty fellow to boot. It is relatively easy to fool a customer over the apparently arcane secrets of technology, whereas "when a table is damaged, its leg is broken, we see it!" Meanwhile, the older kinsman—perhaps a carpenter who actually regards his own calling as much more honest (*timioteri*)—now basks in the approbation of the lad's parents, who feel that he has really helped their son achieve an enviable position in life rather than trapping him in the drudgery of the work he himself does. By a nice irony, he can also bask in the full appreciation of his own many-layered cleverness!

The avoidance of hiring kin is thus always an accommodation between ideals of honest and open loyalty to kin and a recognition that reality is very different and calls for ingenuity and cunning. In an ideal world, one would feel free to hire one's own kin, and especially one's agnates, because both sides would be able to rely on each other's moral determination to respect the obligations thereby incurred; the only constraint, one that I heard explicitly mentioned, is that agnates prefer to avoid reproducing competitors in the same trade. Here again avoidance is justified as solidarity. By the same logic, it is acceptable to express embarrassment at the idea of hiring an unrelated person when a close kinsman is left without work, and this will occasionally induce an artisan to prefer the kinsman. But Rethemniots also know from the school of daily experience that in practice kin make dangerous employees. As they often say, ironically inverting the commonplace view of kinship obligation as central to Greek traditional values, kin are worse than nonkin, because kin always try to exploit a relationship to their own advantage.

Concerns with Kin

This revelation is also an embarrassment at the level of the collective defense of cultural intimacy: it suggests that the family, long upheld by nationalist writers as the foundation stone of Greek culture and society, is not at all the moral sanctum that such writers claim it to be. It is hardly coincidental that one way of describing the self-indulgence of a close agnate who has been taken on as an apprentice draws on the vocabulary and imagery of the Turkishness concealed within the Hellenic exterior: one builder remarked that such a boy would be the "tyrant" of the shop—the one who does as he pleases and gives orders to the other, unrelated boys as though he were personally in charge.[18] A closely related apprentice also "gets into the family, into your family affairs, your economic affairs," and is in a position to spread damaging gossip. That is embarrassing not only for the information that might leak out but also because it means that a kinsman has demonstrated his lack of masculine self-control at the expense of his kin group—the worst failure of all.

Even without the risk of gossip, however, the exploitation of kinship norms is something that most Rethemniots appear to fear at all times. Clearly, as their narratives show, their fear has been repeatedly borne out by events. The opportunism that they describe may be at the expense of employer and employee alike, and they know that these problems are not confined to Rethemnos alone. In another Cretan town, for example, an entrepreneur fired his apprentice, who was his sister's son, when the latter asked for time off to take some school examinations, only to take the boy back when his own brother in Rethemnos forced him to do so on the grounds that the lad had a perfect right to take the examinations without risking his job. Here the complex play of internal family relations illustrates precisely what many artisans fear about entanglements with kin. Where betrayal by outsiders affords an opportunity for displaying insouciant disregard and a what-can-you-expect attitude, betrayal by kin is a correspondingly painful moral and social wound.

A hinterland villager imagined how this hurt would be expressed: "I took my kinsman on at work, I taught him, I helped him, I taught him the craft, he made his way in the world and earned a bit of bread, which he's eating— and now he played this dirty game on me!" A Rethemniot was even blunter, arguing that kin often turned out to be "the biggest layabouts." Such betrayals are not just a rhetorical exaggeration; reluctant employers cannot always resist the blandishments of their close kin, yet they usually regret having done so. As Neni Panourgiá shows for modern Athens,[19] the image of kin solidarity is always more stable at the level of ideology than at that of practice within the intimacies of the group, and this upsets an image of Greek life long cherished as much by anthropologists as by the nationalists of whom they are often so critical. And for those who feel that in an ideal world one would still prefer to take on agnates, when things go wrong there is always the perverse but socially logical possibility of blaming their wives for having "influenced" them to take on affines, members of the wives' natal clans who, as such, are not necessarily agnates of the husbands at all.

Frequently the causes of discord are quite straightforward. A boot-maker was deeply ashamed when an apprentice who was also a distant agnatic cousin stole from the shop and then, when the theft was discovered after originally being imputed to another lad, committed suicide. Neither he nor his son and grandson, cobblers all, ever hired another apprentice, so traumatized were they by the embarrassment of an agnate's dishonesty.

While the pervasive fear of exploitation by kin applies particularly to agnates, even a nonagnate can make for trouble; and the trouble does not have to be as dramatic as theft to create major embarrassments in a society where every male suspects all other men of looking for chances to undermine his authority. A butcher who hired a distant kinsman (the child of a second cousin on the employer's paternal grandmother's side) was obliged to fire him because, although he never stole anything (as the butcher specifically said), "he would come to the shop at whatever time he wanted" and more generally "never accepted the relationship between employer and worker." This failure rankled because the butcher had hired the worker particularly to help a kinsman. In other words, at least from his own point of view, his sense of moral obligation was not reciprocated. But the expectation of real life is that such derelictions will in fact be frequent. An apprentice who is related to his master is likely to expect greater indulgence for his inattention or laziness; a master may think he can demand more grueling hours of sweated labor and be correspondingly furious when his hopes are thwarted.

Indeed, I heard from one builder that in the old days artisans would actually spell out this concern to kinsmen who brought their sons to them in the hope of getting the latter taken on as apprentices. The artisan would resist the appeal of the boy's father thus, according to this man's reconstruction: "Nikos, I'd prefer it if you took the boy to a different master, because with me he's not going to learn anything on account of the fact that he views me as his uncle—he sees me as an uncle or, I don't know, a ritual kinsman; and as he will have the courage that goes with being a ritual kinsman or a relative, I won't be able to give the lad a slap when the occasion demands. My hand won't go that way, and the lad won't learn the work. So we'd better take him to an outsider. That is, he should learn the fear of the outsider so he'll conform more easily." And this same man, when approached by an agnatic first cousin who wanted him to take on his son, claims to have replied, "Petros, I won't take the boy on, because he won't listen to me. As soon as he sees me, he'll stroke me, he'll caress me like a cat, and so on. How can I teach him a craft? Slap him I can't, cuss him out I can't, give him a hard time I can't! And even if I were to give him a hard time, he wouldn't understand. He'd say, 'He's my uncle!'" The apprentice, conversely, is trapped in the relationship as well. He must consider that at any time he wants to leave—to learn from a more accomplished master, for example, or to acquire more refined techniques— he takes the risk of deeply offending his present employer and the entire kin group to which both belong.

There is another, practical aspect to the avoidance of hiring kin as apprentices that deserves some comment here. Hiring kin is a little like turning to one's own kin for baptismal or wedding sponsorship (ritual kinship): it makes for an inefficient use of existing ties rather than for the creation of new ones. One cobbler, reflecting an attitude not unlike American university departments that avoid accepting their own undergraduates for graduate study, suggested that it was better to get experience away from home in any case. Apparently borrowing a metaphor from ceramics, he claimed it was to make sure the apprentice "would be fired [literally, "roasted"] better in life, in work"—an interesting comment for our present purposes in that it links the social with the professional ("in life, in work"). In the words of another artisan, "Just to become a craftsman, everyone should work in the hands of an outsider, should eat an outsider's bread. Because if he goes to someone he knows and does not eat an outsider's bread and doesn't go roistering in the night and get a beating, he doesn't become a person [*anthropos*]. He doesn't become a person!" These explanations clearly display the predominant ideology of personhood and the manner of inculcating masculine identity that it informs. They also recall a classic argument about the incest taboo as a device for expanding alliances.[20] They are nevertheless insufficient here; the avoidance of kin in apprenticeship arrangements is a complex matter, one that reveals a great deal about the practical implications of the system of values in which these arrangements are embedded.

The problem with kin is that they, too, are human; they, too, are subject to the ordinary jealousies that constitute the lived world of everyday experience. Jealousy means that one always has to go one better than one's rival; when the rivalry is between kin, the inequality inherent in employment becomes morally intolerable. The very closeness of the relationship encourages harsher and more direct comparisons. A goldsmith recounted how, in his own agnatic clan, when he had wanted to add silver to his business, his own uncle told him how another member of the clan had wrecked his business by doing exactly that. No doubt the uncle would have defended himself on the grounds that he was simply trying to save his nephew from repeating another kinsman's error; but the nephew saw his intervention in the most cynical terms, arguing that this kind of jealousy was especially rife in Crete. Interestingly, he claimed that the only Rethemnos families of which he knew that they had successfully managed joint ventures over long periods of time were Asia Minor refugees—a category that Cretans often profess to despise but that is associated in the national (and even the local) imagination with ideals of civilization and cosmopolitanism.[21] The collective self-abnegation of the Cretans that we see in such remarks is the clearest possible evidence of how far the global hierarchy of value has come to dominate cultural understanding.

The jealousy that drives Cretan kin apart even as they try to work together, said the goldsmith, is "the evil of the place" *(to kako tou topou)*. Especially in the case of apprenticeship, the risks of employing kin are clear. The ideal relationship between kin is one of mutual respect *(sevas;* verb, *sevome)*. An uncle and nephew, for example, must "respect" each other in this sense; the term suggests less a form of mutual awe than a shared respect for their common identity as close kin. One man recalled that his boss "respected me because he was my uncle" *(me sevotan yati 'tan thios mou)*: these moral obligations are categorical as well as reciprocal. Such binding mutuality sits ill with the inequality inherent in the artisan-apprentice relationship.

It is especially incompatible with the discipline required in training an apprentice. Even leaving aside the apprentice's own reactions, an artisan who hires a close kinsman runs the risk of offending the latter's immediate family if he punishes him or fires him: "If I talk about firing him, then his kinsman will come—either his father or his aunt or his mother, so to speak. . . . His mother will tell me, 'Isn't he kin? You shouldn't have done that.' Whereas when you fire an unrelated person [*kseno*], he doesn't claim to be [entitled to special treatment].... That is, the matter ends there." In this highly masculine context, it is often the apprentice's mother who gets all the blame for undermining discipline: "Well, if you tell the kid who's a relative of yours, 'Go to the house, take a jar of water,' and you don't send the other one, do you know what he tells his mother? 'Mama, Uncle sent me to carry water, while he had the others there learning the craft!'" The expectation is that it will then be the mother who intervenes, disrupting both the master's authority and the rhythm of work in his shop. Even in a male artisan's recollection, it is also women who are expected to object, in particular, to the male reluctance to teach the apprentices.[22]

Dismissal of nonkin can be brusque because nothing is at stake: "When he's not a kinsman, you say, 'You know, you're no use to me; get out!'" But with kin, even a minor complaint to a parent can create bad blood within the family; to an employer's complaint that his nephew had failed to appear for the morning's work, the boy's father or mother will say with as much pity for the child as irritation with the brother-in-law who is making a fuss, "Look, you wretch, he just couldn't get up!" What might be an accusation directed against someone from outside the kin group becomes instead an indulgent excuse.

When apprentices are kin, even the most costly errors may have to be absorbed; but the social cost of sacking a nephew is still greater. A pie-maker cited the dangers posed by an apprentice who ran wild in the nighttime instead of sleeping, then turned up for work incapable of doing very much at all. "There's the danger he'll have an accident; there's the danger he'll give them wrong change from the cash register"; and either way, if the master fires the lad, relations with the disgraced apprentice's parents are liable to become "cold," a situation that eats away at the solidarity of the larger kin group and exposes all its members to collective ridicule.

If one fires a kinsman, moreover, and then lets him come back under pressure from his offended family, there is the added risk of still more heavily compromised efficiency and authority: "he'll pull a long face and won't talk to you." Note that here silence, the prerogative of the employer who does not wish to impart his knowledge, is blamed instead on the disaffected apprentice, sullen because he was fired to start with and also insolent because his employer was forced by the pressure of kinship to take him back. The apprentice, in all probability, will have complained bitterly that his employer—who, as a kinsman, should have acted differently toward him—had refused to "speak to" him and teach him the trade.

The risk of such anger must have been even greater half a century ago, when many fathers paid artisans to take on their sons as apprentices; paying a

Table 1. Categories of artisan-apprentice relationship among males in Rethemnos

Agnates	14	(11.67%)	(includes 5 brothers' sons)
Affines	26	(21.67%)	
Nonagnatic kin	71	(59.17%)	(includes 20 sisters' sons)
Ritual kin	9	(7.5%)	

kinsman, especially an agnate, was virtually to invite complaints of exploitation and of disrespect for the bonds of kinship, which should have precluded payment of any sort—an exploitation of those same bonds that would itself have constituted a good reason for avoiding any such entanglements in the first place. And an apprentice who was also a kinsman might entertain stronger expectations of being taken into partnership and possibly could exert more pressure to make that happen—hardly a formula for ensuring long-term stability.

Since Rethemniots live in nuclear households that are also autonomous economic units, the only kinsman who can normally be trusted with knowledge of the trade is an artisan's own son, and so more distant relatives who seek special consideration are making unreasonable demands. Yet the fact is that Rethemniot artisans do employ kin, and not infrequently at that. Close examination of the kinship links in question, however, reveals an important distinction: the overwhelming majority of these kinsfolk are not members of their employers' clans. In other words, they do not bear the same surname. While there are various ways of interpreting the numbers, by any measure the rarity of clan-mates among artisans' apprentices is remarkable (see table 1).[23] It becomes considerably more so if we discount the closest of all agnatic links: those between father and son and those between two brothers. And since locals often aver that a son categorically cannot be an apprentice (how, after all, could a son, *yos*, also be a foster son, *parayos*?), there is some logic in that exclusion.

Given the high valuation placed on agnation and the male bond of blood in this society, moreover, it is also reasonable that, by extension from the father-son relationship, artisans might prefer to avoid situations in which clan-mates were placed under the demeaning label of foster sons—nonbiological kin categorically considered the epitome of treachery, the antithesis of what one should expect from clan members. Yet such reasons are not usually invoked; indeed, it is hard to elicit specific justifications for a logic that no one wants to acknowledge in the first place. Most artisans, asked whether they particularly preferred to exclude agnatic kin, insisted that they made no distinction between agnatic and uterine kin in this regard, frequently falling back on that old proverb about the avoidance of doing business with one's kin to make the point that *all* categories of kin are best avoided in work situations where they might fail to give satisfaction.

But it is in the proverb, curiously enough, that the key to the covert distinction lies. "With your own person eat, drink, and be merry, don't do business," is the more literal translation of the saw, but the term for "own person" is highly ambiguous. In standard Greek, the phrase might simply mean "with your own kinsman" (indeed, the term may be replaced by *singeni[s]*, "kinsperson")[24] or even "with someone from your own social group in any sense." It can even simply mean "friend," a vague category that in some contexts even excludes kin. In this larger sense, the proverb is widely understood to be an injunction against complicating affective relationships of any sort by mixing them with business. But the Cretan dialect form *(edhiko sou* for *dhiko sou)* has a far more specific meaning—namely, that of agnatic kinsman. To "have *edhići*" is to be a member of a clan large enough to defend one's interests and provide solidary backing against enemies: "A curse on him who has *edhići* of his own and walks with nonagnates [*kseni*]," goes the song.[25] In the often violent feuding systems of the hill villages, the term is absolutely transparent in this regard. One of the few Rethemniots to acknowledge that agnates were the specific target of the proverb did so in a way that beautifully illustrates the usefulness of ambiguity in the proverb, remarking in response to a question, "In older times, they always used to prefer 'outside kin' [*ksenos-inghenis*], because with kin [*singenis*], says a proverb, 'eat and drink, but don't do business.'" "Outside kin," in the context of this man's unusual recognition of the bias against employing agnates, here can only mean kin who have no agnatic ties, and so, in interpretation, it gets conflated immediately with the common generic term for "kin" in use throughout the entire country.

Why are Rethemniots so coy about recognizing the social reality to which the proverb alludes? While they feel moved to make excuses for working with kin in general, they recognize this as something that does occur. One common excuse for hiring a nonagnate such as a sister's son is that one's sister, as a member of the so-called weaker sex *(to adhinato meros)*, has a moral claim on one's help because her dependence on her husband means that, from the perspective of her own agnates, she has no means of her own. This can be read as an extension of the more generic obligation to help kin who are economically weaker than oneself—another reason sometimes given for hiring kin, to whom such assistance then becomes the expression of a moral obligation rather than something to be avoided.

By contrast, people do not like to admit that they specifically avoid hiring patrikin. Whether because this entails admitting the importance of agnation or, conversely, because it would make them look unacceptably indifferent toward those who are ideally their closest kin, the avoidance is almost never presented as intentional but rather as something that requires an excuse. It just "never so happened," artisans explained, that they had an opportunity to hire agnates—the classic appeal to a vague but all-powerful notion of chance that allows people in Greece to deny an unwanted attribution of agency in socially acceptable fashion.[26] In one case, the excuse was offered that the nephew in question was only fifteen years old and was hired just for one summer "so he wouldn't run around in the street" and that "he doesn't learn a thing; he learns not to run around!" If one seeks excuses for hiring kin at all, these seem to become even more pronounced when the apprentices are agnates. The fact that agnatic and bilateral kinship coexist and are partially assimilated to each other in the terminology makes such evasiveness about agnation unobtrusive and therefore effective.

To be sure, some of the principles that govern attitudes to patrikin are also applicable to kin in general: for example, refusal to hire kin of any type does enable artisans to avoid the embarrassment of quarreling with them in front of unrelated and possibly hostile (or at least derisive) neighbors. But by this token, the embarrassment of quarreling with one's patrikin is even greater; the common surname makes the fact of relatedness much harder to hide and threatens to ramify its consequences much farther afield. If admitting collectively to the very existence of such a lowly kinship idiom is embarrassing, moreover, how much more embarrassing it must be to admit that one cannot even play calmly by its solidary rules. To clip an agnate around the ear or send him packing because his work is poor is to expose the whole clan to public humiliation. But to admit that this is even an issue in front of strangers, especially strangers who in some degree represent that hostile yet sometimes unattainable "other within" called "Europe," simply makes matters worse.

This realization emerged very slowly from my inquiries. At first, virtually no one seemed prepared to recognize the pattern of not hiring patrikin specifically. It was not always clear whether my informants even understood what I was asking about, or if they cared whether a particular kinsman was an agnate or not. This was perhaps not entirely accidental, since there is one factor that might have skewed the pattern in the direction of unintentionally avoiding patrikin: in a pattern that appears to have begun at least as early as the 1950s, village men began to marry urban brides, some of them relatively highly educated and from families of good standing in the town, and to live in houses provided by their wives' families, thereby achieving a considerable degree of social as well as geographical mobility. The children of these marriages had few patrikin who were artisans. Most were farmers and shepherds, and to them the children would never be sent for work; that would have represented too much of a return to recently abandoned conditions of rural poverty.

Whatever the reasons, Rethemniots were generally reluctant to acknowledge any tendency to avoid hiring agnates. There were nevertheless a few, usually grudging exceptions to this pattern. Under my rather persistent questioning, a tailor admitted that he knew "one person who does that [i.e., avoids agnates] deliberately" but could not remember exactly what sort of craft (viotekhnia) this man performed—he thought he made some sort of cloth goods. While the tailor made this case sound exceptional, its oddity for him lay more in the other man's frequently and loudly declared insistence on specifically avoiding agnates than in the fact that the latter followed the principle in practice.

In the end, it became clear that most artisans could recognize the avoidance of hiring agnates as something real and present in their working lives but usually would do so only if pressed. At that point, however, their experience easily confirmed the implications of even the most cursory attempt at recollection (see table 1). One ironworker stoutly insisted that no preference was at stake until I asked him to identify every single case of an apprentice working for a kinsman that he could remember. He readily acquiesced, evidently secure in the expectation that some agnates would emerge on his list; but there was not a single one. At this point he agreed that the difference was interesting and asserted, with the air of one who concedes that his interlocutor has pulled off a clever party trick, that he had simply never before come to the point of recognizing it consciously.

Even the builder who distinguished between the sister's son he hired and the brother's son he would not hire had some difficulty articulating the distinction in more general terms; when I asked him (in what is admittedly a leading question) whether the two were of the same degree of kinship to him, he replied, "It's the same." He then wriggled out of the contradiction by recalling that in fact the agnate was not a nephew but a first cousin—that is, further away by one link. Having made that point, he turned to greet a newcomer, and any analytical clarity that might have emerged quickly dissipated in the sociable moment, only to return after a considerable amount of further discussion—at which point the builder did, finally, say that to him a nonagnate was less close than an agnate of equivalent degree. I think he finally relented because he thought I was being extremely slow on the uptake. He may have found my desire for precision tactless; it perhaps suggested that "excessive attention" that Greeks so carefully avoid in all their social interactions[27]— and also because it focuses attention on the culturally intimate fact of a bias toward agnatic kin as well as the Rethemniots' general failure to live up to their categorical moral obligations.

Those few who were more immediately forthcoming about the avoidance of hiring agnates showed thereby that the notion of "misrecognition" would not suffice to explain what was happening. Artisans were clearly able to perceive the bias against hiring patrikin. Most, however, chose, or allowed themselves, to ignore it, at least until it was brought to their attention. The relative ease with which merchants hired agnates allowed them to deny the very idea that such a discrimination could be made. Once, after I had given a public lecture on my ongoing research at the University of Crete and had laid out the question of avoiding patrikin, one artisan who had heard the lecture tried to explain my position to another local man. The latter somewhat grudgingly admitted the bias but then went on to use the merchants as a basis for modifying the picture. As he said, merchants constituted a relatively "closed" profession—by which he apparently meant that they exercised a much higher degree of control over their financial resources. One set of kin I found together in a business worked in a store rather than in an artisanal workshop and, aside from the owner's son, consisted entirely of women: his wife, the wife of another son, and his wife's sister's daughter. The owner could say quite openly that this was economically the only viable way he could maintain such a large staff, because merchants have few professional secrets to guard but must fear for the cash kept on the premises.

Filial Exceptions

My interlocutor at the lecture went on to add that in some artisanal professions, skills passed from father to son constitute a valuable resource, albeit not one that involves huge sums of money. When I pointed out that the situation of an artisan's son was significantly different from that of the same man's brother's son, he agreed readily enough: a brother's son would normally never have been a member of the same household and thus always represents a potential threat to the economic interests of the uncle and the latter's own children. Clearly, it was important to this knowledgeable and engaged member of my audience to preserve the sense of father-son solidarity, and it seems clear that my point about the uncle-nephew relationship actually helped to underscore for him the central importance of the father-son tie.

Indeed, father-son interaction often concerns their shared financial interests. Here is one exchange between a plumber and his son as they worked on a construction site removing old lead piping that the son was about to throw out. The father remonstrated with him:

> *Son:* Why?
> *Father:* Do we throw lead away?
> *Son:* No, we don't throw it away. That's worth one hundred thousand [drachmas].
> *Father:* Five hundred [thousand]!

This simple exchange is verbal, explicit, and entirely consonant with the idea that father and son share a common financial interest.

I heard of only one father—a stair-maker—who concealed his techniques from his own son. He "marked the wood [*esimadheven*] until midday, then, at midday, when he was to go for his meal...he would rub out the marks so his children would not see them!" He, however, was clearly a scandalous exception: he took the usual artisanal secrecy to a degree that conflicted with the most fundamental principle of succession, and this was expressed in revealingly explicit terms: "Just think of it—his own son! And he died without ever telling his son!" In other words, his son would never now inherit the knowledge that was his by right. And the instances where two brothers have a partnership and one of them brings in his son to work in the shop do not notably affect the status of father-son work relationships at all, because the son works directly under his father's, rather than his uncle's, supervision. But sometimes such arrangements break down; one brother may begin to suspect that the other brother and the latter's son might be conspiring against him, and such suspicions are invariably corrosive.

Eghoismos, that ever-lurking source of disruption, is allegedly always ready to break out in response to others' whispering or at the prompting of the brothers' mutually hostile wives. If one brother is better educated, he will certainly not send his son to work for the less sophisticated brother, because he does not want to sacrifice his social advantage by placing himself in the latter's debt. If the brothers are in different crafts, they will try to keep their respective sons with them rather than exchanging forms of knowledge. Aside from other considerations, keeping a son to work for oneself means that one does not have to pay out wages for an assistant, and again possible status differences between the brothers' respective crafts make them both suspicious of each other's motives in agreeing to have one brother's son work for the other brother.

Sons who work for their fathers alone constitute a limiting case and are not to be found very frequently. This is consistent with social experience: the embarrassment that accrues to quarreling agnates in general would be all the greater if the parties were father and son. Yet the more explicit concern is that, since the rapport between father and son should be an indulgent relationship, it is unlikely to prove conducive to the discipline that makes for good learning. That concern is expressed in another proverb: "The master never learned his craft in his father's shop" *(o mastoras dhen emathe tin dekhni stou patera tou to maghazi)*. The strain here comes less from fear of competition in the marketplace, which is unlikely, than it does from the fact that a father may resent his son's taking the initiative or developing new techniques. One artisan recalled how his father, for whom he worked for a while, would irritably demand on such occasions, "And where did *you* learn how to do it?" Any deviation from the father's model becomes a small but hurtful betrayal of precisely what father-son partnerships are intended to protect: the sense of unsullied succession—a succession in which faithful reproduction is the ideal—bound up in the mutual trust and total intimacy that are possible only between, of all agnates, father and son. But the converse of this concern with the risk of betrayal is the general perception that transmission from father to son is in some sense natural. My landlord, recalling that his staircase had been fashioned by a carpenter's son who had never actually worked for his father but had instead gone into another trade (as an electrician), noted as an unremarkable fact the son's uncanny ability to reproduce the father's skill, attributing it to an "instinct" that was perhaps inherited in "the blood." No wonder any deviation from this paternal model would be resented and even feared.

The father-son relationship, when it is expressed through the transmission of craft skills, is the exception that proves the rule. There is even one village in the Rethmini prefecture where cauldron-makers, *tsoukaladhes*, automatically pass on this skill to their sons. Theirs is considered the artisanal profession with the lowest status of all, and only those who are facing economic ruin would adopt it voluntarily—a situation that seems to reinforce the solidarity of those who fall within it and perhaps takes us to the greatest extreme of cultural and social marginalization.[28] Because fathers and their sons share common interests, the usual tensions over money, at least, are absent. But in general, the avoidance of hiring patrikin reproduces itself as an avoidance of even so much as recognizing that one is engaged in avoidance. One avoids hiring kin because, while one is supposed to do everything to favor them, it is their proclivity for exploiting that sense of obligation that means that they, more than all others, cannot be trusted.

The denial of importance is a device for protecting precisely those areas of social relationship that are of particularly intimate significance. Thus, in parallel fashion, the affectation of boredom reproduces itself as a denial that boredom has any meaning in itself: an apprentice is supposed to be eager to learn, but too much of a display of eagerness suddenly makes one a dangerous rival rather than a submissive and willing pupil—a situation that becomes doubly disruptive when the apprentice is a close agnatic kinsman. And both these paradoxes of avoidance—the avoidance of recognizing the avoidance of hiring agnatic kin and the avoidance of recognizing the deep interest of boredom—in turn reproduce a principle that is nicely summarized in a popular Greek proverb that advises one "to be absent from the bad hour [i.e., the moment of violent encounter] in order to live a thousand years." In less gnomic language, that principle is best summarized as follows: avoidance is politic, yet it is so only because the conventions of aggressive male interaction call for an impolitic stance at all times when one is out in the open.

This is the nature of cunning: the body that behaves with politic discretion precisely because it must put on an impolitic display of blithe risk taking. The one risk it cannot afford even to entertain is that of embarrassing its agnates; that would entail the compound embarrassment of revealing the deep engagement of the entire group in a kinship ideology that ranks so far down in the global hierarchy of value. This body belong to a person whose movements must not be constrained by excessive attention, and whose ostentatious disdain for risk both conveys the self-confidence of the socially adroit male and the technically adroit artisan on the one hand and, on the other, limits the extent that this same male artisan can rise in a global hierarchy defined by literacy, bureaucracy, and the carefully explicit accounting of manners, movements, and money. At one extreme lies the feuding agnatic world of the village, thinly concealed in the polite setting of Rethemnos; at the other, the local representatives of the national leadership seize on the exhibiting of tradition as an ideal occasion to deny the relevance of such a world to the European Greece of today. It is on such occasions that the deep craftiness of the national and regional leaders becomes manifest. For it is they who have crafted the pedestal that serves as a post for tethering the remnants of a wild otherness within. By so exhibiting tradition, they also reveal the operation of the global hierarchy of value.

Chapter Eight

Embodying Value

Bodies Devalued: Impolitic Reflections on and of the State of the Nation

In this book I have explored how the body is trained—inculcated, to use Bourdieu's term—into an insubordination that offers short-term personal satisfactions at the expense of longer-term social advantage. It is a body that lives and moves within a fierce but often invisible hegemony. The hegemony is invisible because, from the start, the body has been trained—in a manner that carries the aura of inevitability—to move in concert with rhythms that those social actors who are able to operate more powerfully within the hegemonic system find it convenient to maintain. It suits the bourgeois beautifully that the worker should gesticulate, express anger openly, and retreat to sullen silence when called to account, because such responses confirm what for the bourgeois is the desirable social order.

Some artisans, cannier than most, adopt the quieter mannerisms affected by the bourgeois and even occasionally experience the delight of outsnubbing the snobs when the latter lose their tempers. They bring the self-restraint of the truly tough male and the affectation of disdain into a single, devastating weapon. Refusing to be drawn into a brawl claims the moral high ground—a tactic commonest among the more entrepreneurial artisans, those who are breaching the lower reaches of bourgeois life and who already see their sons and daughters rising with the advantages of a better education. For most artisans, however, especially those engaged in heavier work such as the building and carpentry trades, a rough and surly manner locks them into their assigned place in the prevailing social and cultural hierarchy.

Their mannerisms show that the artisans' place in society is a humble station and that it must remain so because they do not know the behavior appropriate to anything else. Supposedly faithful (or at least resigned) to their station in life, they are, always-already, busily training the next generation in the same systemic self-marginalization. Bourgeois children learn the importance of a modest mien and quiet manners; even when they misbehave at school, they do so in a spirit of downplaying their academic seriousness and at the same time of affecting an easy camaraderie with their teachers—a model no master craftsman would tolerate. Their lives are subject to a discipline of sorts, but that discipline is the price of considerable privilege. It is aimed at freeing the bourgeois from "dependence upon the world and nature."[1]

By contrast, Cretan craft apprentices learn to disguise sneaky cunning in outwardly pliant but sullen bodies; they react to the discipline of the workshop with open resentment. The manners they learn in the process restrict their access to the means of upward mobility. While I am reluctant to overemphasize the contrast between the (very bourgeois) institution of the technical school and the apprenticeship arrangements in a craft workshop, the fact that they are locally perceived as radically divergent from each other—and that this opposition is a common stereotype in Europe and perhaps further afield[2]—suggests that together they represent a local materialization of a globally dominant evaluation system, which together they institutionally reproduce. In this pedagogical context, the masters, too, are debarred from rising socially, because their training techniques—a point many women in particular are able to articulate—reproduce the perceived inadequacies of their social class: gruffness, brutality, and a lack of verbal communication. Masters cannot even ordinarily admit to training their apprentices to be devious because that would also conflict with the social values that the bourgeois state and the encompassing vision of "Europe" represent. From the perspective of sometimes very powerful local bourgeois observers, the artisans are teaching their apprentices nothing at all, and so they end up looking cruel, selfish, or merely inept. They, like their young charges, are thus trapped in the judgmental vise of the global hierarchy of value.

Within these constraints, however, they are indeed training their apprentices for life—a life full of resentment and contest. The training of craft apprentices is one of the many sites at which Greeks commonly reproduce a recognizable collective stance toward the world. It is a stance at once sullenly accommodating at the level of daily practice and yet rhetorically insubordinate and critical of power.[3] At the outset, I described the sense of parallel—or, better, concentric—marginalities that besets the artisans and their apprentices, their sense of being a backward community in a cultural and political backwater; and I argued that it is precisely in such a site, where the inequalities become exaggerated to the point of distortion, that we can most persuasively identify the dynamics whereby hierarchy is produced and reproduced. On this basis, we can begin to identify, not merely the local universe of cultural and social production and its constraints, but also the encompassing forms of cultural habituation and encapsulation of consumer goods and patterned spaces at the regional and even at the national level.[4]

Such temporal depth adds force to the sense of cultural predestination that models of hegemony evoke. We must be careful, however, not to overdetermine this hegemony—to become complicit in it by failing to recognize that there are ways out of its control. It relies to some extent on the indeterminacy created by the absence of order. It requires some disorder as an object of its disdain, much as Hegel's lord required the continuing existence of the slave in order to remain a lord; and this leaves some space for creative manipulation.[5] It is a small space, because most attempts to break out will appear as rude social incompetence and pretension. But it is a space nonetheless. Where is it, and how do people use it?

Education is certainly one route. The butcher's apprentice who becomes the head of an English-language school and the baker's son who goes to university and then joins one of the more educated professions are cases in point, as is the artisan's daughter who opens a day-care center or goes into nursing; there are also possibilities for young men (and women) to gain a professional toehold in electrical and electronic work as well as in the higher echelons of the hotel and catering trades. Such individual shifts do not effectively change the structure within which they acquire their significance; on the contrary, those who make them are ipso facto transformed into bourgeois citizens themselves. It is not clear that the competitive habits inculcated by the artisanal workshop are so much reduced as disguised, and softened, by the new accouterments of educated status; appropriately domesticated, after all, they amplify the idiom of bourgeois capitalism to perfection.

Bourgeois identity is predicated on notions of an order external to the body: it posits a mind that is autonomous and external to the physical embodiment of self and a controlling social system to which the self is expected to submit. Both of these assumptions are anathema to the artisan. So the price of rising in the class system is that one opts out of those familiar habits of speech and gesture that make "tradition" an integral and embodied part of the self; instead, tradition becomes objectified and commodified outside that self. Since it is now the object of management and authorship, those who continue to bear it "within" themselves remain marginalized from the mainstream of modernity. Those who succeed in moving "outside" it, by contrast, have emancipated themselves at the expense of leaving their erstwhile social class behind; they are now actively participating in the perpetuation of that class's marginal status.

In Italy, one sees a very similar effect among the artisans of Rome,[6] where artisans in the central districts of the city face three choices. They may be unable to pay the astronomically rising rents of home and workshop and simply leave for the cheaper suburbs (appropriately known collectively as the *periferia*, or "margin"). They may transform themselves into "artists" *(artisti)* and charge high prices, but they can do this only if the objects they produce either are assimilable to the categories of so-called high art or have acquired the sort of rarity value—usually long after these objects have been made and then discarded—that converts them from garbage to antiques (when both objects and artisans end up perched on a very isolating pedestal indeed).[7] Or they may become small but sometimes remarkably prosperous entrepreneurs *(commercianti)*, in which case their artisanship becomes secondary to their ability to play the consumerist market for status symbols; purveyors of the work of others or disdainful of all but the most specialized artisanship involving objects of high commercial value, they themselves become fully bourgeois in their lifestyle, with summer seaside homes and highly educated children. Those who continue in humbler artisanal professions, notably the carpenters and metalworkers who do the more basic work in people's homes rather than restoring antique "pieces," must either accept employment from those who have succeeded in climbing this status ladder or work in increasingly cramped and often illegal premises that dramatically underscore their seemingly inescapable marginality.

In Rome, apprenticeship has become very rare indeed. The processes that I have described here have moved with ineluctable remorselessness to a conclusion made all the more inevitable by the assumption that it was, in fact, inevitable. This assumption is deeply embedded in the prevailing policies of the European Union but is also anticipated in the tax and social security provisions that had already made apprenticeship a virtually untenable proposition for most artisans and by the chronic housing shortage in Rome as in other major Italian cities. In Rethemnos the cost of housing and work space was less of a problem, although the Archaeological Service and the Town-Planning Service, both organs of the national government, restricted the use of street space and tried to impose some rudimentary zoning. Rethemniot artisans have succeeded in maintaining at least some limited degree of apprenticeship under the conditions I have been describing here. But in both places we find that artisans are increasingly caught up in the paradox of what we might call "the globalization of locality": the emphasis on preserving tradition and heritage, whether as theme parks or as "collectibles." In that process, those artisans who continue in the humbler crafts that formerly constituted the main raison d'être for artisanship and apprenticeship find themselves struggling with growing desperation to make a living out of these practices.

Artisanship is thus moving from a process of production to an object of trade and exhibition. (The annual NOSMBH exhibitions dramatize the process nicely and mark the stages along its march to completion.) Paradoxically, the continuing difficulties of artisans who are unable to make the transition successfully feed the sense that Rethemnos is a town rich in tradition, because their palpable and ubiquitous presence somewhat softens the effect of blatant commodification that we see in more exclusively tourist-oriented places. The case of the filo bakers will illustrate my point. They have started to offer tourists little packages of homemade pastry and filo leaves, but they decided to continue with their backbreaking work up to the point of retirement because local customers are still willing, although to a decreasing degree, to pay for the superior quality of the handmade product. Even some hoteliers have been willing to do so; despite their relative economic autonomy, these local entrepreneurs are often enmeshed in complex kinship and patronage networks and consequently cannot escape the pressure well-connected artisans can exert on them to behave like good neighbors. As those ties weaken and the hoteliers find themselves caught up progressively in the logic of their international business relations, however, their loyalty has noticeably faltered. So the bakers, like those carpenters and ironworkers who have also progressively lost out to factories and imported goods, must try to make do.[8] The bakers' production of these little packages, advertised in several languages on the doors of their establishment, is their small but sweet revenge for the years of being filmed as objects of tourist wonderment even while they usually reaped no benefits from this other than the satisfaction of being seen as living repositories of tradition. But this last effect is itself the product of the shift from process to objectification. Since they are unable to take on apprentices in any way that would make commercial sense, moreover, and since their children have moved into professions requiring a higher level of education, their work will disappear with their retirement: the processes involved will come to an end. And since what they produce is all perishable, so will the objects of their artisanal pride and care, fossilized in memories and books and the occasional journalistic account—all indications of a pride that is itself the clearest sign that this transformation is all but complete.

No doubt there is an element of preemptive nostalgia in thinking about artisanship and apprenticeship in such terms. But nostalgia itself has become the object of much of the commodification now under way; indeed, one might argue that it is precisely this monumentalization of everyday experience that represents the final success, if not of the state, then of the capitalist economy at a stage already long beyond the linkage among capitalism, bourgeois values, and the nation-state. These days, nation-states are themselves the loci of production for a generalized notion of heritage that is itself one of the key components of the global hierarchy of value. Everywhere from France with its *patrimoine* to Thailand with its analogous concept of *moradok*, or from China to Zimbabwe, we see globally generalized the notion that, much as culture is a possession of that collective individual known as the nation, so heritage is its realization as a collective property transfer between generations. Heritage, in this sense, replaces history, much as culture replaces society: in both cases, temporal process is occluded by the sense of a collective eternity.[9] This is the logic of monumentalization, and it is a logic often no more acceptable to local populations than are the products of international companies that attempt to displace local foods and fashions. All these phenomena represent the growing efficiency of the global hierarchy of value.

To understand this transformation more clearly, we can usefully turn to Jane Collier's discussion of modernity in southern Spain.[10] Her argument, broadly stated, runs as follows: Andalusians, heirs to a rationalist perspective in which tradition both defined their collective claims to identity and yet represented an era prior to their capacity for disembodied reason, today reject as adornments of their own bodies and homes the trappings of what they see as a demeaning dependence on tradition, which they prefer to find in the writings of anthropologists and in folklore museums. They must confront a paradoxical "requirement that modern nationalists simultaneously 'think for themselves' and 'obey only their own "inner" voice.'"[11] Here again is the Wittgensteinian duck-rabbit of tradition at its most irreducible: people want to have the best of both worlds, by both claiming tradition as their own and at the same time removing it from the immediate environment of their personal space and identity. The early nationalist folklorists of Europe, notably some Greek writers, placed themselves above the common people, in whose culture they nevertheless saw themselves as participating by abstract right if not in material practice. It was this logic that allowed the early folklorists to claim the right to edit texts to suit their view of the national culture: as participants they knew what the texts were about, while as intellectuals they could intervene in a rational and objective way.[12]

As such ideas spread to the masses, which themselves had become educated and had learned that this meant they were now "rational" and so "modern," the objects classified as traditional retreated from everyday bodily experience into museums and books. This elite version of commodification derives respectability both from the trappings of academic presentation and from an occasionally quite explicit contrast with the gross materialism and vulgarity attributed to the varieties of commodification to be seen in fast-food establishments and Disney World. This, the educated and powerful repeatedly insist, is *our* tradition, and we (the echo of nineteenth-century nationalistic folklore is palpable here) know how to administer it.

The artisans of Rethemnos are certainly no elite. Their pride is only like that of the bourgeois leadership in that, like the latter, it traps them in the circular logic of hegemony. Just as the elite's nationalistic swaggering earns the condescension of the international forces that nevertheless demand it as the price of "protection," the artisans' boastful masculinity signals a charmingly picturesque backwardness that is maintained by their ongoing dependence on powerful politicians. They are charged with the business of reproducing tradition; to the extent that they can do so utilizing premechanical methods, they are also expected to embody it. Their only hope of respectability lies in executing this charge, yet it is precisely their success in doing so—and in reproducing all the ways of acting that are similarly attributed to their social status, including a strongly *gemeinschaftlich* orientation and their dependence on political patrons, aggressive masculinity, and the emphasis on agnatic ties—that condemns most of them to remaining on the margins of a modernity already co-opted by the emergent and rapidly growing middle class, itself hostage to concentric expectations on the larger stage of international relations.

Their marginality mirrors encompassing marginalities; it is not the root cause of these but their vastly magnified and disproportionate effect. In that magnification lies the artisans' significance for our understanding of the encompassing society. Where members of the middle class acquire the means of disguising their dependence or even of dressing it up as the assertion of a modern form of independence, these artisans have no such defenses against the ravages of self-knowledge—except, perhaps, that minimal cloth of respectability that hides from their everyday self-awareness their comprehensive commitment to the solidarities of agnatic kinship. But that small concession, no less than the loincloths of oppressed natives, signifies the extent to which they have been relegated to the cultural margins of the Europe that others claim they embody. Any embarrassment that forbids us to acknowledge what we are is also an acknowledgment that others would like us to be otherwise. In the artisans of Rethemnos, we encounter the derogatory effects of the global hierarchy of value, if not at their very rawest, then at least in a form that admits of little doubt and few hopes for redemption or escape.

The degree to which this happens and the extent to which it is experienced as a dreadful trap vary considerably. For jewelers and electricians, for example, there are ample opportunities to lay claim to fashion consciousness in the first case, "Western" technical knowledge in the second, and modernity in both. Not all artisans wish to travel that route, or have the means to do so. Those with more limited options are forced to define themselves as traditional selves engaged in traditional activities and manufacturing traditional products. They soon find themselves entrapped in that strangely constricting glory for which the pedestal is ever ready and waiting.

In other societies, young people have escaped in a variety of ways. For example, among the Cameroonian carvers described by Nicolas Argenti, those who enter the formal track of apprenticeship have few options to innovate and find that they are enmeshed in a power system that also limits their social advancement to rigidly demarcated channels. Those who instead imitate a variety of styles and objects without the benefit of formal training by masters discover a much greater freedom of social action. Internally, at least, they become the privileged bearers of a modernity that is growing in luster. Whether they in turn will find their handiwork despised by the exemplars they imitate Argenti does not say; the evidence is not yet available. It seems entirely likely that they will do so. In their confrontations with the traditionalists, they are reproducing the destructive dynamic of traditionalism within the community, but it is far from clear that their achievements will win them much advancement externally.

They, too, like the apprentices whose work they seek to mock and displace, are subject to the criteria of the global hierarchy of value. Its passage varies by social and cultural context, but its effects are similar everywhere. For example, in the case of carpenters in Thailand who make furniture in a distinctive Chinese style and whose moral authority comes from the Shanghainese origins of their work and training, the imitation of a supposedly high culture confers prestige but limits the range of innovation in ways that reflect the ambiguous status of the Chinese community—resented for its commercial success but admired for its adherence to tradition—within the larger Thai polity. The apprentices are trained in a severely monitored environment that allows no deviance from the authoritative, as well as authoritarian, models their products represent, and in which the use of machine tools represents a convenience that may bring more ease and money but that sacrifices the status of cultural association.[13]

In Crete, however, the irony is especially bitter. Here, on this island that claims a civilizational antiquity predating even the glories of classical Athens by many centuries, the insertion of its crafty artisans into a rhetoric of European identity constitutes a particularly ironic form of subjection, from which few escape and to which their continuing insubordination effectively binds them ever more tightly. Their predicament reflects, in extreme form, that of their home town, island, and country. It makes no sense to say that the artisans' apprentices are "typical" of Greece in this regard; rather, their bodies incorporate the everyday sources of national and regional resentment in revealingly hyperbolic fashion. It is this exaggeration of commonplace experience that makes their situation such a valuable key to the concentric dynamics that their lives engage.

Some Revealing Contrasts

The contrast between the experiences of the British working-class lads studied by Willis and those of the Rethemniot artisans' apprentices suggests a key difference between the old centers of global power and the corresponding geopolitical margins. In Rethemnos, those who fail to develop the guile that accompanies their artisanal identity—the apprentices who, by asking direct questions and by appearing most focused on a literal application of whatever they manage to learn—most closely resemble the studious "ear'oles" of Willis's account. It is these more school-oriented boys, not the sullen rebels, who usually and most conspicuously fail to achieve master artisan status, whereas the English "ear'oles" are the active achievers within the system of educational values sanctioned by the state. Some Rethemniots, like the butcher's nephew who became an English-language-cramming school headmaster, are successful in laying a material claim on modernity; others, however, earnest though they may be (or because they are *too* earnest), fall back and remain as subordinate workers in the larger workshops, their hopes of becoming successful artisans dashed forever by incremental failures in their initial response to training.

In a self-avowedly modernist setting, educational qualifications confirm achievement already recognized and socially validated.[14] In those situations, as Willis acutely notes, refusal to play the game is a "radical act" that "refuses to collude in its own educational suppression."[15] Within that modernist project, however, those who are charged with reproducing tradition do not have that option; their uncouthness and insubordination are an intrinsic part of the role that has been assigned to them. Although this role debars them from access to the symbolic capital of modernity, it is the only means they have of holding on to the symbolic capital of traditionalism, which is the basis of whatever respect they can earn. They are thus not so much refusing to collude as unable *not* to collude. In this sense, they are worse off than the British lads: their particular entrapment is reinforced by the overlapping and hierarchically organized concentricities of value judgment that, in the final analysis, are also the predicament of their regional and national culture. These concentricities amplify the bitterness of their subjection.

Something of the same predicament comes across in Dorinne Kondo's sympathetic account of how the confectionery made by the artisans she studied has now come to seem "too traditional" and of how the status of artisanal apprentice has suffered a similar and parallel eclipse. The production of this confectionery in an atmosphere of silence was explicitly linked by her informants to their stereotypes of Japanese tradition.[16] Here, as in Rethemnos, we do not encounter what Willis saw as "the individual labourer's blindness to the special nature of the commodity which he sells which is at the heart of the ideological legitimation of capitalism."[17] As Kondo's analysis would lead us to expect, the Rethemniot artisans are far from uniform in their response to the reductive individualism of both the local value system and the state's reading of capitalism. On the contrary, and perhaps more acutely in Rethemnos even than in Tokyo, we encounter a variety of tactical variations on what is nonetheless, to a great extent, common to all the artisans: a determined attempt to preserve and accentuate that added value that tradition supposedly confers, an added value that is reproduced in each artisan as a deep-seated unwillingness to part with the requisite specialized knowledge. That reluctance is in turn matched by the realization that failure to impart the knowledge to the cleverer apprentices would doom the entire enterprise of tradition itself. In this last response, we also sense an appalled sadness and panic, at least on the part of the more articulate, at the prospect that the mantle of local tradition, like that of the classical heritage of the country at large, is fast slipping from their shoulders and into the plastic-lined dustbin of history.

The issue is not simply that of the changing fortunes of national heritage politics. It is also a larger process: the commodification of a now-globalized hierarchy of cultures and values. When politically weak national cultures could only produce limited quantities of commodified goods, these at least might acquire some rarity value. They became curios of an exoticized peasant world. But when factories began to mass-produce a simplified iconography of tradition, the artisans who had hitherto been the producers of these fetishized workaday objects—objects now rapidly multiplied and dispersed across the emporia of the entire world—were mostly not invited to participate in that factory production, which in any event would have represented a radical deskilling for them. Instead, they were reduced to performing relatively menial or utilitarian forms of production for local consumers. They no longer made goods that were profitably traditional; much of what they did was not recognizably traditional at all. As a result, they were left with only the dubious *status* of traditional artisans—a symbolic currency that the encompassing processes of commodification on the one hand and deskilling on the other have whittled away at an alarming speed.[18]

In the Greece of technocratic leaders and the European Union, these artisans continue, although in steadily decreasing numbers, to reproduce that dwindling status in the form of skills and modes of social interaction that also have little place in the new national culture. The "technocratic" label so often applied to Prime Minister Simitis, for example, while perhaps understood by some as a recognition of his crafty guile, is for most Greeks a beacon of what they want their national culture to become. Yoked to the mantle of tradition, Greeks had hitherto been locked in an "obsession with ancestors" that, like the artisans' traditionalism, brought immediate short-term benefits at the price of a well-disguised long-term dependency. Today, ever fewer Greeks want that miserable trade-off for themselves or for their children.

But artisans continue to work in Rethemnos, and they still manage to attract a handful of apprentices; the tourists still descend in their indifferent or condescending hordes, leaving a short while later clutching a few factory-made souvenirs of neoclassical design or perhaps a bottle or two of local wine; and, for all the strides the modernizers in government made in the closing years of the twentieth century, Greece remains a troubling vantage point from which to observe the operations of global ideas about value. The very paucity of artisans and their reduction to a truly marginal irrelevance have become part of the palimpsest of social change and struggle that is the lived space of Rethemniots: like the urban architecture of the Old Town, scarred by the battles over conservation and modernization, but, unlike the architecture, swept aside by the torrent of change.

The vantage point that Greece offers is indeed troubling, to be sure; but that is why it is important. The power dynamic in nostalgic attributions of tradition has not always been evident; indeed, people's insistence on the symbolic value of tradition has often effectively disguised the burden that it represents for its bearers. Greece, symbolic heart of what most people unthinkingly conflate as "the West," elevates that problem to a national level. But Greece is also commodified at an *international* level, and this is where the artisans' present-day status becomes especially significant. They remain, a dwindling but irrepressible presence, to remind the observer-consumer that Greece is, after all, a land of tradition.

That they are not the major producers of that tradition is irrelevant to the ways in which visitors experience their presence or to the ways in which they experience their roles. The Greeks as a nation, similarly, have not been the major producers of "their own" contributions to Western identity. This induces a curiously diagnostic difference between Greece and other countries that boast a long tradition of artisanship.

I have noted significant differences between the practices discussed here and those reported from Britain, France, Japan, and other countries. The cultural specificities that account for these contrasts are not epiphenomenal to capitalism. They are produced by the same forces that engendered the capitalist economy and the nation-state polity, and they are managed by interests that now operate beyond the visible controls associated with both. The national self-presentation that obeys the dictates of an exoticist commodity market depends on local-level refractions of a highly globalized exoticism, presented as the constituent "traditional cultures" of the nation-state. Locally produced traditions thus refract opposed but complementary processes. They refract the exoticist logic of the global market through local cultural practices and understandings, through which artisanal producers invest both objects and social relations with meanings that may be invisible outside the community; they also refract local specificity through an array of "national cultures" eager, for the most part, to participate in this global market of cultural forms.[19]

It becomes easier, in this light, to see how and why Greeks have been generally reluctant to let go of their demeaning dependency on their ancient ancestors. It is not that they are the dupes of more intelligent masters; it is that, for reasons associated with their very emergence into modern nationhood, they have few defenses against those who pose as their protectors and benefactors. Not all artisans fail to appreciate the irony in which they are caught; but again there is very little they can collectively do about it, no matter how successfully individuals play the system to their personal advantage.

The Body (Im)politic: Experiencing Marginality and Hegemony

Not all Greeks are artisans, still less artisans in small towns like Rethemnos; but the experiential dimension of artisanal life in Rethemnos encapsulates in extreme form the logic of traditionalism in this symbolically overdetermined nation-state. Some Greeks who have read this book in manuscript form or heard me speak about the research generously admitted that they recognized many familiar aspects of their own surroundings, and more particularly of the traditionalism in which they have been constantly inculcated and immersed. I do not want to claim, it hardly needs to be said, that the ethnography of Greece is richer in data of this sort than is that of other countries, but I do think it fair to argue that the particular *positioning* of Greece's cultural dynamics on the world stage is especially diagnostic of how heritage politics reinforces a worldwide hierarchy of social, political, and—especially—cultural values. Consequently, we should also expect that the experiences, the *viomata*, of the artisans engaged in the reproduction of traditional Greek selves (if not always of traditional Greek craft objects) exhibit in particularly raw form the often cruel effects of that hierarchy on people's lives. Such is the complex of interrelationships that I have tried to identify in this study.

Ethnography that focuses on social experience tends to emphasize local perspectives, because that is the level at which most fieldwork takes place. Focus on embodiment has produced an even more intense narrowing of the social range of contexts, perhaps partly in opposition to the opposite tendency toward institutional generalization to which other anthropological work has sometimes seemed prone with the rise of interest in "multi-sited ethnography" and the processes of globalization.[20] Clearly, important work has addressed the effects of national disasters and international cataclysms, but here, too, analysis has generally focused exclusively either on institutional structures or on the experiences of those caught therein. It has rarely captured the tension between these extremes.

Yet today's world is a world of nation-states, which both infuse the local and are in turn pervaded by the global. Transformations of meaning among the multiple levels thereby engaged are frequent and complex. In this study, I have illustrated some of the ways in which anthropologists can identify the dynamics whereby these levels inflect each other. That they do so is the result of long historical processes that have seeped into collective experience through the constant iteration of metonymies of collective identity: the nation as a family, the town as a state, the people as a workforce of erstwhile slaves. The complicity in their own subjugation to which some workforces have consented as a result of well-documented processes such as deskilling in capitalist economies is not confined to work alone. With the emergence of modern nation-states in the dependent penumbra of expanding colonial power, cultural values have been deployed to embed selfhood in an ever more global hierarchy. The emergence of local, regional, and national identities historically provided that framework of concentricities through which the hierarchy acquired the force of clarity and definition, resonating in the experiences of working bodies as a sense—a sensibility—made inexorably common to all.

While I agree with earlier writers that apprenticeship is not simply a matter of the transmission of technical knowledge, investigating what actually does get transmitted or blocked conveys a clearer understanding of the role of apprenticeship in meshing local society with these processes of social and cultural encompassment. In the final analysis, it is in daily, embodied experience that such change actually takes effect. Behind the abstractions of class, for example, there are substantial differences in access to resources, and these frame and direct the self-performances that channel political, cultural, and moral authority. Pierre Bourdieu and Jean-Claude Passeron note that in France the more privileged bourgeois students were able to escape the controlling formalism of school education because of the cultural resources available to them at home.[21] Relative ease with experimentation and inventiveness distinguished them, in a self-fulfilling pattern, from those with lower-class backgrounds and correspondingly restricted resources for dealing with the content of cultural lessons in particular. The more richly endowed in such resources they were, the more independent they were of the schoolroom for their mastery of the elite culture. They disdained rote learning, predictable allusions, and standard classics in favor of an eclectic style and a marked preference for the avant-garde.

It would be all too easy, on this basis, to conclude that it was freedom from formalism that constituted the diagnostic prerogative of the children of wealthy and established parents in a country that exemplifies the idea of the *mission civilisatrice* worldwide. Among the Rethemniot artisans, however, a high value is similarly accorded to the creative management of norms and rules. Like the upper bourgeois studied by Bourdieu and Passeron, these men value and celebrate freedom from the precision of bureaucratic constraints. In defiance of audit culture logic, their mastery of improvisation marks them off from a bureaucratic state considered by many of their compatriots, including numerous functionaries of the state itself, to be morally bankrupt and conceptually inept.

Yet there is an important difference between the French bourgeois students' affectations of aristocratic ease and disdain for effort on the one hand and the Rethemniot artisans' insouciant displays of self-confident disdain for formal rules on the other. The individualism of the educated French upper bourgeois is an individualism of open rupture with the past. It represents freedom to reject the very underpinnings of established style. At the other end of the hierarchy, the Rethemniot artisan must always, in the final analysis, be seen to reproduce; what he reproduces is "tradition"; and so he remains trapped in a circular logic in which his very individualism becomes a variety of conformism.

In large measure this comes about, I suggest, because he occupies a very different space in the concentric frameworks that together constitute the global hierarchy of value, and it is here especially that I want to enter a plea for adding consideration of this encompassing hierarchy to analyses of both social class structure and the anthropology of experience. While both the French intellectual and the Cretan artisan distinguish themselves by their daring, the French intellectual controls the criteria by which its effects will be judged to a much greater degree than does the Cretan artisan. That discrimination permits radically different "spins" on displays of a nominally similar, individualistic ethos. Where Western European bourgeois intellectuals and executives can respectively formulate and propagate a seemingly universalistic ranking of distinctions—for which Paris was always, after all, famous—artisans in the periphery can display their talents only within a decidedly localized and antimodernist space. The Rethemniot artisans do not control the criteria of taste for the "tradition" that they supposedly embody, produce, and represent.

Their personal experiences are thus embedded in a set of hierarchically ordered, concentric, and interlocking disabilities; these extend far beyond the ramifications of class, and many of them originate—as here—in the political relations among nation-states. Paradoxically, however, it is the macro-scale focus of much class analysis that has obscured the corrosive local workings of encompassing hierarchies of cultural value. The marginalities of Greece, Crete, and Rethemnos—along with the artisans' own social class and background, to be sure—together limit the possibilities for redefining their situation. Far more than class alone, these concentric hierarchies channel and to a large extent define the position of the artisans in a country long exposed to external trade, cultural influence, and political pressure. It is not that the artisans' life choices are totally overdetermined; it is, rather, that their class identities are to a striking degree determined by encompassing hierarchies of cultural value that they reproduce through the practices of apprenticeship. I would add that it is therefore all the more extraordinary that, in the final analysis, their lives are not totally determined by this concatenation of outside forces and influences with internal social constrictions.

For the possibility of real change is not entirely eliminated. One reason for this is that the global political environment is itself changing; for example, France's once commanding cultural leadership of the world can no longer be assumed, while assumptions of Greece's centrality to the project of Western civilization have largely faded as well. Greek indignation at the collapse of classical *paideia* in the West seems at least partly motivated by a widespread sense that, having both forced Greece into its neoclassical guise and attributed extravagant virtues to its own reading of ancient Greek civilization, the West now owes it to Greece to maintain that particular structure of knowledge. The West is not so minded; the denizens of its chancelleries, who could once pen iambic pentameters in elegant Attic Greek (and partly owed their positions to that arcane capacity), no longer care, or even know very much, about Plato or Aristophanes.

Another reason for avoiding too deterministic an interpretation of these processes lies in the unpredictability of any progression of events that must depend on the whims and whiles of agency. A single violent act, political upheaval, or popular book may yet change the balance of cultural power, by deflecting the world's attention to new concerns at the expense of the old. The emergence of audit culture may represent just such a moment, threatening both Cretan artisans *and* Western European bourgeois intellectuals with relegation to the farthest margins of an efficiency-driven society. The leaders of an efficiency-driven society, unable to see their own predilections as cultural but instead attributing universal validity to them, may want to use both "tradition" and "high culture" (along with ethics, rationality, and taste) as rhetorical tethering posts for the importunately local and exceptionalist. They will then assign a certain condescending value to these marginalized entities and people by treating their "inefficiency" as "picturesque." In this book, I have hinted at the beginning of that process in the exoticization of the picturesque for the tourism trade.

Such connections emerge in closely observed ethnography, a point that has been obscured by the division of labor (and ideology) between much of political science and anthropology, respectively. World-shattering events and local-level ethnography have often seemed entirely irrelevant to each other. When anthropologists have commented on world events, they have usually done so (although there are exceptions)[22] on the basis of generalizations about national cultures. These, while often grounded in the authors' detailed, firsthand cultural knowledge, do not engage the ethnography of experience in order to explore alternative readings of national and international structures of power at the level of the ethnography itself. Instead, they mine existing ethnographic knowledge for clues to decipher the present moment. Yet it is only at a highly localized level that the effects of global process can be brought under genuinely intense inspection. Ethnography pinpoints universalism's capillary pervasion of embodied experience at specific times and places.

Precisely because the global is so easily conflated with the universal, it is vital to ground its appearances in those times and places. The global always arrives with a local, as well as with a larger, history: someone has let it in through the back door of class or national solidarity, developed a profitable relationship with its bearers, or redesigned it for local consumption. One would not have to be a conspiracy theorist, and indeed one might not be able to track specific incentives and motives, in order to acknowledge that both the arrival of mass-produced consumer goods from abroad and the refashioning of tradition at home must have something to do with the play of local, as well as external, interests and pressures.

It would be hard to understand the predicament of Rethemniot artisans without documenting the growing globalization and homogenization of public ideas about tradition and locality, without acknowledging the concentricity of marginalities within which the artisans' every act is embedded and interpreted, or without paying attention to the dynamics of gender and kinship in the social organization of their knowledge. At the same time, however, one cannot understand globalization in general independently of case histories such as the story outlined in this book. The exponents of globalization may have designed its packaging in advance; but its local consumers have already unwrapped and recast it for their own ends.

The issues that emerge as central to the analysis of the social experience of cultural change at the beginning of the twenty-first century, amid all the talk of globalization, necessarily include class, power, hierarchy, and value. These issues are neither local nor global alone; they are both at the same time, and much more besides. Moreover, they are fundamentally cultural as much as they are social; they are about value, and value is defined in terms that, while often appearing necessary, are arbitrary in the sense that they are historically accidental and culturally contingent. The appearance of necessity comes from the force of the historical events that generated those particular valuations. In the case of Rethemnos, the peculiar circumstances of the birth of the Greek nation-state, its subsequent incorporation of Crete, and its current relationship with the encompassing European Union are especially salient aspects of cultural and political history for understanding the local dynamics of traditionalism today. Such specificities will produce different cultural responses in different places.

It is important not to view these processes as a total determination of people's destinies. I have resisted the idea that artisans' apprentices can never escape the logic that I have been describing here, although to do so is extremely difficult and does little to change the overall arrangements of power and value. Some apprentices, as I have tried to show, have been able to create very divergent lives for themselves, but in the process they have, if anything, strengthened the grip of these encompassing structures. Much the same can be said of the country as a whole—a country that garners praise, precisely because it is becoming more "European," from a curious combination of the conservative elite and the technological avant-garde. Some voices continue to resist these changes; the Neo-Orthodox movement is a prominent example, as are the remnants of the old hard-core Left who long for the political East much as a few intellectuals look to the cultural East. But resistance entails a considerable risk of further marginalizing the country within the neoliberal ecumene. This is a risk that some are not altogether sorry to entertain, as they weigh it against the loss of spirituality, dignity, and autonomy that they attribute to modernization.[23]

A few artisans, such as the much-traveled English-speaking boot-maker who chose to remain an artisan, are keen to spell out the articulation of experience with ideology. Most, however, true to their deep taciturnity, waste few words on ideological abstractions. But all are engaged in the replication of their collective identity both in their embodied selves and in the objects they manufacture. By studying their daily vicissitudes, we can more fully appreciate the complex articulation of social experience with the historically grounded, concentric frames of cultural identity and evaluation within which they live. In the process, we can and must also try to resist the temptations of once again splitting the local and the global asunder, a dualism that violates local actors' experience of this same concentricity. We should also assiduously beware of treating the local and the global as the only two levels of demonstrable relevance—a simplification that does great violence to the artisans' experience and overlooks the deep historical sedimentation and metonymic ordering of social complexity in their lives.

Understanding globalization means understanding its agents, some of whom are paradoxically engaged in what appear to be radically localizing activities, while others may pay court to more regional concerns of various kinds. The Rethemniot artisans' dignity is tested and dramatized in a local place and validated in terms of an island's pride, but it is also devalued and discounted within the emergent global hierarchy. The tensions that subsist among these multiple levels are the consuming, compelling, confusing reality of the artisans' all-but-inescapably crafty lives. More than the techniques of their craft, it is these tensions that the artisans in turn pass on to the coming generations of cringing youths who still, remarkably, aspire to follow in their turbulent wake.

Chapter One

1. The critical term here is *tekhni* (classical Greek *techn<ē*), in which what we might take as the two meanings of "art" and "craft" merge comfortably. Etymological cognates must be understood in this context. Thus, as Thomas Malaby (2002a: 592) notes, Prime Minister Constantine Simitis's reputation as a "technocrat" *(tekhnokratis)* "resonates particularly well in Greek," presumably because—despite Simitis's political modernism (see Diamandouros 1994), and unlike the etymologically cognate but ideologically more conformist English term—it connotes a potent mix of the ability to "fix" problems and the exercise of real power. Greeks may take Simitis's openly progressivist stand, which incorporates an explicit commitment to changing "mentalities" (perhaps an unfortunate term; see Lloyd 1990; Herzfeld 1997b: 78–80), at face value, but they may also see this as a form of dissembling intended for foreign consumption. A representative example of Simitis's political style (posted at http://www.primeminister.gr/speeches/20010331.htm) exhibits, perhaps not surprisingly, both a new vision of Greece's relationship with Europe as a whole and some long-established rhetorical strategies for resisting European pressure. It represents, at the highest political level, the collective Greek ambivalence about the country's cultural place in the world that I attempt to analyze here in some of the most intimate spaces of Greek social life.

2. For example, in his study of working-class boys at an English school, Paul Willis ([1977] 1981: 23) quotes one of the "lads" saying proudly, "We're getting to know it now . . . and we know where to have a crafty smoke." In Greek, *me doulevis* (literally, "you're working me") means "you are trying to deceive me," suggesting an implicit but close identification among craft, labor, and craftiness.

3. See Pardo 1996: 11; in a slightly more elaborate form *(la bell'arte di arrangiarsi)*, this phrase ironically evokes *le belle arti*, "the fine arts," and so makes a mockery of the distinction between high art and low life.

4. See especially the comparative account advanced by Helms (1993).

5. This is a significant part of Thompson's (1979) "rubbish theory."

6. Cf. Gramsci's (1988: 348) equation of common sense with hegemony. In anthropology, there is a long tradition of probing local versions of common sense as

the key to underlying structures of moral authority; see especially Douglas 1975: 276–283.

7. For the connections between national identity and the ownership of a reified culture, see especially the highly original writings of Richard Handler (1985, 1988) on this topic. See also Herzfeld 1987a, 1997a, 1997b, 2002b.

8. The political and economic meaning of the global hamburger—the tangible success its ubiquity demonstrates—is undeniable; but that hamburger does not necessarily mean the same thing to everyone everywhere (Watson 1997). Hannerz and Löfgren (1994: 205) make the related and similarly important point that international influences, artifacts, and styles can be drafted into the service of nationalizing culture; theirs is a further warning against taking surface implications at face value.

9. See Kleinman 1999: 90, on "local worlds"; Miller 1997, on the culture of capitalism.

10. Anthropologists find themselves especially troubled by the recent debates about the ethics of research. Even the well-intentioned critique of nationalism can have negative consequences for subnational groups struggling for recognition and political freedom against hostile regimes (see especially Jackson 1995). If the principal concern of protecting human experimental subjects is to escape the chilling routinization of the audit culture (see especially Shore and Wright 2000), care must be taken to ensure that the rhetoric of ethics does not end up subverting its own underlying intentions by providing an alibi for political manipulation that simultaneously suppresses critical research. In the Greek context Gefou-Madianou (2000) has cogently analyzed the fine line that local scholars must tread in negotiating the relationship between ethical concerns and the context of national politics; see also Herzfeld 1997b: 165–170 for a complementary but differently situated view of the corresponding situation of, especially, foreign researchers.

11. But marginal cultures are no longer the discipline's *sole* preoccupation. On the contrary, such ethnographic studies now increasingly exist in complementarity with ethnographic studies of elites (e.g., de Pina-Cabral and Pedroso de Lima 2000; Marcus 1992; Nugent and Shore 2002), of national and supranational bureaucracies (e.g., Hertz 1998; Herzfeld 1992; Shore 2000; Zabusky 1995, 2000), and of political institutions and leaders (e.g., Abélès 1989, 1990, 2000; Holmes 2000). Much of this work is done in "the West," further undermining the old division of labor between "observers and informants," and this has been accompanied by a sustained rethinking of the locus of anthropological research (Gupta and Ferguson 1997; Marcus 1998). In this context, the significance of more "traditional" sites of anthropological investigation is actually enhanced, as these sites are brought—as here—into a consideration of transnational dynamics that is also arguably more faithful to the intrinsic comparativism of anthropology than anything that has gone before.

12. The Italian ethnologist Ernesto De Martino was an early advocate of this perspective, which is at once both a methodological technique and an instrument of political and social critique: "But not all the things that we have made slight in importance deserved to become that, and in any case the 'slight' and the 'serious' do not belong to things in themselves but can always once again be redistributed in the network of reality in the function of certain 'current questions' that stimulate the choice of the 'important past'" (De Martino [1961] 1994:13–14; translation mine).

13. Especially germane here is Robert Ulin's (1996: 20) remark, in the context of his exploration of how French wines and their makers came to occupy different positions in a value hierarchy at once aesthetic and social, that the tradition-modernity dichotomy "was pushed by European statecraft and the globalization of European society and economy to apply dialectically to the colonies and the peripheries of Europe itself."

14. The protection of women's concern for preserving their reputations may not always, however, be a strong motivation at all. Even in the mid–twentieth century it was already fading (Lambiri-Dimaki 1965). On the other hand, many Cretans still pride themselves on their ethical as much as on their artisanal traditionalism.

15. Cockburn 1983: 19, on compositors in Britain. On the Ottoman guild (Greek *sindekhnia* [formal] or *sinafi* [informal; alternative forms: *isnafi, esnafi;* from Turkish *esnaf*]), see Khatzimikhali 1953; Papageorgiou 1986: 11–12 (see also the further references given in his useful bibliography). Elements of hazing still mark the early steps of apprenticeship in some Greek artisanal trades, but they no longer have the systematic character that a few elderly craftsmen can still recall.

16. The phenomenon I call "crypto-colonialism" is a situation in which, as the price of freedom from colonial rule, some countries accepted the tutelary control of Western nations, especially in the adoption of a bureaucratically conceived, fundamentally positivistic understanding of the territorial nation-state. In the Greek case, this entailed a particularly ruthless "cleansing" of indigenous cultural forms (see Herzfeld 2002a, 2003).

17. On Thailand, see especially Barmé 1993, and cf. Rhum 1996: 347–349; on Greece, Koliopoulos 1987; St. Clair 1972: 8, 36–38; and on Greek management of the terminology of heroism and brigandage during the War of Independence (1821–1833) and again during the Civil War (1944–1949) and its aftermath, Herzfeld 1982: 60–70, 1997c: 278. In both cases, the nomenclature exemplified the generic use of philology for irredentist and nationalist ends. From the beginning of the nineteenth century until at least the mid–twentieth century, this use of philology foreshadowed the globalization of local heritage that steadily emerged, following largely European models, in the last quarter of the twentieth century.

18. Peleggi 2002; see also Herzfeld 2002a.

19. On the rise of aesthetic neoclassicism in Greece and the corresponding representation in Western Europe, see especially Athanassoglou-Kallmyer 1989; Bastéa 2000; Jenkyns 1980; on the role of the German universities in shaping Western conceptions of the classical past, see Bernal 1987: 189–240; on the philhellenes and the shaping of Greek ethnology, see Herzfeld 1987a, 2002a.

20. See, comprehensively, Bastéa 2000.

21. Not all Neo-Orthodox theologians and apologists espouse the views of Christos Yannaras (1972, 1978, 1992), who has argued that the association of the church with the structures of the modern Greek state subjected it to processes of routinization that exposed its hierarchy to the pernicious materialism and crass mind-body dualism that he associates with Western thought and political practice, but he is probably the most articulate of such critics.

22. As the argument of this book would lead us to expect, local people often reproduce these notions that demean them. Malaby (2002a: 592) offers a usefully

contextual view of how both perspectives (European and local) played in one Greek town at the time of the currency change.

23. Yalouri (2001) explores a wide range of current interpretations of the Acropolis in Greece.

24. Veïkou 1998: 259; she is speaking of the way people known for desirable personal qualities and achievements attract the damage attributed to the evil eye.

25. Thus, in the Ano Milopotamos dialect (spoken in many of the villages that are more notoriously prone to endemic reciprocal animal rustling), *ksa sou* means "Suit yourself!" while *ksa mas emas* means, loosely translated, "We can take care of ourselves—don't *you* worry your little heads!" The notion of "social worth" entered the vocabulary of Greek ethnography at an early point, in the key study by J. K. Campbell (1964: 268).

26. *Childe Harold's Pilgrimage*, canto 11; cited in St. Clair 1972: 18.

27. Prevelakis's memoir, *A Tale of a Town*, has enjoyed considerable fame. Nakou's *Madame Do-Re-Mi* (1955) is discussed in Tannen 1983. On the several relevant novels by Nenedakis, see Herzfeld 1997c.

28. This term, *tourkospita*, literally "Turk-houses," is perhaps suggestive of *paliospita*, "brothels," and its syntactical construction clearly reinforces the sense of contrast in local speech with the more decorous *venetsianika spitia*, "Venetian houses," used by those who have a more positive attitude to these domestic spaces of ambiguous date. See Herzfeld 1991a: 57, 160.

29. The phrase "the social life of things" comes, famously, from Appadurai 1986. That work is part of a rich anthropological literature on questions of value (see also Carrier 1995a), much of it a deeply suggestive antidote to the temptation to globalize theoretical notions of value instead of putting them to work on the deconstruction of globalization itself. English unfortunately has no word as general as the Latin *res*, which includes everything on my list here. On cultural capital, see especially Bourdieu 1984 but also, although in a different jargon, Thompson 1979. Helms 1993 and Douglas and Isherwood 1979 are also relevant to these concerns.

30. On the relationship between aggressive comportment and the expectation of restraint, see Campbell 1964: 97; Herzfeld 1985: 51. On the politics of nonchalance, see Malaby 2002b.

31. For details of these evasions, see Herzfeld 1991a: 149–152. For discussions of the role of secrecy and indirection in Greek social interaction, see Campbell 1964: 192, 210; du Boulay 1974: 189, 206–207; Hirschon 1992.

32. Kiskiras 1968.

33. Herzfeld 1985: xi–xii.

34. Campbell 1964: 50.

35. See the sensitive and experience-rich essay by Joseph Blum (2000). See also Willis [1977] 1981: 127.

36. On the reformulation of the locus of research, see Gupta and Ferguson 1997. On the limits of the globalization concept, see, critically, Watson 1997.

37. Hobsbawm and Ranger 1983.

38. On the ideological battles over historic conservation in Rethemnos, see

Herzfeld 1991a. For details of my research in Rome, see Herzfeld 2001; the work on Bangkok is still in progress, but see also Askew 1996.

39. See, for example, Handler and Gable 1997.

40. One famous exception is the Navajo response to the preservation in museums of sandpaintings intended for ritual reasons to be destroyed (see Parezo 1983: 20–21, 29–30, 148–156, for a rather roseate view of this conflict).

41. Some actors, however, like the Andalusians studied by Collier (1997: 3–6, 212–215), can co-opt tradition in a way that actually gives them access to the practical aspects of the modernist vision.

42. See Douglas 1966 for the fullest exposition of this important argument.

43. The Greek phrase "we'll go illegal" *(tha vghoume sti paranomia)* is a clear marker of long-standing attitudes toward the state (see, e.g., Campbell 1964; Herzfeld 1985, 1992; Sutton 1996). I am indebted to Eleftheria Deltsou for alerting me to the current use of the phrase in this context.

44. Malaby (2002b: 305), for example, notes how west Cretans often regard their supposedly endemic forms of aggressive and demonstrative masculinity as "embarrassingly 'un-European.'"

45. Willis [1977] 1981: 3, 67.

46. The difference between this system and its antecedents may in any case be quite small. Not only does Willis ([1977] 1981: 84) point out that "progressivism is a broadening of its [the older method's] terms, not an overthrow of traditionalism," but the evidence of Lilika Nakou's *Madame Do-Re-Mi* (1955) shows that in Rethemnos schoolroom disorder and challenges to authority are nothing new.

47. Willis ([1977] 1981: 74) remarks that "the axis of moral authority underlying its [i.e., the school's] certainties and its style is quite different from the profane confusions, compromises and underlying spirit of resistance in working class culture." Although apprentices' parents sometimes feel morally beholden to the artisans who employ their sons, the resulting inequality is nevertheless a temporary and contextual obligation within a shared class status and culture, not a distanced relationship reinforced by the institutional pomposity of formalism as in the case of the school studied by Willis. The technical high school in Rethemnos (on which see chaps. 4 and 8) does not represent as large a gap in class status as is commonly the case with schools in working-class districts in England, but the persistence of bureaucratic forms and weakly institutionalized sanctions against misbehavior nonetheless suggests some degree of convergence. On the other hand, it is worth noting that, as Lave (1982: 182) predicted in more generic terms, the distinction between formal and informal education breaks down here, in particular because the institution that lays claim to the mantle of formality is clearly far less well equipped to enforce discipline than are the artisans of what used to be regarded as the "informal" sector.

48. This scenario is closer than Willis's ultimately activist recommendations, especially his concluding chapter ([1977] 1981: 185–192), to the argument advanced by Bourdieu and Passeron (1977, 1979), whom he nevertheless cites elsewhere with evident approval.

49. Willis [1977] 1981: 62.

50. Kondo 1990: 222. Had Willis argued for a degree of intentionality on the part of those responsible for running the school, as, for example, Malarney (1996) does in his account of "state functionalism" in Vietnam, his account would have been one of willful determinism rather than of a self-reproducing machine. This is a key difficulty with the notion of misrecognition.

51. Kondo 1990: 112–115, 222–224.

52. Indeed, local ideologues emphasize the alleged *contrast* between European individualism and Japanese conformity (see especially chap. 7), a contrast that the prevalence in Japan of stereotypical models of selfhood such as that described by Kondo presumably reinforces to the extent that Greeks know about it at all.

53. See Herzfeld 1987a: 137.

54. See Classen 1993; Connerton 1989; Cowan 1990; Horn 1994; Jackson 1989; Jenkins 1994; Kleinman 1980; Kleinman and Kleinman 1994; Kondo 1990; Linke 1999a, 1999b; McCall 2000; Seremetakis 1993a, 1993b; and many more.

55. Douglas 1970. For a sympathetic but critical appraisal, see Fardon 1999: 110–116.

56. Such work includes the recovery of history from dance (McCall 2000) and the tracing of identity through sensory markers (Classen 1993; Seremetakis 1993a).

57. On the conflict over schooling and bodily discipline, see Starrett 1998. For an interesting account of the (not altogether straightforward) relationship between Islamic schooling and the discipline of apprenticeship, see Marchand 2001: 100–109. On the effects of economic restructuring and fiscal centralization on the lives of Egyptian artisans, see Koptiuch 1999.

58. The term "multi-sited ethnography" (see Marcus 1998) has gained a good deal of currency, but it suffers from the same oversimplification of the notion of fieldwork *location* as does the term "globalization." When are sites separate, different, or otherwise distinguishable? Michael Fotiadis (1985; and see also Fotiadis 1993) has raised this question for archaeology, where it is epistemologically crucial; social and cultural anthropologists would do well to follow suit. See also Gupta and Ferguson 1997.

59. See Carrier 1995b for a collection of studies that explore the concept of occidentalism.

60. On the preservation of local craft industry as an issue of heritage politics, see Han 1995. For a highly internationalized view of Japanese and Korean living cultural treasures (artisans), see the UNESCO website at http://www.unesco.org/culture/heritage/tangible/treasures/html_eng/method.shtml. See also Yang 1994.

61. See Terrio 2000.

62. See especially Sutton 1994, 1996. See also Argyrou 1996. Deltsou (1995, 1996) offers some well-contextualized discussion of the rhetorical and political dynamics associated with the terms "tradition" and "modernity" in the context of the Greek nation-state. Although such issues are not restricted to the Greek-speaking world, it is perhaps indicative of what I have argued here concerning Greece's peculiar centrality to issues of European authenticity that so much work on the subject should have been done in Greek communities. Thanks in part to the globalizing logic of crypto-colonialism,

however, striking and far from coincidental parallels can be found in Thailand; see Askew 1996; Peleggi 2002; Rhum 1996.

63. As feminist scholars have remarked of the term "man," the semantically unmarked status of certain terms indexes power because it signifies the capacity to resist being identifiable (see, e.g., Lakoff 1975).

64. Wittgenstein 1963: 194.

65. For recent, authoritative accounts of survivalism and its aftermath, see Stocking 1987, 1995; Tambiah 1990. On the persistence of survivalist logic in later paradigms, see Fabian 1983.

66. See Fabian 1983.

67. Hill 1992.

68. The deployment of the doctrine of Catholic Mutualism to prop up class relations in Francoist Spain offers another excellent illustration. See Maddox 1993: 125–130; Mintz 1982.

69. For a critical assessment of the processes of recognition, see Eco 1976: 221–224.

70. For a trenchant critique of "mentalities," see Lloyd 1990. See also my discussion of the consequences of this concept for thinking about European models of individualism (Herzfeld 2002b: 147–149). It is a common term in everyday Greek discourse, and its currency and authoritative-sounding orotundity facilitate the permeation of people's self-perception by values that demean them.

71. As Danforth (1984) points out, following Fabian (1983) but extending his argument beyond the discourse of anthropologists to that of some of the power structures within which they have operated, such internal exoticism—as typical of official attempts to conserve tradition as it is of academic folklore—serves as both the expression and the instrument of elite domination. See also Greenhouse 1996: 99; Herzfeld 1991a: 16; Malaby 2002b: 304; Malaby 2003b. Consider also Stewart's (1991) very similar argument about the rhetoric of official versus folk religion in Greece.

72. The Greek terms are, respectively, *viotekhnis* (from *vios*, "life," and *tekhni*, "craft") and *viopalestis* (from *palevo*, "struggle"); while the former term emphasizes the practical nature of the craft professions, the latter instead underscores the (agonistic) social orientation of artisans—and other workers—toward nature, the social world, and the very conditions of existence.

73. This phrase, ironically, comes straight from the full name of NOSMBH.

74. See the important discussion in Faubion 1993.

75. See David Horn's (1994) analysis of the Italian development of "criminal anthropology" by writers such as Cesare Lombroso and its subsequent elaboration under Mussolini. For broader studies, see Gilman 1985; Mosse 1985; Poliakov 1971.

76. Elias 1978.

77. Brownell 1995; Kleinman and Kleinman 1994.

78. Goffman 1959, especially pp. 106–121 on backstage patterns of interaction. Goffman (1959: 128; my emphasis) argues that "backstage conduct is one which allows minor acts which might easily be taken as *symbolic of intimacy* and disrespect for others and for the region, while front region conduct is one which disallows such potentially offensive behavior." He suggests that this conduct corresponds to what psychologists call

"regressive" behavior. Neither his formulation nor the psychological model he invokes, however, goes far enough in acknowledging the social centrality of such patterns, which do not so much "symbolize" as actually create the intimacy that provides the very grounds on which official decorum can exist. The cultivation of uncouth masculinity that I describe here, for example, provides the labor force, the cannon fodder, and the mythological free spirit that constitute some of the most recognizable experiential materials whereby ordinary people understand the official Greek nationalist discourse and historiography.

Chapter Two

1. Terrio 2000: 155.

2. For the metaphor of "sedimentation," see Connerton 1989. On the inculcation of dispositions, see Bourdieu 1977; for a detailed and insightful ethnographic exploration of collective dispositions, see Terrio 2000: 152–156; for rich further illustration, consult Cowan 1990; while Starrett (1998: 36–39) nicely contextualizes within the larger history of Cartesian and colonial preoccupations with pure knowledge the failure of early anthropological theory to recognize the educational significance of embodied learning.

3. Kondo 1990: 246–247, 287–289.

4. There is a suggestive parallel in the verbal dueling that is common in Crete, especially in the highland villages (see, e.g., Herzfeld 1985: 141–149), in which what matters is less to produce a completely fresh verse couplet than to riposte in a way that ridicules the style of the original couplet and so questions its inventiveness; occasionally these retorts are effective enough to provoke outbursts of physical violence because their mockery undermines the victim's manhood.

5. On Cretan understandings of risk and chance, see especially Malaby 1999, 2002b, 2003a.

6. The sense of concentricity is very strong, and many examples could be provided (see also Herzfeld 1985: 9–10, 19, 37). Consider especially this reflection on the preference for endogamy, whether local, regional, or national. An elderly Rethemniot of Asia Minor origin is speaking: "I married in [i.e., someone from] my village. I didn't want to marry someone from another [kseno] place. Because in myself I am so ethical I married someone from my place, from my village, so no one could [say anything against me, or ask,] 'Why did you marry someone from your village?' or whatever. I want to show that I am a true Greek! That I haven't married a 'foreign' [kseni] woman. No! Because I am a real Cretan, that's why I did this thing!"

7. Kasfir 1987: 37. The Tiv declaration that "everywhere is my country" superficially resembles an oft-quoted ancient Greek proverb: "Wherever there is a land, it is my fatherland." That proverb, however, while originally linked to a view of Hellenism as a culture unconnected to descent or territory, has acquired in the context of the modern Greek nation-state (which is, after all, a relatively recent invention) the sense that Greeks are adaptable emigrants who carry their Greek homeland inside them. Kasfir attempts to link degrees of originality and invention to types of political control. His analysis is an interesting experiment that nevertheless begs two important questions. First, any such correlations must take account of the fact that resemblance is itself subjective and culturally defined, while "artistic freedom" (Kasfir 1987: 41) is a version of individualism, a Eurocentric concept that cannot be read into artifacts without risking violence to the

aesthetic of their producers. Second, Kasfir attributes central importance to patronage in defining the range of aesthetic variation, but patronage presumably affects artistic production only when it is directly concerned with it. That, however, is not always an important form of patronage. It has rarely been so in the Greece of modern times, a country that has in other respects operated for most of its history as a nation-state under conditions of extensive political patronage (see, e.g., Campbell 1964). Scoditti (1982), writing of the Melanesian society of Kitawa, describes a context in which apprentice woodcarvers receive very explicit instruction but are not allowed to vary the spatial arrangement of symbols; this rigidity, which places spatial arrangement above symbolic interpretation, requires an aesthetic discipline that subordinates style to strongly hierarchical and ritually embedded considerations of appropriateness.

8. The localized orientalism implicit in treatments of the Balkans (on which, see especially the critique by Todorova [1997]) also spilled over into political attitudes toward Eastern Europe both before and after the collapse of the Communist regimes there. The history of approaches to aesthetics in the region cannot be understood independently of this political economy of culture.

9. See Barnard 1977; Brubaker 1989; Herzfeld 1990; Kenna 1985; Uspensky 1976.

10. Jackson 2002: 126.

11. This is the central theme of Herzfeld 1985.

12. See Befu's (2001) extended treatment of this point.

13. Holmes 2000; Taylor 1990.

14. See Kostis Papadakis's (1994) locally produced—and thus doubly relevant—study of Chrysostom's ideas about education. While we should beware of overdrawing parallels between religious and work discipline even in societies where they are more explicitly linked in everyday discourse than is the case on Crete (see, e.g., Marchand 2001: 109, for a strong contrast between slack religious observance and a strong work ethic among Yemeni minaret builders), it would be surprising had the long tradition of links between monastic and secular life in the Greek Orthodox tradition left no mark on ideas and practices concerned with the disciplining of the working body.

15. Bourdieu (1977: 82 on *hexis* and 164–171 on *doxa*) uses these terms in a manner that is strikingly close to the meanings given by Chrysostom. We should not forget that, for the Orthodox Church, *anthropologia* is the study of humanity, not as an object of scholarly critique, but as an ethical exercise (see Ellverson 1981). Some terminological convergence is to be expected and in this case indicates a direct relationship between monastic ideals of bodily discipline and our growing understanding of the articulation of meaning with embodied experience.

16. The problem here is precisely, as Asad (1993: 27–54) notes, that anthropological definitions of religion are so deeply rooted in Christian models that their analytic and comparative utility is seriously compromised. The problem is compounded when, as here, the object of analysis is the relationship among the practices of a people whose religion is a form of Christianity strongly associated with the very terminology of anthropology itself. See, further, Herzfeld 1987a: 32.

17. There is a direct parallel between the condition of *anthropi*, "human beings," flawed creatures whose sinful state is dramatized in the story of the expulsion from Eden,

and Greeks, who, as *Romii* rather than as glorious Hellenes, must live with the cultural imperfections that flow from the ignominious collapse of the Byzantine Empire. See Herzfeld 1987a: 33–36. What Asad (1993) says about the Christian foundations of most anthropological definitions of "religion," moreover, is especially pertinent here, where it would be all too easy to overlook the specific characteristics of Eastern Orthodox Christianity in contrast to the Western versions of Christianity, especially those influenced by the Aristotelian and Cartesian mind-body dualism and excoriated by some theologians of the now-ascendant Neo-Orthodox persuasion (notably Yannaras 1992). If Greece is a crucial site for decentering the European bias in studies of nationalism, as I have argued here and elsewhere, Orthodoxy is similarly important for testing the extent to which analysis can be said to presuppose a generically Christian definition of religion rather than one determined specifically by Western Christian doctrine.

18. On the Orthodox-inspired plan of the houses of left-wing Asia Minor refugees in Piraeus, see Hirschon 1989: 139; on the modeling of the nuclear family on the Holy Family, see Campbell 1964: 354; and on the cosmological underpinning of bureaucrats' excuses, see Herzfeld 1992: 127–157. See also, on Catholic Italy, Kertzer 1980: 162–168, 1996: 41, 74.

19. See Campbell's (1964: 190, 32) vivid description of how Sarakatsani react to violence against children, for example.

20. Papadakis 1994: 81.

21. Du Boulay 1974: 82.

22. The fullest discussion of Original Sin in the social attribution of responsibility is Campbell 1964: 324–329; on its secular extensions in the Greek cultural universe, see Herzfeld 1987a: 35–36.

23. The Neo-Orthodox movement, which has become extremely influential politically among members of both major political parties, seeks a return to Byzantine theological roots that predate the bureaucratization of the church through its sometimes very close relationship with the official structures of the state. A major representative of this movement, and one of the most unequivocally critical of what he regards as the hegemonic materialism of the West, is the philosopher-theologian Christos Yannaras (Giannaras) (e.g., 1992). See also n. 29, below.

24. For a valuable critique of the distinction between folk and official religion, see especially Stewart 1991: 8–16, 144–153.

25. Willis [1977] 1981: 56.

26. Exalting manual labor in this fashion is itself a mode of inculcation that confirms and perpetuates hegemony (Gramsci 1988: 306–307, 312). The Gramscian model of hegemony is deployed by Willis ([1977] 1981) to explain the prevalence among working-class youths of the idea that manual labor is worthier than mental; see the application of a similar argument to hierarchical ideologies of gender in Cowan 1990. On the so-called culture of poverty, see Lewis 1966, 1971, and critiques by, among others, Leacock (1971) and Tyrwhitt (1967).

27. See Danforth 1976.

28. On the role of Cartesian rationalism in the management of colonial dominion, for example, see Rabinow 1989. See also Lloyd 1990; Tambiah 1990.

29. The most explicit of such attacks are to be found in the writings of Christos Yannaras (e.g., 1972, 1978, 1992). Not all Neo-Orthodoxy is anti-Western, but strongly anti-Western feelings were fanned by American and British military operations in predominantly Orthodox and neighboring Serbia among a Cretan population already ideologically (on the Left) and theologically (on the Right) deeply suspicious of Western intentions. Because of its criticism of the formal church and the Cartesian (or "Protestant") rationality that the church has embraced in the pursuit of temporal authority, Neo-Orthodoxy also potentially represents a real threat to the authority of the state, although—indeed, perhaps because—it has adherents in both of the main political parties.

30. Asad 1993: 27–54.

31. Coy 1989c; Bureau and de Saivre 1988; Chevallier 1991; Delbos and Jorion 1984; Kondo 1990; Lave and Wenger 1991; Singleton 1998.

32. Coy 1989b: 2–3.

33. Singleton 1989: 13.

34. Buechler 1989.

35. Singleton 1989.

36. This is a stereotype that Kondo was concerned to contest, although there is some debate about how far she succeeded in doing so. See also, comprehensively, Befu 2001.

37. Jenkins 1994.

38. Lave and Wenger 1991.

39. In her early and important critique of binary oppositions between formal and informal modes of learning, Lave (1982: 182) argued that craft transmission was not the whole or even the major focus of artisan-apprentice interaction. Argenti (2002) similarly explores continuities that subvert another dualism, that between apprenticed and nonapprenticed woodcarvers in a Cameroonian society. In undermining that simplistic binary opposition, these continuities also index the power dynamics that the distinction sustains.

40. E.g., Coy 1989a; Jenkins 1994; Stoller and Olkes 1987.

41. See the critique by Karp and Kendall 1982.

42. Lave and Wenger 1991.

43. The novelist Dimitris Khatzis (1977) provides a vivid portrait of an apprentice who describes himself as a *khazopouli*—one who likes to lounge around watching the world go by. The term is redolent of the adjective *khazos*, "stupid," but also of the verb *khazevo*, "to gaze aimlessly," and thus again suggests the same mixture of foolishness and guile. (Veïkou [1998: 255–258] offers a splendid account of the term *khazos* as a social evaluation that does not stigmatize but does index social marginality.) Khatzis's hero also compares the literal-minded efficiency of a German-run factory (where the lad allows his bosses to condescend to him, secure in the knowledge that he actually knows more than they do) with the haphazard hours of a master carpenter whose style recalls many of the features I have described here for the artisans of Rethemnos.

44. The image of the idealized Hellene is an issue of self-presentation. See Goffman 1959; Herzfeld 1997b: 9; Hirschon 1992.

45. Here, see Strathern's (2000: 5 and 15 n. 9) extremely interesting comment on the need to define the location of indifference in the analysis of bureaucratic practice.

46. The conventional, Weberian view is that modernity (here represented in the financial sphere by the banks) is antithetical to risk. This perspective has been analytically criticized by Malaby (2002b, 2003a). Recasting aversion to risk as a way of *performing* modernity works well here, as it shows how the elite distances itself from classes it regards as representing outmoded tradition and unacceptable risk.

47. Here there is again an obvious parallel with the international context in which alleged Greek predilections for conspiracy theories earn them the punitive derision of those against whom the theories are directed, thereby producing well-oiled self-fulfilling prophecies on both sides.

48. See Terrio 2000; Ulin 1996; Yanagisako 2002. I am indebted to Arthur Kleinman for the American examples.

49. Blum (2000) describes the devastating effects of deskilling in the United States.

50. See, for example, the discussion of how European Union rhetoric produces "the transformation of contingency into necessity, and necessity into virtue" (Weiss and Wodak 2000: 80), in advancing a neoliberal model of globalization.

51. In a perhaps not quite unconscious echo of neoliberal ideology, Cretan highlanders told me that this kind of competitiveness was beneficial, not destructive; see Herzfeld 1985: 62, 232–238.

52. Being very struck by similar agglomerations of shops all doing the same kind of business in Bangkok, I asked about whether this created excessive competition. My question was usually treated as barely comprehensible; local merchants argued that customers needed to be able to compare goods of the same sort in a common area, and this conviction is also reproduced now in the spatial organization of shopping malls.

Chapter Three

1. Because such disavowals may be part of a performance convention in which self-assertiveness is viewed negatively, and are almost always concessions to etiquette even where boasting is expected (Bauman 1977: 22), they are displays of competence in their own right.

2. Examples are to be found in Coy 1989c; Delbos and Jorion 1984; and Singleton 1998.

3. I owe this observation to James L. Watson.

4. Friedl 1962: 75.

5. See, for example, Leitch's (1996: 242–245) splendid account of Carrara marble workers' embodied sense of battling the mountain that they quarry.

6. See the rather caustic debunking by Damer (1988).

7. Such, at least, is the local rhetoric, although many anthropologists seem to have taken this at face value as a description of social relations. George Foster's (1965) "limited good" model offers an excellent illustration of the approach; but see du Boulay and Williams 1987.

8. Such affectations of simplicity—often rather insistently announced even as a

guest is struck by the host's opulent generosity—provide a means for wealthier bourgeois to defend their status against encroachment by the newly rich who lack the necessary sense of refinement. Ostentatious simplicity of this sort ironically reproduces the demonstratively quiet modesty of the truly strong men of Rethemnos and its hinterland; in each case, an ostentatious silence announces that one has skillfully mastered the means of access to the highest level of one's class identity and that one may even be about to transcend it. It is revealing to compare the French bourgeois concern with modesty, which, although on an even grander scale, follows similar principles (Le Wita 1994: 57).

9. See Herzfeld 1991a: 60–61, for a discussion of "simplicity" as a bourgeois affectation.

10. The introduction of the plural form of address into spoken Greek appears to be derived from French and nicely encapsulates the "civilizing process" that such pro-Western neoclassicists as Admantios Koraes hoped to encourage among their allegedly less sophisticated compatriots.

11. It is not clear whether the socially greater offense was the act of theft or the failure to get away with it.

12. One commentator even sourly suggested that many of the young men were currently earning rich wages as gigolos!

13. The type of cunning that theft suggests is regarded as more laudable in men than in women. Although stealing has distinctly male connotations in Cretan rural society (see also Angioni 1989), Maher's (1987: 136–145) data from Turin show that elsewhere in southern Europe at least, "stealing with the eyes" (a commonly attributed tactic of Rethemniot male craft apprentices) is a mark of class insubordination rather than of gender alone. On Crete, however, relations among women working together appear generally to be much less hierarchical than those among men, women have joined the public workforce (as opposed to working at home) much more rarely, and those who do enter the workforce emphasize artistry rather than craft as their main professional goal and characteristic. Thus, the almost exclusive association of masculinity with working-class identity in Rethemnos impedes the widespread development of a parallel pattern of female insubordination in the workplace; it appears more identifiably within domestic spaces (see Herzfeld 1991b: 85–93).

14. The implications of "not allowing" someone to act are distinctly political; the phrase often figures in explanations of Greek diplomatic failures ("they [the Great Powers] would *not let us* act"). Here the context might appear more benign, but we should remember that acts of hospitality and generosity can always serve to imply symbolic control and moral superiority; see Herzfeld 1987b.

15. See Brown and Gilman 1960 and critiques by Kendall (1981) and Sifianou (1992). See also Chock's (1987) discussion of irony and stereotypes.

16. Greenfeld 1992: 15–17. The term "resentment" may strike some readers as too psychologistic, but it does convey the way that the attitudes underlying the push for independence are often represented by the principal actors and their chroniclers themselves. Indeed, the idiom of "not being allowed" to act freely can be read as residual expressions of *ressentiment* by those who feel that national independence is incomplete or has been compromised.

17. Scott's (1985) widely (and justly) admired model of resistance has come in for a measure of (also very interesting and well-considered) criticism; see especially Abu-Lughod 1990; Reed-Danahay 1993.

18. Cf. the Bangkok scene reported by Mills (1999).

19. The amount of dialectal variation on Crete is still relatively high, and those hailing from the higher villages of Milopotamos sound particularly rustic to people born in or near Rethemnos.

20. I am particularly indebted to Eleftheria Deltsou and Vassiliki Yiakoumaki, who both, independently of each other, drew my attention to this further semantic reverberation.

21. A *kalfas* is an apprentice who already has enough experience to work on his own. For the initial stage, the term *tsiraki* (from Turkish *çirak*) is still sometimes used; occasionally people will speak as though *parayos* (foster son) were the second stage, between *tsiraki* and *kalfas*. For a detailed historical account of how this progression worked in mainland Greece, see Papageorgiou 1986.

22. See the brief representations in the novel by Nakou (1955), the memoir *Tale of a Town* by Prevelakes (1976), and my discussion (Herzfeld 1997c) of the writings of Nenedakis.

23. The term *meraki* is of Turkish origin; see Herzfeld 1997c: 271. There is also the sense that enjoyment, sometimes also known as *kefi* (on which see especially Cowan 1990), allows the independently minded artisan the opportunity of limiting the actual amount of work undertaken, since the expression *kano to kefi mou* can be loosely translated as "I do as I wish"; on this, see Kardulias 2000: 278. That attitude allowed Kardulias's informant to adapt gracefully to a situation in which, having neither a son to succeed him (he had learned from his own father) nor any likelihood of finding an apprentice, he had to face a gradual diminution of his activity as old age began to slow him down. But there is also a sense here of what Malaby (2002b) calls "instrumental nonchalance," in which *kefi* is the antithesis of calculation; in cases such as that described by Kardulias, it becomes a way of asserting defiance and independence of action in the face of inexorable physical and hence also economic decline: appearances to the contrary, it is a denial of calculation and an assertion of bravado.

24. Nenedakis 1976: 67; see also Herzfeld 1997c: 264.

25. The form *dhioti* is *katharevousa* (purist Greek) for the more usual demotic (every-day) *yati* and adds authority and emphasis to the rhetorical claim to lucid reasoning here.

26. Cardona (1989: 90–93) has usefully suggested that the practice of imitation in artisanal knowledge transmission incorporates the transmission of appropriate terminology; abstract knowledge is thus dependent on an embodied mode of learning.

27. Lave and Wenger 1991: 85.

28. See especially Bourdieu 1982.

29. The Greek word *kalamaras* (plural, *kalamaradhes*), "pen pusher," is derived from *kalami*, the reed that was the main part of old pens; this is a commonly heard and usually contemptuous term on Crete and Cyprus and received a degree of notoriety in Greece through Kazantzakis's liberal use of it (see especially *Freedom or Death* [1956] and *Zorba the Greek* [1952], both of which celebrate some of the masculine attitudes described here, albeit in highly intellectualizing terms).

30. Willis [1977] 1981: 96. As Willis (149) points out, furthermore, in the British working-class context pen pushing stands for a reversal of the sexual prowess and physical strength associated with masculinity, just as it does in Crete.

31. Blum (2000) presents his ethnography as a critique of the social effects of neoliberal restructuring policies in the United States and globally.

32. Willis [1977] 1981: 148.

33. See especially her discussion of the evocation of exoticism through the use of "Aztec" motifs (Terrio 2000: 241–248).

34. See Shore and Wright 2000; Strathern 2000. Anthropology itself faces the same risks, but at least it does not carry the same level of cultural glory.

35. See Comaroff 1985: 221, 242–245; Comaroff and Comaroff 1997: 234–273; Orlove 1997.

36. See the critique of economism in Bourdieu 1977: 172; compare his intensified appeal to the potentially quite economistic model of cultural capital in *Distinction* (1984), where, clearly, it appears to make particularly good sense, because as readers we are led to expect precisely this kind of metaphor.

37. This is the logic of the "audit culture" that has recently been applied so savagely to British and Australian higher education in particular (see especially Shore and Wright 2000).

38. I have conducted research on the gentrification of central Rome in 1999–2000 and am working on publishing the findings in detail; meanwhile, see Herzfeld 2001. Much of the drive to remove potentially troublesome, economically weak populations from historic city centers has passed from the hands of openly authoritarian states (such as the Fascist state under Mussolini) into those of the citizens of proudly self-proclaimed democracies, under whose tutelage gentrification's more diffuse sources and the great economic power that often supports it arguably make it all the harder to combat.

39. Willis remarks that the "damnation" of British working-class lads "is experienced, paradoxically, as a form of true learning, appropriation and as a kind of resistance" ([1977] 1981: 113). They develop a sense of self-valuation by opposing what they see as the dominant value system. The Cretan artisans' apprentices, by contrast, are directly induced into "traditional" roles, of which a spirit of insubordination is all but explicitly part and parcel.

Chapter Four

1. This is a familiar pattern in European labor history; see especially the argument advanced by Phillips and Taylor (1980: 84–86) that in Britain men, especially when threatened with deskilling by their industrial masters, refused to attribute skill to women at all but instead fought to relegate the labor contributed by women to the undifferentiated and subordinate category of women's work. On Crete, women's skills, while often recognized as such, are not embedded in a masculine ethos of struggle; they are treated as simply irrelevant to the larger battle between industrial deskilling and heroic traditionalism, because they are inextricably bound to a domestic and subordinate form of tradition.

2. On male agonistic displays in coffeehouses, see Campbell 1964: 97. Papataxiarchis (1991: 167) emphasizes for a village on Lesbos that men who meet in

coffeehouses are "friends of the heart"; in the company of such friends, men often escape the sometimes disconcerting demands of kinship solidarity. In the Cretan highland villages the pattern is similar but is already somewhat predetermined in that coffeehouses are identified with agnatic clans and draw most of their clientele from the proprietors' patrilineal kin (Herzfeld 1985: 59–60). Cowan's (1990: 60, 218–219) account of the Greek women's *parea* (group of friends) offers a suggestive basis for comparison, although regional variation in patterns of solidarity and obligation must be taken into account in any comparative analysis. Papataxiarchis (1991: 165–166) gives an interesting account of how the sense of *parea* emerges among unrelated men.

3. In applying the concept of feminization, I follow Ferguson's (1984) usage. Speaking of the pre–World War II past, artisans often describe apprentices as "little slaves." The sense of servility also perhaps evokes images of how Greeks today have learned to think that the Turkish (i.e., Ottoman) authorities treated their Greek subjects and is to be contrasted with the term for "dignity" *(aksioprepia)*, an etymological cognate of the terminology of value and social worth.

4. I should also emphasize that these conventions take on added salience in places like western Crete, where agnatic kinship and succession are unusually important and to which the encompassing national society attributes an especially dramatic devotion to masculinity. Such local peculiarities account for much of the difference between Reizakis's (2001) useful account of social poetics on Chios and my own ethnographic reporting from Crete; and what she describes also confirms by contrast, I suggest, that patrilineality and masculine aggression serve to marginalize those who continue to embrace them in the present, self-consciously modernist age—especially when they do so by using feminization as a way of marginalizing other males. It is not so much that Cretan women never experience the play of freedom Reizakis describes for their Chiot counterparts as that many Cretans feel to a considerable extent tied to the traditionalist tethering post defined by a strong association between their island and heroic masculine ideals as celebrated by Kazantzakis and others (see Reizakis 2001: 27, 31).

5. See Cowan 1990; Willis [1977] 1981.

6. The questions were posed both in written form on the screen and with voice-over and were supplemented whenever respondents appeared to want to engage me in conversation about what they were seeing. The method produced, not a set of quantifiable data, but something much more important: a means of evaluating my own interpretations of gesture and expression. I particularly asked respondents to interpret hand or arm and eye movements as well as overall posture, inquiring whether they thought the apprentices were learning as they worked. I also suggested that they try to imagine what the master and apprentice might actually be saying. The twenty Irakliots and three Khaniots I interviewed in their hometowns were mostly middle-class people (teachers and students and business people), although some were of quite recent rural origin. They did not know the individuals whose actions they were observing, a situation required both by ethics and by my wish to focus particularly on locally entertained cultural expectations and stereotypes without the effects of long mutual acquaintance. See my initial description of this method in Fernandez and Herzfeld 1998: 99–101.

7. Hirschon's (1992) article has the advantage of carrying a discussion that was already familiar from rural contexts (see especially du Boulay 1974; Friedl 1962) into the context of people who live in urban and cosmopolitan settings, showing that training in

agonistic social relations exhibits what to advocates of a modernist view of the state or of an evolutionary "civilizing process" (Blok 1981, 2001; Elias 1978) might seem to be a surprising degree of cultural persistence. Lancy (1980: 271) has documented the ways in which, among the Kpelle of Liberia, children act out roles that allow them to experiment with the idea of becoming apprentice blacksmiths; they learn the social roles along with the external displays of technique that they must then, if they are indeed apprenticed to blacksmiths, learn through the harsh and often taciturn mode of instruction that accompanies most forms of craft apprenticeship around the world.

8. On wife beating, see especially Campbell 1964: 152; although I occasionally heard of it in rural Crete, it seems to have become rarer (or, because it was viewed as uncivilized, more embarrassing) by the time of my fieldwork in the 1970s and later—one positive effect, one might say, of the global hierarchy of value. On the conceptualization of women as objects of male contest, see Herzfeld 1985: 152–162.

9. De Certeau (1984: xix) usefully defines tactics as lacking the dimensions of power and determinate structure that he attributes, by contrast, to strategy. Thus, what Rethemniot apprentices learn about social life consists of tactical ingenuity (a stand that, in de Certeau's words, has "no base where it can capitalize on its advantages, prepare its expansions, and secure independence with respect to circumstances") rather than of strategic command; every transient success risks placing the actor at the mercy of his victim in the longer term.

10. On that mission, see especially Fabian 2000.

11. See, for example, du Boulay 1974: 172–173, 191. One is also reminded of the ancient story of the Spartan lad who allowed a stolen fox cub to gnaw out his entrails rather than reveal his crime; what mattered more than all else was to remain undetected to the end. I am not necessarily suggesting direct cultural continuity here; such a heavy emphasis on dissimulation is common in many peasant cultures (see, e.g., Gilsenan 1976).

12. Structural nostalgia is the longing for a past characterized by mutual respect and reciprocity, or by other forms of harmony and balance, and is also structural in the sense that it remains as an institutionalized ache from generation to generation. See Herzfeld 1997b: 22, 90.

13. We shall later see (chap. 6) that business partnerships are said to break up because the partners' wives quarrel, a reproduction in the world of daily commerce of an older view of the instability of extended households.

14. For an account of female insubordination and practical powerlessness, see Herzfeld 1991b.

15. Lanoue 1991: 55.

16. See discussions in Herzfeld 1997c: 221–222; Malaby 2002b: 293, 2003a: 15, 83–88.

17. Bourdieu's usage of "misrecognition" (1977: 5–6) appears to be a relative, nonevaluative rendition of the Marxist definition of ideology as false consciousness. Willis ([1977] 1981: 177) similarly sees as evidence of misrecognition the fact that, in the case of British schools processing working-class boys, "some of the real functions of institutions work counter to their stated aims." Certainly there is a clash between the stated aims of these institutions and the actual effects on the boys' consciousness and actions, but whether this is a functionally productive misrecognition and whether those in charge

realize or even deliberately develop its effects remain unclear. In the Rethemniot case, acknowledging the *convention* whereby artisans refuse in a generic sense to recognize as intentional the process of inculcating social attitudes that I describe here does not commit analysis to any assessment of how far particular artisans *actually* failed to realize that they had intended it to have such brutalizing and superficially counterproductive effects.

18.   The most famous example of this model is that advanced by Lévi-Strauss (1963a: 281); see my critique (Herzfeld 1987a: 60) and Fabian's related argument about the objectivist underpinnings of the structuralist project (1983: 61).

19.   See especially Friedl 1962: 80; Hirschon 1992: 50.

20.   Lanoue (1991: 55), in making this observation, also recognizes the risks that the master takes by leaving so much to the ambiguities of nonverbal and indirect communication. This might simply be the result of a calculated weighing of the benefits and losses of spending time on instruction, but I suspect that it in fact indicates that masters more or less deliberately expose themselves to such risks in order to toughen up their more promising apprentices through the danger and actual experience of failure.

21.   Lanoue 1991: 55.

22.   Papadakis 1994.

23.   Within the inner spaces of cultural intimacy, ostensibly hostile criticisms can become expressions of deep affection. Greek men often address their closest friends with what are literally very insulting adjectives. This forms part of the constant mutual testing that is a feature of Greek male interaction; it is also an affirmation of the generic sense that, among humans defined by their necessary and entirely amiable imperfections, saints may be the worst kind of company. It also offers a target for those who wish to be offended (although they thereby risk ridicule), and it suggests ready-made explanations for the ease and frequency with which quarrels erupt.

24.   Such aural sensitivity is characteristic of people who work with their bodies. In some cases, such as the Carrara marble quarrymen described by Leitch, it can literally make the difference between life and death (1996: 243–244).

25.   Maher 1987: 136. The Turin seamstresses discussed by Maher were trapped in a subaltern position in relation to elite women, in part by their insubordinate manners. They would occasionally rise to the position of senior craftswoman *(première* or *coupeur)*, but those who made it to that rank feared the competition of their juniors; and these senior members of the ateliers had to learn to deal deferentially with clients about whom they amassed considerable amounts of personal information. They were also subject to sometimes brutal forms of discipline but recalled their social solidarity with pleasure and understood that the work entailed a "passion" (138), analogous to the Cretan artisans' "love" for theirs. In all these respects, the Turin seamstresses' apprentices experienced their roles much as do the male apprentices of Rethemnos. The major difference is that marriage debarred them from rising to the highest ranks and indeed usually got them fired. They were thus trapped in a different form of class hegemony, one intensified by the comparable hegemony of gender (see Cowan 1990: 11–14), although, like their male Cretan counterparts, a few of them, exceptionally, succeeded in escaping its constraints (Maher 1987: 143). In the end, however, their relative sexual freedom, which contravened a strongly gendered class hierarchy further strengthened by its endorsement by state

institutions and laws, limited their chances of upward social mobility at least as powerfully as the reproduction of aggressive masculinity today limits that of young Rethemniot artisans.

26. As do their Cretan counterparts, Japanese artisans express frequent concern about the danger that well-trained apprentices can too easily set up in competition with their erstwhile masters. See Singleton 1989, 1998. The notion of "stealing with the eyes" appears so commonplace in some countries that, for example, the Italian anthropologist Giulio Angioni (1989) could use it as the title of an essay without ever actually discussing it—an ironic reversion to the kind of unconscious acquisition of knowledge about which he was writing!

27. Indeed, until very recently reciprocal theft formed the principal basis of mutual recognition and alliance formation among powerful local shepherds from different villages and was seen as a positive activity in relation to rivals worthy of co-optation as well as, in the past, wealthy landowners, Turks, and anyone who dared to break the well-defined rules of the animal-theft game. See Herzfeld 1985: 31.

28. An analysis of the lamenting appears in Herzfeld 1993.

29. Hsu 1999: 57, 53.

30. Since modernity is conventionally associated with bureaucratic surveillance, especially by a nation-state, it is easy to see how such practices of performative secrecy appear to exclude their exponents from the general aura of modernity. But the Greek state, not unlike that of the United States and indeed that of many another country ideologically and historiographically claimed as the product of rebellion against authority, must also deal with an inbuilt proclivity on the part of its citizens to cite an alleged national character trait of love of independence as the excuse for defying the state's authority as constituted in the present.

31. It is, of course, impossible to know how far he *really* thought they were absurd. He may, after all, have been saving face by blaming his wife for her "female" fears—a standard male technique for evading responsibility for social disasters, as we shall see in the conventional response to the collapse of business and craft partnerships (this is almost always blamed on the wives' mutual jealousy). He may also have been employing a standard device for the protection of cultural intimacy: refusing to admit to something as embarrassing as either wrongdoing on his part or the very possibility that he—or any other Greek—might have anything to fear from its consequences.

32. Campbell (1964: 354–356), for example, discusses the metaphor and model provided by the image of the Holy Family. Yet both he and many other ethnographers provide small but suggestive hints of frequent domestic discord, without expatiating on what is clearly a sensitive topic not only for families and local communities but also for a nation-state grounded in metaphors and ideals of domestic harmony. It was not until Panourgiá (1995) opened this topic up in full that it became an acceptable topos in the anthropological analysis of Greek society, even though it has been one in Greek literature for decades.

33. For the context, see Herzfeld 1991a: 43.

34. See Campbell 1964 and du Boulay 1974: 222 for the fullest descriptions of this stereotype. Its importance in Greek society has certainly faded with urbanization but may still be encountered—at least as an ideal type—in rural settings.

35. See the discussion of their compositional skills in Herzfeld 1985: 136–149. At the same time, they appreciate the value of *controlling* verbality. Indeed, these traits often go together, as we find in other societies that have been socially and politically marginalized by an encompassing national culture (see, e.g., Labov 1972).

Chapter Five

1. For another Greek example, among builders in the Peloponnese, see Konstantinopoulos 1987: 80. Those master builders, like the Cretan artisans, are quite explicit about the importance of forcing their apprentices to "steal" the requisite skills from them. For Yemen, Marchand (2001: 138) remarks that questions might "be construed as a challenge to the Master's authority, and also ... because of the nature of this form of knowledge, it cannot be 'talked about' anyway." Cretan artisans evidently see serious questions less as a challenge than as an irritating nuisance and perhaps also as a sign of a lack of self-sufficiency and initiative and thus as a weakness that must be eradicated in the apprentice.

2. This is probably the most explicit linkage of "stealing with the eyes" with animal theft that I ever heard in the area surrounding Rethemnos (the speaker resided in a large community not far from the zone that is particularly well known for animal rustling), and it is highly revealing of the Cretans' awareness of their collective—if far from evenly distributed—cultural idiosyncrasies. It is also likely that my informant was aware of my earlier interest in reciprocal animal theft, but this does not, in my view, weaken the strength of the association suggested in this remark.

3. Even in the 1990s, rural and sometimes small-town Greeks had an abiding distrust of banks and generally suspected that depositing money in them was very risky. Indeed, in a society where mutual distrust is socially as widely assumed to be normal as it is in rural and small-town Greece, the idea of bank "credit" (*pistosi*, from *pisti*, "trust," "belief") is understandably counterintuitive for many people.

4. The donkey is thought to be the ultimate embodiment of social worthlessness since it is an animal that can suddenly turn difficult or aggressive, and on which it is thus difficult to depend. Quite powerful people can be so described. I once heard the term used of the colonels' regime of 1967–1974 in a Dodecanesian village where most residents seemed to be among their admirers; in such a case, presumably, the term suggested the power of the colonels' brutal unpredictability rather than any form of weakness.

5. As, for example, happened in Italy (see Horn 1994), the dictatorship of Ioannis Metaxas brought in its train a number of social measures that were designed to protect workers' interests and bring the workers themselves under much tighter state surveillance. See Close 1990; Vatikiotis 1998.

6. See Herzfeld 1985 and the extended discussion in Herzfeld 1997b.

7. See Bourdieu 1977: 7.

8. For another example, in which a sure sense of touch allows an artisan to affect a carefree lack of interest in temporal precision, see Kardulias 2000: 280; such performances are not only about male self-confidence but also about the importance in social life of being able to adapt to the social pressures of the moment. These include the general disapproval of focusing too precisely on monetary matters (the "ethos of

imprecision" in Rethemniot commercial relations), which may explain why Kardulias was unable to get his potter friend to explain his pricing calculations in any detail.

9. Needham 1972: 237–238.

10. Angioni 1989: 9.

11. Malaby's (2002a) evocation of the tactile welcome Greeks accorded the arrival of the euro currency in their lives suggests that even at a moment of profoundly bureaucratic and "European" rationalization, they continue, within the more intimate recesses of their lives, to value a physically grounded competence over the formality and abstraction that the international power brokers, or "Eurocrats" (on whom, see Shore 2000: 130–146, 100–111), evidently envisaged.

12. Maher 1987: 136.

13. See the useful discussion in Danforth 1989: 78.

14. Until very recently, smoking was a sign of adult masculinity; women—especially in the rural communities—did not smoke at all, and young men avoided doing so in front of their elders, especially their fathers (see Campbell 1964: 160). Neither restriction seems to apply in the towns today.

15. Literally, "taken out"—a term that suggests an act of display, designed to enhance status.

16. See my discussion of this attitude in Rethemnos in Herzfeld 1991a: 168–174.

17. On Greek evil-eye practices and attitudes, see most recently the useful and comprehensive critical study by Veikou (1998). See also Dionisopoulos-Mass 1976; Herzfeld 1981, 1986.

18. Even success that is entirely attributable to chance—for example, at cards—may provoke anger and, sometimes, charges of cheating and in some cases may lead to violent challenges that, if unmet, would offset the winner's advantage with a loss of social standing; see, for example, Campbell 1964: 97. In Rethemnos, those who have done well for themselves often complain of the backbiting that prevents them from doing even better.

19. As with excuses, the issue is not one of credibility—belief not being ultimately a verifiable property—so much as *acceptability*. See Herzfeld 1992: 129.

20. See Malaby 1999. We see this same attitude dramatized in some male dance forms (see Cowan 1990: 173–180). It underlies the highly risk-prone activities of animal theft—surely one of the most extreme manifestations of Greek masculinity-as-risk-taking (Herzfeld 1985: 140). Both activities entail playing for high stakes by placing the male body in arenas where poor performance can result in crippling ridicule.

21. Bernard 1967.

22. Dimitris Dimitrakos, *Eleftheros Typos*, 17 July 1993, p. 4.

23. "G. Kork.," *Eleftherotypia*, 17 July 1993, p. 7.

24. Fatalism, defined as a preemptive resignation to the whims of destiny (and not simply as after-the-fact attributions of disaster to the whims of fate), is probably an orientalist fantasy wherever it occurs, in which guise it serves to relegate colonized (and colonizable) others to the role of followers; see Herzfeld 1987a: 36, 49–50.

25. Malaby (1999) uses the metaphor of the "aleatory" quality of social life with particularly ironic effect, since his study focuses heavily on gambling.

26. Weber's view of modernity appears to entail the reduction of risk. Malaby (2002b, 2003a) argues against this characterization of modernity, suggesting that it is the management rather than the abolition of chance that is at stake in modernist projects. Empirically he is right, but in the context of negotiating social relations the drive for conceptual and pragmatic certainty (or predictability) does constitute a significant part of the rhetorical self-justification of such systems as state bureaucracies even though—as if to confirm Malaby's insight—their members do often create deliberate uncertainty in pursuit of their own interests.

27. I would also argue that the simplistic bureaucratic mode of accounting that Strathern and others (2000) appropriately call "audit culture" is no less parodic; it renders modernity as a caricature of Weberian rationality and of moral accountability alike.

28. The Greek term for "transcendence"—a watchword of Political Spring (a right-wing party founded by former Foreign Minister Antonis Samaras)—is *ipervasi*. It is a philosophical neologism that nonetheless acquired the aura of a real buzzword during the early 1990s, when Samaras broke with the conservative-neoliberal New Democracy party over what he saw as its insufficient zeal on the issue of how the emergent Republic of Macedonia should be named. The name of his party is creatively ambiguous in Greek: *aniksi* means both "spring" and "opening"; in other words, it is the opening of the balmy weather of summer but also of new political opportunities. "Transcendence," however, is also the description sometimes offered of the way in which fifth-century B.C. Athens developed perspectives on identity and the human condition that went beyond the purely local; see Humphreys 1978: 209–241.

29. The most comprehensive attempt to pursue and modulate such arguments has been propounded by Gilmore in several publications (notably 1990: 45–46, 228), largely on the basis of his research in Andalusia during the Franco era.

30. See Cockburn 1983; Taylor 1983: 214.

31. This is an example of what Bateson (1972: 166) called "deutero-learning," learning how to learn—a modeling of the knowledge acquisition process that can be applied across a wide range of activities, of which artisanship is only one.

32. Argenti 2002: 526 n. 39.

33. The evolutionism of Marcel Mauss shares this nostalgia in significant degree and exhibits a variant of what I have elsewhere called "structural nostalgia" (Herzfeld 1997b: 111), which is reproduced in some of the dominant social theories of the twentieth century.

Chapter Six

1. Lave and Wenger 1991: 40–41.

2. Initiation rituals of this kind appear to occur no longer. For an example from another part of Greece, and apparently modeled on baptism, see Konstantinopoulos 1987: 82.

3. It is hardly coincidental that in Serbian rural societies, where such extended families do subsist in the celebrated institution of the *zadruga*, their eventual breakup is conventionally blamed on the failure of the brothers' wives to get along. See Byrnes 1976.

4. I deliberately invoke the metaphor of Original Sin here; it is deeply rooted in

Greek popular theodicy (see Campbell 1964: 327–329) and ramifies into secular cultural historiography as well (Herzfeld 1992: 5–10, 1997b: 48).

5. See Papataxiarchis 1991.

6. The local term for slave girls (*dhoules*) parallels the common pre–World War II habit of calling male apprentices *sklavakia* (little slaves).

7. Here I am extending an older model of the developmental cycle in anthropological studies of the family, as exemplified in the work of Goody and his associates (1958).

8. They may invoke the metaphor of blood to resolve the apparent paradox that closeness of kinship, by causing "blood to boil," provokes both huge surges of affection and sudden bursts of hatred. See Herzfeld 1987a: 172.

9. On animal theft and its entailment in systems of reciprocity and alliance, see Herzfeld 1985. Campbell (1964: 145–146) shows how Sarakatsani commonly expect that affinal relations will be contracted between members of mutually hostile households.

10. This view should be read as a rhetorical strategy in a society where people often and no less easily express the opposite sentiment.

11. For example, this is the explanation given for the fact that sometimes the authorities manage to discover illegal building activities during the night, usually in violation of historic conservation regulations; see Herzfeld 1991a: 92.

12. In Rethemnos this is both a literal place—a street that is regarded as the central market area of the town—and a metaphor for the arena of public self-display.

13. Note here again that the idea of fatalism as passive resignation is antithetical to Greek popular social philosophy.

14. The statement that one cannot know what another person is thinking is quite conventional in Greek everyday speech but in practice never seems to prevent people from trying to second-guess others' intentions.

15. Here I build on Argenti's (2002: 503) persuasive insight into the relationship between mimesis in craft and selfhood on the one hand and the progressive "liberation" of an apprentice's self on the other. As Argenti goes on to show, the self-liberation thus set in motion can lead to entrapment in what, in the larger context of a society undergoing change, is the constraining force of traditional power structures and aesthetics, as artisans who conversely have not undergone formal apprenticeship but who do have greater access to external sources of aesthetic inspiration challenge the authority of the traditionalists (520–521). Argenti's observation, *mutatis mutandis*, converges closely with my attempt here to demonstrate the Rethemniot artisans' entailment in the global hierarchy of value.

16. The speaker had been invited by NOSMBH to conduct seminars in his craft but had asked that organization to provide him with appropriate Italian tools—which NOSMBH refused to do.

17. This is a crucial and sometimes painful moment in the developmental cycle of pastoral families; see Campbell 1964: 163.

18. Among merchants, for whom the money itself becomes the most easily stolen commodity and for whom there are few skills that one could realistically "steal with one's eyes," patterns of trust are significantly different; news of intraclan theft would deeply embarrass clan members and so it rarely or never happens. It is noteworthy that the

former tailor also praised his father for teaching his own apprentices, contrasting this ideal behavior with the jealousy displayed by the majority of master artisans toward their young helpers. In this way, at least in memory, a loyal son transforms what others might have interpreted as a sign of weakness into one of manly self-confidence and praiseworthy professionalism. This individual, however, had since become a merchant and was therefore engaged in a radically different set of priorities, giving him greater expectations of cooperation among agnates in general.

19. This is the structural converse of historically documented contexts in which artisans' sons were actually classified as apprentices; among these situations, which the weavers of western France from the mid–eighteenth to the early twentieth centuries exemplify (Liu 1994: 234–235), the control of craft knowledge by particular households was more vital to survival than any consideration of building external alliances.

20. The ambiguity of the foster son metaphor is especially apparent when people speculate about possible etymological cognates. *Parayos* literally means "offside son" (cf. English "paranormal," etc.); the more generic *parapedhi* (foster child) actually sounds more affectionate, as when an Irakliot woman watching my video questionnaire used it to indicate the ideal view a boss should have of his apprentices. At a lecture I gave at the University of Crete on my research on apprenticeship (see also chap. 7), however, one member of the audience wryly remarked that one could not envisage the term *parakori* (foster daughter) being used for a female apprentice. This response is a clear indication of the negative affect so characteristic of relations between artisans and their male apprentices, which is not expected to appear between a woman and her female apprentices.

21. Literally, "it doesn't bother me." The verb *niazi* can also have connotations of concern or interest of an affective nature.

22. The phrase she chose to describe her craft was that it was "not a craft business [*viotekhniki*], it's not productive; my work is artistic [*kallitekhniki*]." She also departed from male norms in expressing a strong preference for employing kin (indeed, she would never again employ a nonkinswoman after this one particularly traumatic experience) and relies now on the solidarity of female kin (she was especially happy to employ a sister's daughters). Perhaps predictably, she is verbally very explicit in her instructions to these female apprentices.

23. This is what Malaby (2002b) describes as "instrumental nonchalance."

24. Banfield's (1958) model of "amoral familism" postulates a negative self-view among southern European peasants that locates their values squarely near the bottom of the global hierarchy of value; cf. du Boulay and Williams 1987.

25. The Greek term for "work ethic" is *erghasiaki sinidhisi*, which, rooted in a different social and religious background, has slightly different implications from the English term. *Sinidhisi* is usually translated as "consciousness" in the political sense; it is also used to translate "conscience." It means awareness of one's social obligations.

26. Persuading the workforce to consent in a revaluation that damages its own standing, as in the case of deskilling in American labor (Burawoy 1979; see also Blum 2000), necessarily implies that a set of encompassing values already legitimates the terms of the change. Among Greek artisans, the self-deprecating view of the Greeks as lacking a work ethic reproduces a moral hierarchy already established through political and

historical processes that have pervaded Greek sensibility far beyond the domain of labor relations alone.

Chapter Seven

1. Such formulations are hardy perennials in the discourse of European claims to superiority, as one can see in the ways in which European Union officials frame their understanding of commercial competition, with Europe posited as the home of democracy and culture in an assumed contrast with both Japan and the United States (see Weiss and Wodak 2000: 80–81). On cultural fundamentalism, see Herzfeld 1997a; Jackson 2002: 107–126; Stolcke 1995.

2. This kind of disclaimer follows a common rhetorical modality in Greece ("not that I wish to praise myself, *but* . . . "); see also Chock 1987 for a discussion of the elaboration of such ironic forms among Greek Americans.

3. On the other hand, the designs, sometimes quite elaborate, scratched into the plaster façades of local houses by desperately poor rural-urban migrants in the 1960s and 1970s are not taken seriously and indeed seem to be regarded by the conservation authorities as an abomination rather than as an aesthetic record of working-class struggle; see Herzfeld 1991a: 37.

4. The terminology is especially salient in Crete, where the terms *fili* and *yenos* (classical Greek *genos*), which signify the Greek people as a collectivity defined by shared blood, merge semantically with *yenia* ("agnatic clan," also from *genos*).

5. On electoral patterns and concealment, see Herzfeld 1991a: 125–127. On the role of the patriline in the constitution of Greek national identity, see, variously, Herzfeld 1982, 1987a, and 1997b.

6. Here Prevelakis's *The Tale of a Town* (1976) is especially evocative of the prevailing attitude.

7. The importance of implicit meanings is clear also from the ambiguity, to be described below, of a key proverb about working for one's kin.

8. I owe this insight to James L. Watson. For another patrilineal context in which transmission of the craft moves from father to son, see Marchand 2001: 139, where we nevertheless learn that, ideals notwithstanding, stability of even this tightly introverted association over several generations is not only socially difficult but long recognized as a problem in Arab society. For the structurally analogous case of a matrilineal society in which the normative apprentice is the sister's son of the master carver, see Scoditti 1982: 76–77.

9. See, for example, Kozyris 1993; see discussion in Herzfeld 1997b: 98–105.

10. See, for clear evidence on this point, Bringa 1995.

11. The poet Bounialis (Nenedakis 1979) preserves a memory of the older view of the Ottomans as liberators; the anti-Westernism expressed by a number of poets who witnessed the crumbling of Christian power in the eastern Mediterranean and the concomitant strengthening of the Ottoman presence is also a template for the *ressentiment* that informs the more defensive idioms of nationalism today.

12. See Herzfeld 1985: 86–87; Makris 1992: 65.

13. For a particularly dramatic example, see Herzfeld 1985: 84–90.

14. Again, see Chock 1987.

15. See especially Lekatsas 1977.

16. See Campbell 1964: 95 for an early and comprehensive treatment of the concept of obligation.

17. Literally, "he hears," a common gloss for obedience.

18. He used a Greek variant of a Turkish title for "tyrant" *(dhervenaghas)* in order to conjure up implications of arbitrary and unwarranted power. It is perhaps significant that he chose not to employ the more usual term, *tiranos,* a word of undeniably classical pedigree *(turannos).*

19. Panourgiá (1995) describes the circle of her own family intimates and provides a rare portrait of internal dissension.

20. See especially Lévi-Strauss 1963b.

21. On this ambivalence about Asia Minor refugees elsewhere in Greece and the mutual cultural tension with their host communities, see especially Hirschon 1989: 30–33.

22. See chapter 4 on the reaction of a woman informant viewing the videotaped interactions between masters and apprentices.

23. The figures in table 1 were computed on the basis of the transcribed interviews only; ambiguous attributions of any kind were discounted, as were data clearly derived from other locations, and brother-brother and father-son dyads were excluded by the local cultural logic that denies them the status of apprenticeship relations. While there may be some inaccuracies in the specific identification of relevant cases, the overall proportions give an accurate portrait of the situation.

24. I am indebted to Ada Kalogirou for this version.

25. See Khandambakis 1986: 42 and numerous other collections.

26. See Herzfeld 1992: 128; and on strategic manipulations of related ideas, see Argyrou 1993.

27. This larger sense of overwhelming interest offers a more generalizable sense of the nature of such accusations than the more restrictive category of jealousy, as Spooner (1976) observed with regard to similar concepts in Iran.

28. There are, nevertheless, other situations elsewhere in Greece in which sons work with, and learn from, their fathers by local convention. See, for example, Kardulias 2000: 278; see also Sklavenitis 1996: 84 for an example of a community of potters in western Crete where the craft seems to have been continuously transmitted in the male line for several generations.

Chapter Eight

1. The phrase is from Le Wita's (1994: 72) study of the French bourgeoisie, but it has much larger applicability.

2. On the problems associated with this stereotype as an analytic tool, see Sigaut 1991: 39–40.

3. This is the argument of my article "It Takes One to Know One" (Herzfeld 1995), in which I endeavored to sketch an early version of the model of an experiential ontology that (literally) incorporates concentric identities.

4. See Hannerz and Löfgren 1994; Zabusky 2000. We might productively add to this perspective the intentional uses of sport (Brownell 1995), dance (Doi 2002), and participatory ritual (Bowie 1997; Kligman 1981) by various nation-states in the highly controlled production of belonging through what Malarney (1996) has acutely recognized as the managed teleology of "state functionalism." A government that manages the production of consumer goods designed to act on the human body in predictable ways may well be able thereby to disguise its intervention to a degree that will enhance the effectiveness of its control.

5. See Scott's (1985: 288–289) updating of this image.

6. I conducted research in Rome in 1999–2000 and again in the summer of 2001, with assistance from the J. S. Guggenheim Memorial Foundation and the National Endowment for the Humanities, neither of which should be held responsible for the views expressed here; I also received support as a *professore visitatore* at the University of Rome "La Sapienza" during part of this period.

7. The allusion is to Michael Thompson's "rubbish theory" (Thompson 1979).

8. Compare here what Reed-Danahay (1996: 61–65) reports for the concept of *débrouillardise* from rural France.

9. Here, Daniel's (1996) distinction between "history" and "heritage" may be a useful tool. Gellner (1983: 37) was, as far as I am aware, the first to point out that the transformation of local communities into nation-states entailed a conversion of social relations into cultural collectivities; see also Herzfeld 1992: 28–29 on the associated semiotic transformations in the way people understand their implication in larger identities.

10. Collier's *From Duty to Desire* (1997) is an important theoretical contribution, grounded in her Andalusian ethnography, to our understanding of how notions of tradition and modernity are experienced within local worlds.

11. Collier 1997: 212.

12. See in particular my discussion of writers such as Lelekos and Zambelios (Herzfeld 1982: 40–42, 81–86).

13. See the detailed account by Vipas Prachyaporn (2001).

14. Bourdieu and Passeron 1977, 1979.

15. Willis [1977] 1981: 128.

16. Kondo 1990: 232, 254–255.

17. Willis [1977] 1981: 131.

18. On the effects of deskilling, see especially Willis's well-placed jibe about the ways deskilled laborers can be moved among widely differing jobs in "many conglomerates which indeed include unlikely combinations such as meat-packing and space age exploration" ([1977] 1981: 133). See also Phillips and Taylor 1980 for an account of the impact of deskilling on gender roles and ideology in Britain. A rich sociological literature (e.g., Braverman [1974] 1998; Burawoy 1979) addresses the manipulative fostering of consent to deskilling under the emergence of neoliberal capitalism.

19. The metaphor of refraction, which originates in the work of Evans-Pritchard (1956) on the relationship between the numinous and the social, has a peculiar applicability to attempts, as here, to disinter a particular historical moment (or set of

ethnographic situations) from allegedly commonsensical assumptions about universal principles.

20. An important exception to the pattern (interestingly, by a group of sociologists rather than anthropologists) was achieved by Michael Burawoy (2000) working with a group of his students. This work persuasively demonstrates the importance of an ethnographic focus for detaching analysis from the preemptive logic of globalization and international bureaucracy.

21. Bourdieu and Passeron 1979: 17–21.

22. See, for example, Bowie 1997; Das 1995; Kleinman and Kleinman 1994; Tambiah 1996.

23. Autonomy is, as Hirschon (1992) demonstrates, a key element of the selfhood that the ideology of the state, grounded like most European nationalisms in a model of possessive individualism (see Handler 1985, 1988), expands into a compelling collective self-image as a people unquenchably independent in spirit.

Bibliography

Abélès, Marc. 1989. *Quiet Days in Burgundy: A Study of Local Politics.* Translated by Annella McDermott. Cambridge: Cambridge University Press.

———. 1990. *Anthropologie de l'état.* Paris: Armand Colin.

———. 2000. *Un ethnologue à l'assemblée.* Paris: Odile Jacob.

Abu-Lughod, Lila. 1990. Romance of Resistance: Tracing Transformations of Power through Bedouin Women. *American Ethnologist* 17: 41–55.

Anderson, Benedict. 1983. *Imagined Communities: Reflections on the Origin and Spread of Nationalism.* London: Verso.

Angioni, Giulio. 1989. Rubar cogli occhi: Fare, imparare e saper fare nelle tecnologie tradizionali. In Giorgio Cardona, ed., *La trasmissione del sapere: Aspetti linguistici e antropologici*, 7–16. Rome: Bagatto Libri.

Appadurai, Arjun. 1986. Introduction: Commodities and the Politics of Value. In Arjun Appadurai, ed., *The Social Life of Things: Commodities in Cultural Perspective*, 3–63. Cambridge: Cambridge University Press.

Argenti, Nicolas. 2002. People of the Chisel: Apprenticeship, Youth, and Elites in Oku (Cameroon). *American Ethnologist* 29: 397–533.

Argyrou, Vassos. 1993. Under a Spell: The Strategic Use of Magic in Greek Cypriot Society. *American Ethnologist* 20: 256–271.

———. 1996. *Tradition and Modernity in the Mediterranean: The Wedding as Symbolic Struggle.* Cambridge: Cambridge University Press.

Asad, Talal. 1993. *Genealogies of Religion: Discipline and Reasons of Power in Christianity and Islam.* Baltimore: Johns Hopkins University Press.

Askew, Marc. 1996. The Rise of *Moradok* and the Decline of the *Yarn:* Heritage and Cultural Construction in Urban Bangkok. *Sojourn* 11(2): 183–210.

Athanassoglou-Kallmyer, Nina A. 1989. *French Images from the Greek War of Independence (1821–1830): Art and Politics under the Restoration.* New Haven: Yale University Press.

Banfield, Edward C. 1958. *The Moral Basis of a Backward Society.* Glencoe: Free Press.

Barmé, Scot. 1993. *Luang Wichit Wathakan and the Creation of a Thai Identity.* Singapore: Institute of Southeast Asian Studies.

Barnard, Leslie. 1977. The Theology of Images. In Anthony Bryer and Judith Herrin, eds., *Iconoclasm*, 7–13. Birmingham: University of Birmingham, Centre for Byzantine Studies.

Bastéa, Eleni. 2000. *The Creation of Modern Athens: Planning the Myth.* Cambridge: Cambridge University Press.

Bateson, Gregory. 1972. *Steps to an Ecology of Mind: A Revolutionary Approach to Man's Understanding of Himself.* New York: Ballantine Books.

Bauman, Richard. 1977. *Verbal Art as Performance.* Rowley, Mass.: Newbury House.

Befu, Harumi. 2001. *Hegemony of Homogeneity: An Anthropological Analysis of Nihonjinron.* Melbourne: Trans Pacific Press.

Bernal, Martin. 1987. *Black Athena: The Afroasiatic Roots of Classical Civilization.* Vol. 1. New Brunswick: Rutgers University Press.

Bernard, H. Russell. 1967. Kalymnian Sponge Diving. *Human Biology* 39: 103–130.

Blok, Anton. 1981. Rams and Billy-Goats: A Key to the Mediterranean Code of Honour. *Man,* n.s., 16: 427–440.

———. 2001. *Honour and Violence.* Cambridge: Polity Press; Malden: Blackwell.

Blum, Joseph A. 2000. Degradation without Deskilling: Twenty-Five Years in the San Francisco Shipyards. In Michael Burawoy, ed., *Global Ethnography: Forces, Connections, and Imaginations in a Postmodern World,* 106–136. Berkeley: University of California Press.

Bourdieu, Pierre. 1977. *Outline of a Theory of Practice.* Translated by Richard Nice. Cambridge: Cambridge University Press.

———. 1982. *Ce que parler veut dire: L'économie des échanges linguistiques.* Paris: Fayard.

———. 1984. *Distinction: A Social Critique of the Judgement of Taste.* Cambridge: Harvard University Press.

———. 1991. *Language and Symbolic Power.* Cambridge: Polity.

Bourdieu, Pierre, and Jean-Claude Passeron. 1977. *Reproduction in Education, Society and Culture.* Translated by Richard Nice. London and Beverly Hills: Sage.

———. 1979. *The Inheritors: French Students and Their Relation to Culture.* Translated by Richard Nice. Chicago: University of Chicago Press.

Bowie, Katherine. 1997. *Rituals of National Loyalty: An Anthropology of the State and the Village Scout Movement in Thailand.* New York: Columbia University Press.

Braverman, Harry. [1974] 1998. *Labor and Monopoly Capital: The Degradation of Work in the Twentieth Century.* New ed., New York: Monthly Review Press.

Bringa, Tone. 1995. *Being Muslim the Bosnian Way: Identity and Community in a Central Bosnian Village.* Princeton: Princeton University Press.

Brown, Roger, and A. Gilman. 1960. The Pronouns of Power and Solidarity. In Thomas A. Sebeok, ed., *Style in Language,* 253–276. Cambridge: MIT Press.

Brownell, Susan. 1995. *Training the Body for China: Sports in the Moral Order of the People's Republic.* Chicago: University of Chicago Press.

Brubaker, Leslie. 1989. Byzantine Art in the Ninth Century: Theory, Practice, and Culture. *Byzantine and Modern Greek Studies* 13: 23–93.

Buechler, Hans. 1989. Apprenticeship and Transmission of Knowledge in La Paz, Bolivia. In Coy 1989c: 31–50.

Burawoy, Michael. 1979. *Manufacturing Consent: Changes in the Labor Process under Monopoly Capitalism*. Chicago: University of Chicago Press.

———, ed. 2000. *Global Ethnography: Forces, Connections, and Imaginations in a Postmodern World*. Berkeley: University of California Press.

Bureau, René, and Denyse de Saivre, eds. 1988. *Apprentissage et cultures: Les manières d'apprendre*. Paris: Karthala.

Byrnes, Robert, ed. 1976. *Communal Families in the Balkans: The Zadruga: Essays by Philip E. Mosely and Essays in His Honor*. Notre Dame: University of Notre Dame Press.

Campbell, J. K. 1964. *Honour, Family, and Patronage: A Study of Institutions and Moral Values in a Greek Mountain Community*. Oxford: Clarendon Press.

Cardona, Giorgio. 1989. Aspetti linguistici della trasmissione del sapere tecnico. In Giorgio Cardona, ed., *La trasmissione del sapere: Aspetti linguistici e antropologici*, 89–98. Rome: Bagatto Libri.

Carrier, James G. 1995a. *Gifts and Commodities: Exchange and Western Capitalism since 1700*. London: Routledge.

———, ed. 1995b. *Occidentalism: Images of the West*. Oxford: Clarendon Press.

Chevallier, Denis, ed. 1991. *Savoir faire et pouvoir transmettre*. Paris: Éditions de la Maison des Sciences de l'Homme.

Chock, Phyllis Pease. 1987. The Irony of Stereotypes: Toward an Anthropology of Ethnicity. *Cultural Anthropology* 2: 347–368.

Classen, Constance. 1993. *Worlds of Sense: Exploring the Senses in History and across Cultures*. New York: Routledge.

Close, David. 1990. *The Character of the Metaxas Dictatorship: An International Perspective*. London: Centre of Contemporary Greek Studies, King's College London.

Cockburn, Cynthia. 1983. *Brothers: Male Dominance and Technological Change*. London: Pluto Press.

Collier, Jane Fishburne. 1997. *From Duty to Desire: Remaking Families in a Spanish Village*. Princeton: Princeton University Press.

Comaroff, Jean. 1985. *Body of Power, Spirit of Resistance: The Culture and History of a South African People*. Chicago: University of Chicago Press.

Comaroff, John L., and Jean Comaroff. 1997. *Of Revelation and Revolution*. Vol. 2, *The Dialectics of Modernity on a South African Frontier*. Chicago: University of Chicago Press.

Connerton, Paul. 1989. *How Societies Remember*. Cambridge: Cambridge University Press.

Cowan, Jane K. 1990. *Dance and the Body Politic in Northern Greece*. Princeton: Princeton University Press.

Coy, Michael W. 1989a. Being What We Pretend to Be: The Usefulness of Apprenticeship as a Field Method. In Coy 1989c: 115–135.

———. 1989b. From Theory. In Coy 1989c: 1–30.

———, ed. 1989c. *Apprenticeship: From Theory to Method and Back Again*. Albany: State University of New York Press.

Damer, Seán. 1988. Legless in Sfakia: Drinking and Social Practice in Western Crete. *Journal of Modern Greek Studies* 6: 291–310.

Danforth, Loring M. 1976. Humour and Status Reversal in Greek Shadow Theatre. *Byzantine and Modern Greek Studies* 2: 99–111.

———. 1984. The Ideological Context of the Search for Continuities in Greek Culture. *Journal of Modern Greek Studies* 2: 53–87.

———. 1989. *Firewalking and Religious Healing: The Anastenaria of Greece and the American Firewalking Movement.* Princeton: Princeton University Press.

Daniel, E. Valentine. 1996. *Charred Lullabies: Chapters in an Anthropography of Violence.* Princeton: Princeton University Press.

Das, Veena. 1995. *Critical Events: An Anthropological Perspective on Contemporary India.* Delhi: Oxford University Press.

de Certeau, Michael. 1984. *The Practice of Everyday Life.* Translated by Steven Rendall. Berkeley: University of California Press.

Delbos, Geneviève, and Paul Jorion. 1984. *La transmission des savoirs.* Paris: Maison des Sciences de l'Homme.

Deltsou, Eleftheria. 1995. O "istorikos topos" ke i simasia tis paradhosis ya to ethnos-kratos. *Ethnoloyia* 4: 107–126.

———. 1996. Tradition and Modernity: A Discourse of the Past and the Future. *European Journal for Semiotic Studies* 8: 759–774.

De Martino, Ernesto. [1961] 1994. *La terra del rimorso: Contributo a una storia religiosa del Sud.* Milan: Il Saggiatore.

De Pina-Cabral, João, and Antónia Pedroso de Lima, eds. 2000. *Elites: Choice, Leadership and Succession.* Oxford: Berg.

Desjarlais, Robert R. 1992. *Body and Emotion: The Aesthetics of Illness and Healing in the Nepal Himalayas.* Philadelphia: University of Pennsylvania Press.

Diamandouros, P. Nikiforos. 1994. *Cultural Dualism and Political Change in Postauthoritarian Greece.* Estudio/Working Paper 1994/50. Madrid: Instituto Juan March de Estudios e Investigaciónes.

Dionissopoulos-Mass, Regina. 1976. The Evil Eye and Bewitchment in a Peasant Village. In Clarence Mahoney, ed., *The Evil Eye,* 42–62. New York: Columbia University Press.

Doi, Mary Masayo. 2002. *Gesture, Gender, Nation: Dance and Social Change in Uzbekistan.* Westport: Bergin and Garvey.

Douglas, Mary. 1966. *Purity and Danger: An Analysis of Concepts of Purity and Taboo.* London: Routledge and Kegan Paul.

———. 1970. *Natural Symbols: Explorations in Cosmology.* New York: Pantheon Books.

———. 1975. *Implicit Meanings: Essays in Anthropology.* London: Routledge and Kegan Paul.

Douglas, Mary, and Baron Isherwood. 1979. *The World of Goods.* New York: Basic Books.

du Boulay, Juliet. 1974. *Portrait of a Greek Mountain Village.* Oxford: Clarendon Press.

du Boulay, Juliet, and Rory Williams. 1987. Amoral Familism and the Image of Limited Good: A Critique from a European Perspective. *Anthropological Quarterly* 60: 12–24.

Eco, Umberto. 1976. *A Theory of Semiotics.* Bloomington: Indiana University Press.

Elias, Norbert. 1978. *The Civilizing Process.* Vol. 1. New York: Urizen Books.

Ellverson, Anna-Stina. 1981. *The Dual Nature of Man: A Study in the Theological Anthropology of Gregory of Nazianzus.* Acta Universitatis Upsaliensis. Studia Doctrinae Christianae Upsaliensia, 21. Uppsala: Uppsala University.

Evans-Pritchard, E. E. 1940. *The Nuer: A Description of the Modes of Livelihood and Political Institutions of a Nilotic People.* Oxford: Clarendon Press.

———. 1956. *Nuer Religion.* Oxford: Clarendon Press.

Fabian, Johannes. 1983. *Time and the Other: How Anthropology Makes Its Object.* New York: Columbia University Press.

———. 2000. *Out of Our Minds: Reason and Madness in the Exploration of Central Africa.* Berkeley: University of California Press.

Fardon, Richard. 1999. *Mary Douglas: An Intellectual Biography.* London: Routledge.

Faubion, James D. 1993. *Modern Greek Lessons: A Primer in Historical Constructivism.* Princeton: Princeton University Press.

Ferguson, Kathy E. 1984. *The Feminist Case against Bureaucracy.* Philadelphia: Temple University Press.

Fernandez, James W., and Michael Herzfeld. 1998. In Search of Meaningful Methods. In H. Russell Bernard, ed., *Handbook of Methods in Cultural Anthropology,* 89–219. Walnut Creek: Altamira.

Foster, George McClelland. 1965. Peasant Society and the Image of Limited Good. *American Anthropologist* 67: 293–315.

Fotiadis, Michael. 1985. "Site" as Model of Archaeological Practice. Paper presented at the 7th Theoretical Archaeology Group Meeting, Glasgow.

———. 1993. Regions of the Imagination: Archaeologists, Local People, and the Archaeological Record in Fieldwork, Greece. *Journal of European Archaeology* 1: 151–168.

Friedl, Ernestine. 1962. *Vasilika: A Village in Modern Greece.* New York: Holt, Rinehart, and Winston.

Gefou-Madianou, Dimitra. 2000. Disciplines, Discipline and Reflection: Anthropological Encounters and Trajectories. In Marilyn Strathern, ed., *Audit Cultures: Anthropological Studies in Accountability, Ethics and the Academy,* 256–278. London: Routledge.

Gellner, Ernest. 1983. *Nations and Nationalism.* Ithaca: Cornell University Press.

Gilman, Sander L. 1985. *Difference and Pathology: Stereotypes of Sexuality, Race, and Madness.* Ithaca: Cornell University Press.

Gilmore, David D. 1990. *Manhood in the Making: Cultural Concepts of Masculinity.* New Haven: Yale University Press.

Gilsenan, Michael. 1976. Lying, Honor, and Contradiction. In Bruce Kapferer, ed., *Transaction and Meaning: Directions in the Anthropology of Exchange and Symbolic Behavior,* 191–219. ASA Essays, 1. Philadelphia: Institute for the Study of Human Issues.

Goffman, Erving. 1959. *The Presentation of Self in Everyday Life.* Garden City, N.Y.: Doubleday.

Goody, Jack, ed. 1958. *The Developmental Cycle in Domestic Groups.* Cambridge: Cambridge University Press.

Gramsci, Antonio. 1988. *An Antonio Gramsci Reader: Selected Writings.* Edited by David Forgacs. New York: Schocken.

Greenfeld, Liah. 1992. *Nationalism: Five Roads to Modernity.* Cambridge: Harvard University Press.

Greenhouse, Carol. 1996. *A Moment's Notice: Time Politics across Cultures.* Ithaca: Cornell University Press.

Gupta, Akhil. 1998. *Postcolonial Developments: Agriculture in the Making of Modern India.* Durham: Duke University Press.

Gupta, Akhil, and James Ferguson. 1997. Discipline and Practice: "The Field" as Site, Method, and Location in Anthropology. In Akhil Gupta and James Ferguson, eds., *Anthropological Locations: Boundaries and Grounds of a Field Science,* 1–46. Berkeley: University of California Press.

Han, Seung-Mi. 1995. From Regional Craft to National Art: Politics and Identity in a Japanese Regional Industry. Ph.D. diss., Harvard University.

Handler, Richard. 1985. On Dialogue and Destructive Analysis: Problems in Narrating Nationalism and Ethnicity. *Journal of Anthropological Research* 41: 171–182.

———. 1988. *Nationalism and the Politics of Culture in Quebec.* Madison: University of Wisconsin Press.

Handler, Richard, and Eric Gable. 1997. *The New History in an Old Museum.* Durham: Duke University Press.

Hannerz, Ulf, and Orvar Löfgren. 1994. The Nation in the Global Village. *Cultural Studies* 8: 198–207.

Helms, Mary W. 1993. *Craft and the Kingly Ideal: Art, Trade, and Power.* Austin: University of Texas Press.

Hertz, Ellen. 1998. *The Trading Crowd: An Ethnography of the Shanghai Stock Market.* Cambridge: Cambridge University Press.

Herzfeld, Michael. 1981. Meaning and Morality: A Semiotic Approach to Evil Eye Accusations in a Greek Village. *American Ethnologist* 8: 560–574.

———. 1982. *Ours Once More: Folklore, Ideology, and the Making of Modern Greece.* Austin: University of Texas Press.

———. 1985. *The Poetics of Manhood: Contest and Identity in a Cretan Mountain Village.* Princeton: Princeton University Press.

———. 1986. Closure as Cure: Tropes in the Exploration of Bodily and Social Disorder. *Current Anthropology* 27: 107–120.

———. 1987a. *Anthropology through the Looking-Glass: Critical Ethnography in the Margins of Europe.* Cambridge: Cambridge University Press.

———. 1987b. "As in Your Own House": Hospitality Ethnography, and the Stereotype of Mediterranean Society. In D. D. Gilmore, ed., *Honor and Shame and the Unity of the Mediterranean,* 75–89. Special Publication no. 22. Washington, D.C.: American Anthropological Association.

———. 1990. Icons and Identity: Religious Orthodoxy and Social Practice in Rural Crete. *Anthropological Quarterly* 63: 109–121.

———. 1991a. *A Place in History: Social and Monumental Time in a Cretan Town*. Princeton: Princeton University Press.

———. 1991b. Silence, Submission, and Subversion: Toward a Poetics of Womanhood. In Peter Loizos and Evthymios Papataxiarchis, eds., *Contested Identities: Gender and Kinship in Modern Greece*, 79–97. Princeton: Princeton University Press.

———. 1992. *The Social Production of Indifference: Exploring the Symbolic Roots of Western Bureaucracy*. Oxford: Berg.

———. 1993. In Defiance of Destiny: The Management of Time and Gender at a Cretan Funeral. *American Ethnologist* 20: 241–255.

———. 1995. It Takes One to Know One: Collective Resentment and Mutual Recognition among Greeks in Local and Global Contexts. In Richard Fardon, ed., *Counterworks: Managing the Diversity of Knowledge*, 124–142. London: Routledge.

———. 1997a. Anthropology and the Politics of Significance. *Social Analysis* 41: 107–138.

———. 1997b. *Cultural Intimacy: Social Poetics in the Nation-State*. New York: Routledge.

———. 1997c. *Portrait of a Greek Imagination: An Ethnographic Biography of Andreas Nenedakis*. Chicago: University of Chicago Press.

———. 2001. Competing Diversities: Ethnography in the Heart of Rome. *Plurimondi* 3(5): 147–154.

———. 2002a. The Absent Presence: Discourses of Crypto-colonialism. *South Atlantic Quarterly* 101: 899–926.

———. 2002b. The European Self: Rethinking an Attitude. In Anthony Pagden, ed., *The Idea of Europe: From Antiquity to the European Union*, 139–170. Cambridge: Cambridge University Press; Washington, D.C.: Woodrow Wilson Center Press.

———. 2003. Mia ghnisia elliniki traghodhia. *Neos Ellinismos ke Arkheotita, 18os-19os Eonas: I Kathimerini, Epta Imeres, I Kathimerini* [newspaper, Athens, Greece], special number 2-32 (9 February): 17–19.

Hill, Jane H. 1992. "Today There Is No Respect": Nostalgia, "Respect," and Oppositional Discourse in Mexicano (Nahuatl) Language Ideology. *Pragmatics* 2: 263–280.

Hirschon, Renée. 1989. *Heirs of the Greek Catastrophe: The Social Life of Asia Minor Refugees in Piraeus*. Oxford: Clarendon Press.

———. 1992. Greek Adults' Play, or, How to Train for Caution. *Journal of Modern Greek Studies* 10: 35–56.

Hobsbawm, Eric, and Terence Ranger, eds. 1983. *The Invention of Tradition*. Cambridge: Cambridge University Press.

Holmes, Douglas R. 2000. *Integral Europe: Fast-Capitalism, Multiculturalism, Neofascism*. Princeton: Princeton University Press.

Horn, David G. 1994. *Social Bodies: Science, Reproduction, and Italian Modernity*. Princeton: Princeton University Press.

Hsu, Elisabeth. 1999. *The Transmission of Chinese Medicine*. Cambridge: Cambridge University Press.

Humphreys, S. C. 1978. *Anthropology and the Greeks*. London: Routledge and Kegan Paul.

Jackson, Jean E. 1995. Culture, Genuine and Spurious: The Politics of Indianness in the Vaupés, Colombia. *American Ethnologist* 22(1): 3–27.

Jackson, Michael. 1989. *Paths toward a Clearing: Radical Empiricism and Ethnographic Enquiry.* Bloomington: Indiana University Press.

———. 2002. *The Politics of Storytelling: Violence, Transgression and Intersubjectivity.* Copenhagen: Museum Tusculanum Press.

Japan Cultural Properties Protection Commission. 1967. Ningen Kokuho [Living National Treasures of Japan]. N.p.: Japan Cultural Properties Protection Commission.

Jenkins, Timothy. 1994. Fieldwork and the Perception of Everyday Life. *Man*, n.s., 29: 433–455.

Jenkyns, Richard. 1980. *The Victorians and Ancient Greece.* Cambridge: Harvard University Press.

Kante, Nambala. 1993. *Forgerons d'Afrique noire: Transmission des savoirs traditionnels en pays malinke.* Paris: L'Harmattan.

Kardulias, P. Nick. 2000. The "Traditional" Craftsman as Entrepreneur: A Potter in Ermioni. In Susan Buck Sutton, ed., *Contingent Countryside: Settlement, Economy, and Land Use in the Southern Argolid since 1700*, 275–289. Stanford: Stanford University Press.

Karp, Ivan, and Martha B. Kendall. 1982. Reflexivity and Fieldwork. In Paul Secord, ed., *Explaining Human Behavior*, 249–273. Los Angeles: Sage.

Kasfir, Sidney Littlefield. 1987. Apprentices and Entrepreneurs: The Workshop and Style Uniformity in Sub-Saharan Africa. *Iowa Studies in African Art* 2: 25–47.

Kazantzakis, Nikos. 1952. *Zorba the Greek.* Translated by Carl Wildman. New York: Simon and Schuster.

———. 1956. *Freedom or Death.* Translated by Jonathan Griffin. New York: Simon and Schuster.

Kendall, Martha B. 1981. Toward a Semantic Approach to Terms of Address. *Journal of Language and Communication* 12: 237–254.

Kenna, Margaret E. 1985. Icons in Theory and Practice. *History of Religions* 24: 345–368.

Kertzer, David I. 1980. *Comrades and Christians: Religion and Political Struggle in Communist Italy.* Cambridge: Cambridge University Press.

———. 1996. *Politics and Symbols: The Italian Communist Party and the Fall of Communism.* New Haven: Yale University Press.

Khandambakis, Yeoryios. 1986. *To rizitiko traghoudhi apo tis piyes tou.* 2d ed. Chania: n.p.

Khatzimikhali, Angeliki. 1953. Morfes apo ti somatiaki organosi ton Ellinon stin Othomaniki aftokratoria: I sinteknies—ta esnafia. In *L'Hellénisme contemporain (1453–1953)*, 279–303. Athens: n.p.

Khatzis, Dimitris. 1977. *To dhiplo vivlio.* 2d, rev. ed. Athens: Kastaniotis.

Kiskiras, Io. 1968. *I simvasis mathitias en ti venetokratoumeni Kriti (met' anekdhoton enghrafon ek tou Archivio di Stato tis Venetias).* Athens.

Kleinman, Arthur. 1980. *Patients and Healers in the Context of Culture: An Exploration of the Borderland between Anthropology, Medicine, and Psychiatry.* Berkeley: University of California Press.

———. 1995. *Writing at the Margin: Discourse between Anthropology and Medicine.* Berkeley: University of California Press.

———. 1999. Bioethics and Beyond. *Daedalus* 128(4): 69–97.

Kleinman, Arthur, and Joan Kleinman. 1985. Somatization: The Interconnections in Chinese Society among Culture, Depressive Experiences, and the Meanings of Pain. In Arthur Kleinman and Byron Good, eds., *Culture and Depression*, 429–490. Berkeley: University of California Press.

———. 1994. How Bodies Remember: Social Memory and Bodily Experience of Criticism, Resistance, and Delegitimation following China's "Cultural Revolution." *New Literary History* 25: 707–723.

Kligman, Gail. 1981. *Căluş: Symbolic Transformation in Romanian Ritual.* Chicago: University of Chicago Press.

Koliopoulos, John S. 1987. *Brigands with a Cause: Brigandage and Irredentism in Modern Greece, 1821–1912.* Oxford: Clarendon Press.

Kondo, Dorinne K. 1990. *Crafting Selves: Power, Gender, and Discourses of Identity in a Japanese Workplace.* Chicago: University of Chicago Press.

Konstantinopoulos, Christos G. 1987. *Mathitia stis kombanies ton khtiston tis Peloponnisou.* Athens: Yeniki Grammatia Neas Yenias.

Koptiuch, Kristin. 1999. *A Poetics of Political Economy in Egypt.* Minneapolis: University of Minnesota Press.

Kozyris, P. John. 1993. Reflections on the Impact of Membership in the European Economic Community on Greek Legal Culture. *Journal of Modern Greek Studies* 11: 29–49.

Labov, William. 1972. *Language in the Inner City: Studies in the Black English Vernacular.* Philadelphia: University of Pennsylvania Press.

Lakoff, Robin. 1975. *Language and Woman's Place.* New York: Harper and Row.

Lambiri-Dimaki, Ioanna. 1965. *Social Change in a Greek Country Town: The Impact of Factory Work on the Position of Women.* Athens: Center of Planning and Economic Research.

Lancy, David F. 1980. Becoming a Blacksmith in Gbarngasuakwelle. *Anthropology and Education Quarterly* 11: 266–274.

Lanoue, Guy. 1991. Life as a *Guaglió:* Public and Private Domains in Central and Southern Italy. *Ethnologia Europaea* 21: 47–58.

Lave, Jean. 1982. A Comparative Approach to Educational Forms and Learning Processes. *Anthropology and Education Quarterly* 13: 181–187.

Lave, Jean, and Etienne Wenger. 1991. *Situated Learning: Legitimate Peripheral Participation.* Cambridge: Cambridge University Press.

Leacock, Eleanor Burke, ed. 1971. *The Culture of Poverty: A Critique.* New York: Simon and Schuster.

Leitch, Alison. 1996. The Life of Marble: The Experience and Meaning of Work in the Marble Quarries of Carrara. *Australian Journal of Anthropology* 7: 235–257.

Lekatsas, Panayis. 1977. *I mitriarkhia ke i singrousi tis me tin elliniki patriarkhia.* Athens: Kastanioti.

Lévi-Strauss, Claude. 1963a. *Structural Anthropology.* Translated by Claire Jacobson and Brooke Grundfest Schoepf. New York: Basic Books.

———. 1963b. *Totemism.* Translated by Rodney Needham. Boston: Beacon Press.

Lewis, Oscar. 1966. *La Vida: A Puerto Rican Family in the Culture of Poverty—San Juan and New York.* New York: Vintage Books.

———. [1959] 1971. *Five Families: Mexican Case Studies in the Culture of Poverty.* New York: New American Library.

Le Wita, Béatrix. 1994. *French Bourgeois Culture.* Translated by J. A. Underwood. Cambridge: Cambridge University Press.

Linke, Uli. 1999a. *Blood and Nation: The European Aesthetics of Race.* Philadelphia: University of Pennsylvania Press.

———. 1999b. *German Bodies: Race and Representation after Hitler.* New York: Routledge.

Liu, Tessie P. 1994. *The Weaver's Knot: The Contradictions of Class Struggle and Family Solidarity in Western France, 1750–1914.* Ithaca: Cornell University Press.

Lloyd, G. E. R. 1990. *Demystifying Mentalities.* Cambridge: Cambridge University Press.

Macpherson, C. B. 1962. *The Political Theory of Possessive Individualism: Hobbes to Locke.* Oxford: Clarendon Press.

Makris, Julie. 1992. Ethnography, History and Collective Representations: Studying Vendetta in Crete. In João de Pina-Cabral and John Campbell, eds., *Europe Observed,* 56–72. Basingstoke: Macmillan.

Maddox, Richard. 1993. *El Castillo: The Politics of Tradition in an Andalusian Town.* Urbana: University of Illinois Press.

Maher, Vanessa. 1987. Sewing the Seams of Society: Dressmakers and Seamstresses in Turin between the Wars. In Jane Fishburne Collier and Sylvia Junko Yanagisako, eds., *Gender and Kinship: Essays toward a Unified Analysis,* 132–159. Stanford: Stanford University Press.

Malaby, Thomas M. 1999. Fateful Misconceptions: Rethinking Paradigms of Chance among Gamblers in Crete. *Social Analysis* 43: 141–165.

———. 2002a. Making Change in the New Europe: Euro Competence in Greece. *Anthropological Quarterly* 75: 591–597.

———. 2002b. Odds and Ends: Risk, Mortality, and the Politics of Contingency. *Culture, Medicine, and Psychiatry* 26(3): 283–312.

———. 2003a. *Gambling Life: Dealing in Contingency in a Greek City.* Urbana: University of Illinois Press.

———. 2003b. Spaces in Tense: History, Contingency, and Place in a Cretan City. In Keith S. Brown and Yannis Hamilakis, eds., *The Usable Past: Greek Metahistories,* 171–190. Ranham, Md.: Lexington Books.

Malarney, Shaun Kingsley. 1996. Limits of "State Functionalism" and the Reconstruction of Funerary Ritual in Contemporary Northern Vietnam. *American Ethnologist* 23: 540–560.

Marchand, Trevor Hugh James. 2001. *Minaret Building and Apprenticeship in Yemen.* Richmond: Curzon.

Marcus, George E. 1992. *Lives in Trust: The Fortunes of Dynastic Families in Late Twentieth-Century America.* Boulder: Westview Press.

———. 1998. *Ethnography through Thick and Thin.* Princeton: Princeton University Press.

Mbembe, Achille. 1992. Provisional Notes on the Postcolony. *Africa* 62: 3–37.

McCall, John C. 2000. *Dancing Histories: Heuristic Ethnography with the Ohafia Igbo.* Ann Arbor: University of Michigan Press.

Megas, Georgios A. 1963. *Greek Calendar Customs.* 2d ed. Athens: n.p.

Miller, Daniel. 1997. *Capitalism: An Ethnographic Approach.* Oxford: Berg.

Mills, Mary Beth. 1999. *Thai Women in the Global Labor Force: Consuming Desires, Contested Selves.* New Brunswick: Rutgers University Press.

Mintz, Jerome R. 1982. *The Anarchists of Casas Viejas.* Chicago: University of Chicago Press.

Mosse, George L. 1985. *Nationalism and Sexuality: Respectability and Abnormal Sexuality in Modern Europe.* New York: Howard Fertig.

Nakou, Lilika. 1955. *I kiria Do-Re-Mi.* Athens: Diphros.

Needham, Rodney. 1972. *Belief, Language, and Experience.* Oxford: Blackwell.

Nenedakis, Andreas. 1976. *To khiroghrafo tis Skholis Kalon Tekhnon.* Athens: n.p.

———, ed. 1979. *O kritikos polemos, 1645–1669.* Athens: n.p. [Edition of Marinos Tzane Bounialis's poem.]

Nugent, Stephen, and Cris Shore, eds. 2002. *Elite Cultures: Anthropological Perspectives.* London: Routledge.

Orlove, Benjamin, ed. 1997. *The Allure of the Foreign: Imported Goods in Postcolonial Latin America.* Ann Arbor: University of Michigan Press.

Panourgiá, E. Neni K. 1995. *Fragments of Death, Fables of Identity: An Athenian Anthropography.* Madison: University of Wisconsin Press.

Papadakis, Kostis El. 1994. *Themata aghoyis tou pedhiou kata ton Iero Khrisostomo (singritiki pedhaghoyiki prosengisi tis praghmatias 'Peri Kenodhoksias ke opos dhi tous ghoneas anatrafin ta tekna' kato apo to prisma tis dhiakhronikis pedhaghoyikis skepsis).* 2d ed. Rethimno: n.p.

Papageorgiou, Giorgos. 1986. *I mathitia sta epangelmata: 16–29 ai.* Athens: Yeniki Grammatia Neas Yeneas.

Papataxiarchis, Evthymios. 1991. Friends of the Heart: Male Commensal Solidarity, Gender, and Kinship in Aegean Greece. In Peter Loizos and Evthymios Papataxiarchis, eds., *Contested Identities: Gender and Kinship in Modern Greece,* 156–179. Princeton: Princeton University Press.

Pardo, Italo. 1996. *Managing Existence in Naples: Morality, Action and Structure.* Cambridge: Cambridge University Press.

Parezo, Nancy J. 1983. *Navajo Sandpainting: From Religious to Commercial Art.* Tucson: University of Arizona Press.

Peleggi, Maurizio. 2002. *The Politics of Ruins and the Business of Nostalgia.* Bangkok: White Lotus.

Phillips, Anne, and Barbara Taylor. 1980. Sex and Skill: Notes towards a Feminist Economics. *Feminist Review* 6: 79–88.

Poliakov, Leon. 1971. *Le mythe aryen: Essai sur les sources du racisme et des nationalismes.* Paris: Calmann-Levy.

Prevelakis, Pandelis. 1976. *The Tale of a Town.* London: Doric Publications.

Rabinow, Paul. 1989. *French Modern: Norms and Forms of the Social Environment.* Cambridge: MIT Press.

Reed-Danahay, Deborah. 1993. Talking about Resistance: Ethnography and Theory in Rural France. *Anthropological Quarterly* 66: 221–229.

———. 1996. *Education and Identity in Rural France.* Cambridge: Cambridge University Press.

Reizakis, Marina. 2001. Playing for One's Life—Playing for One's Name: Power and the Game of Life in a Greek Village. *Focaal: European Journal of Anthropology* 37: 27–37.

Rhum, Michael R. 1996. "Modernity" and "Tradition" in "Thailand." *Modern Asian Studies* 30(2): 325–355.

Salmona, Michèle. 1994. *Les paysans français: Le travail, les métiers, la transmission des savoirs.* Paris: L'Harmattan.

Scoditti, Giancarlo M. G. 1982. Aesthetics: The Significance of Apprenticeship on Kitawa. *Man*, n.s., 17: 74–91.

Scott, James C. 1985. *Weapons of the Weak: Everyday Forms of Peasant Resistance.* New Haven: Yale University Press.

Seremetakis, C. Nadia. 1993a. Memory of the Senses: Historical Perception, Commensal Exchange and Modernity. *Visual Anthropology Review* 9(2): 2–18.

———. 1993b. *Ritual, Power, and the Body: Historical Perspectives on the Representation of Greek Women.* New York: Pella.

Shore, Cris. 2000. *Building Europe: The Cultural Politics of European Integration.* London: Routledge.

Shore, Cris, and Susan Wright. 2000. Coercive Accountability: The Rise of Audit Culture in Higher Education. In Marilyn Strathern, ed., *Audit Cultures: Anthropological Studies in Accountability, Ethics and the Academy,* 57–89. London: Routledge.

Sifianou, Maria. 1992. *Politeness Phenomena in England and Greece.* Oxford: Clarendon Press.

Sigaut, François. 1991. L'apprentissage vue par les ethnologues: Une stéréotype? In Denis Chevallier, ed., *Savoir faire et pouvoir transmettre,* 33–42. Paris: Éditions de la Maison des Sciences de l'Homme.

Singleton, John. 1989. Japanese Folkcraft Pottery Apprenticeship: Cultural Patterns of an Educational Institution. In Coy 1989c: 13–30.

———, ed. 1998. *Learning in Likely Places: Varieties of Apprenticeship in Japan.* Cambridge: Cambridge University Press.

Sklavenitis, Khristoforos. 1996. Keramika kendra ke laiki angioplastes tis dhitikis Kritis. In Irini Gavrilaki, ed., *Keramika erghastiria stin Kriti apo tin arkeotita os simera,* 81–100. Rethimno: Istoriki Laoghrafiki Eteria Rethimnis.

Spooner, Brian. 1976. Concluding Essay 1: Anthropology and the Evil Eye. In Clarence Mahoney, ed., *The Evil Eye,* 279–285. New York: Columbia University Press.

Starrett, Gregory. 1998. *Putting Islam to Work: Education, Politics, and Religious Transformation in Egypt.* Berkeley: University of California Press.

St. Clair, William. 1972. *That Greece Might Still Be Free: The Philhellenes in the War of Independence.* London: Oxford University Press.

Stewart, Charles. 1991. *Demons and the Devil: Moral Imagination in Modern Greek Culture.* Princeton: Princeton University Press.

Stocking, George W. 1987. *Victorian Anthropology.* New York: Free Press.

———. 1995. *After Tylor: British Social Anthropology, 1888–1951.* Madison: University of Wisconsin Press.

Stolcke, Verena. 1995. Talking Culture: New Boundaries, New Rhetorics of Exclusion in Europe. *Current Anthropology* 36: 1–24.

Stoller, Paul, and Cheryl Olkes. 1987. *In Sorcery's Shadow: A Memoir of Apprenticeship among the Songhay of Niger.* Chicago: University of Chicago Press.

Strathern, Marilyn, 2000. New Accountabilities: Anthropological Studies in Audit, Ethics and the Academy. In Marilyn Strathern, ed., *Audit Cultures: Anthropological Studies in Accountability, Ethics and the Academy,* 1–18. London: Routledge.

Sutton, David E. 1994. "Tradition" and "Modernity": Kalymnian Constructions of Identity and Otherness. *Journal of Modern Greek Studies* 12: 239–260.

———. 1996. Explosive Debates: Dynamite, Tradition, and the State. *Anthropological Quarterly* 69: 66–78.

Tambiah, Stanley Jeyaraja. 1990. *Magic, Science, Religion, and the Scope of Rationality.* Cambridge: Cambridge University Press.

———. 1996. *Leveling Crowds: Ethnonationalist Conflicts and Collective Violence in South Asia.* Berkeley: University of California Press.

Tannen, Deborah. 1983. *Lilika Nakos.* Boston: Twayne.

Taylor, Barbara. 1983. "The Men Are as Bad as Their Masters . . . ": Socialism, Feminism and Sexual Antagonism in the London Tailoring Trade in the 1830s. In Judith L. Newton, Mary P. Ryan, and Judith R. Walkowitz, eds., *Sex and Class in Women's History,* 187–220. London: Routledge and Kegan Paul.

Taylor, J. L. 1990. New Buddhist Movements in Thailand: An Individualistic Revolution, Reform and Political Dissonance. *Journal of Southeast Asian Studies* 21: 135–154.

Terrio, Susan J. 2000. *Crafting the Culture and History of French Chocolate.* Berkeley: University of California Press.

Thompson, Michael. 1979. *Rubbish Theory: The Creation and Destruction of Value.* New York: Oxford University Press.

Todorova, Maria. 1997. *Imagining the Balkans.* New York: Oxford University Press.

Tyrwhitt, Jaqueline. 1967. The Culture of Poverty. *Ekistics* 23(134): 3–5.

Ulin, Robert. 1996. *Vintages and Traditions: An Ethnohistory of Southwest French Wine Cooperatives.* Washington, D.C.: Smithsonian Institution Press.

Uspensky, Boris. 1976. *The Semiotics of the Russian Icon.* Lisse: Peter De Ridder.

Vatikiotis, P. J. 1998. *Popular Autocracy in Greece, 1936–41: A Political Biography of General Ioannis Metaxas.* London: Frank Cass.

Veïkou, Christina. 1998. *Kako mati: I kinoniki kataskevi tis Optikis Epikinonias.* Athens: Ellinika Grammata.

Vipas Prachyaporn. 2001 [2544]. Chiang mai: Khwaamruu le tua ton. M.A. thesis, Thammasat University, Bangkok.

Watson, James L., ed. 1997. *Golden Arches East: McDonald's in East Asia*. Stanford: Stanford University Press.

Weiss, Gilbert, and Ruth Wodak. 2000. Debating Europe: Globalization Rhetoric and European Union Employment Policies. In Irène Bellier and Thomas M. Wilson, eds., *The European Union: Building, Imagining and Experiencing the New Europe*, 75–92. Oxford: Berg.

Willis, Paul. [1977] 1981. *Learning to Labor: How Working Class Kids Get Working Class Jobs*. Reprint, Morningside Edition. New York: Columbia University Press.

Wittgenstein, Ludwig. 1963. *Philosophical Investigations*. 2d ed. Translated by G. E. M. Anscombe. Oxford: Blackwell.

Yalouri, Eleana. 2001. *The Acropolis: Global Fame, Local Claim*. Oxford: Berg.

Yanagisako, Sylvia. 2002. *Producing Culture and Capital: Family Firms in Italy*. Princeton: Princeton University Press.

Yang, Jongsung. 1994. Folklore and Cultural Politics in Korea: Intangible Cultural Properties and Living National Treasures. Ph.D. diss., Indiana University.

Yannaras, Christos. 1972. *Orthodhoksia ke Dhisi—I theoloyia stin Elladha simera*. Athens: Athena.

———. 1978. *I neoelliniki taftotita*. Athens: Grigori.

———. 1992. *Orthodhoksia ke Dhisi sti neoteri Elladha*. Athens: Domos.

Yiakoumaki, Vassiliki. 2002. "The Nation as Acquired Taste": On Greekness, Consumption of Food Heritage, and the Making of the New Europe. Ph.D. diss., New School University.

Zabusky, Stacia E. 1995. *Launching Europe: An Ethnography of Cooperation in European Space Science*. Princeton: Princeton University Press.

———. 2000. Boundaries at Work: Discourses and Practices of Belonging in the European Space Agency. In Irène Bellier and Thomas M. Wilson, eds., *The European Union: Building, Imagining and Experiencing the New Europe*, 179–200. Oxford: Berg.